Relating Difficulty

The Processes of Constructing and Managing Difficult Interaction

LEA's Series on Personal Relationships
Steve Duck, Series Editor

Relating Difficulty

The Processes of Constructing and Managing Difficult Interaction

Edited by

D. Charles Kirkpatrick
Steve Duck
Megan K. Foley
University of Iowa

LAWRENCE ERLBAUM ASSOCIATES, PUBLISHERS
2006   Mahwah, New Jersey   London

Lawrence Erlbaum Associates, Inc., Publishers
10 Industrial Avenue
Mahwah, New Jersey 07430
www.erlbaum.com

Cover design by Tomai Maridou

Don't Fall Apart on Me by Bob Dylan. Copyright © 1983
by Special Rider Music. All rights reserved. International
copyright secured. Reprinted by permission.

Library of Congress Cataloging-in-Publication Data

Relating difficulty: The processes of constructing and man-
aging difficult interaction / edited by D. Charles
Kirkpatrick, Steve Duck, Megan K. Foley
        p. cm.
Includes bibliographical references and index.
ISBN 0-8058-5411-8 (cloth : alk. paper)
ISBN 0-8058-5412-6 (pbk. : alk. paper)
1. Interpersonal conflict. 2. Interpersonal communica-
tion. 3. Interpersonal relations. I. Kirkpatrick, D.
Charles (Dan Charles) II. Duck, Steve. III. Foley, Megan
K.
BF637.I48.R45 2006
158.2—dc22   2005053042
                                                  CIP

Books published by Lawrence Erlbaum Associates are printed
on acid-free paper, and their bindings are chosen for strength
and durability.

Printed in the United States of America
10 9 8 7 6 5 4 3 2 1

Contents

Preface

Because this book is about difficult relationships, its subject matter should be immediately recognizable to almost anybody. Difficult people are a feature of regular experience, and difficult relationships are all too common and regrettable. However, despite the growth in relationship research in the last 25 years there has been very little research effort devoted to understanding the nature of difficulties in relating. The tendency to focus on the positive side of relationships, the growth of dating, and the increases in intimacy that occur across time has only relatively recently been balanced by an effort to understand the dark side of relationships (Cupach & Spitzberg, 1994; Spitzberg & Cupach, 1998), and the ways in which relationship challenges may be managed (Duck & Wood, 1995). Nevertheless, the possibility that some relationships are inherently difficult and the nature of the factors that make any kind of relationship difficult have been relatively neglected until recently when Fritz Harden and Omdahl (2006) published a book on difficult relationships in the workplace. Whereas much previous work still tends to typify relationships or people as the sources of difficulty, the present book moves toward an emphasis on the whole process of relating.

Relating Difficulty is an attempt to understand the nature of difficulty in relationships and to place it in a broad context of human experience. We are interested in demonstrating a number of different places and ways in which difficulties are experienced in relating and also coming to some understanding of the nature of relational difficulty both in the abstract and in performance. The book therefore contains a number of conceptual and empirical chapters that address these issues and concludes with a final summary attempting to articulate the main points that characterize difficulty across these different relational contexts and processes.

In the first chapter, the editors attempt to characterize relationship difficulty, and we demonstrate that there is something unsatisfactory about attributing that difficulty to the inherent qualities of individuals or to relationship forms rather than to relating itself. Although there are some personality traits that might render individuals unwelcome companions in relationships, the nature of difficulty itself is an inherently relational concept that relies very strongly on the presumption that there are cultural norms of appropriateness for the performance of social behavior. Indeed, without the recognition that relationship quality is a cultural evaluation (Montgomery, 1988), it is not possible to envision relationship difficulty in the first place, nor is it possible to decide which features of behavior will render the judgment applicable.

Subsequent chapters give several different examples across the spectrum of human behavior, which lead to the experience of difficulty in relating.

Scott D. Bradshaw analyzes shyness, demonstrating that the necessity of open conversation with relationship partners makes life difficult for those people to whom that does not come easily. Recognizing that the shy person's partner is not a passive participant in relationships, Bradshaw offers a searching analysis of the long-term and short-term consequences of shyness on both the partner and the shy person. The future challenge is to understand how shyness affects not only the conduct of specific interactions but also the formation, implementation, and maintenance of longer-term relationships. We must not overlook the fact that relationships are dynamic temporal entities in which the nature of difficulty can change diachronically. It appears that shy persons can overcome many of the initial difficulties and can form satisfying and lasting relationships, but that these relationships are not necessarily in all respects equivalent to those formed by other people.

Megan K. Foley deals with the troubling issue of partner violence in abusive relationships, a case where the nature of the relational difficulty is immediately apparent—and immediately repellent—but nonetheless complex to understand. She identifies the four primary places where scholars, activists, and members of violent relationships locate this difficulty: the abused partner, the abusive partner, relational interaction, and societal discourses. Because none of these can adequately account for intimate partner violence on its own, she then offers a framework that traces the relationships between these sites where the difficulty of intimate partner violence may emerge. Determination of accountability for the difficulty of violence in relationships depends in turn on determination of agency and control.

Michael J. Lovaglia and Jeffrey W. Lucas explore the nature and dynamics of power management in relationships at work and the ways in which it can lead to difficulty. Distinguishing between formal power and the power that comes from relational status and informal prestige and honor, the authors review a number of issues concerning the way in which power works in social interaction. They note that the exercise of power in itself can cause problems but that the major difficulties come from the inequalities of power that are exercised in hierarchies present in work relationships. In particular, there are special difficulties for interaction created when the hierarchies represented by formal power structures cut across informal hierarchies created through status and honor.

Graham Allan and Christian Gerstner examine the social consequences of allocating material goods in the family and the ways in which that can create difficulty between the members. Not only are there economic constraints on certain kinds of relationships, but the redistribution of wealth at death can create significant and troubling interactions between the survivors. Furthermore, in divorce cases many of the struggles are about the division of resources. The chapter focuses on these and a number of other illustrative examples of how the uses and distribution of money become problematic in relationships, and lead to distress between partners or members of the family. In many cases, the use of money is a proxy for the use of other kinds of power. Economic control can lead to difficulty in a way that is often overlooked by psychologists and communication scholars, who do not question the nature of social structure that is presumed within the performance of particular kinds of relationships.

Mary Claire Morr Serewicz describes the context and dynamics of the in-law relationship, whose difficulties have been a source of wry humor for many generations and in many cultures. This form of relating is a particularly difficult one for people to handle because it is essentially involuntary, and the in-laws come with the spouse even in cultures where the individual is allowed to choose the spouse. The person is confronted with an expectation that he or she should love persons to whom the spouse is deeply attached but with whom he or she has had no previous long-term experience or basis for any affection. In addition to these problems, there is a lack of clarity about the role of in-laws in relationship to the nondescendent spouse, and the intertwining of issues of relating here renders both parties to the relationship somewhat perplexed.

Erin M. Sahlstein explores the role of management issues in several different types of long-distance relationships. Given that closeness—both metaphorical and real—is typically presumed to be an essential component of satisfactory relating, those relationships that have to be conducted at a distance are particularly likely to experience difficulties and be seen as less than satisfactory. The chapter discusses a number of ways in which people overcome these difficulties, but it also presents the interesting case that part of the problem comes from the fact that the participants are simultaneously conducting long-distance relationship and other proximal relationships, which they evaluate in comparison. In addition to considering long-distance dating romances, the chapter deals with military marriages and commuter relationships and illustrates the particular strains of these examples of long-distance relating.

Elizabeth L. Paul writes about the increasing prevalence of casual hookups on college campuses, where the ostensible purpose is simply sexual activity with a previously unknown partner or at least a partner with whom there is no present or intended romantic involvement. Despite the prevalence of this kind of relating, there appear to be a number of significant difficulties for the people who conduct them. These difficulties essentially revolve around the image of self that results from the interaction. The person who engages in frequent hookups rapidly discovers that reputation as a romantic partner has been damaged by gossip—particularly if they are women—but as the author indicates this is not the only source of difficulty in these kinds of relationships.

Eric K. Foster and Ralph L. Rosnow have contributed a chapter on gossip that explores the positive and negative purposes that gossip can serve in social interaction. In part, the difficulty of gossip is its very ambiguity and the sense that gossip is not best counted as a static representation of social knowledge but rather that its flow and location are constantly changing within a dynamic social network. A significant theoretical contribution of the chapter is to assess the way in which these changes in the network influence and are influenced by the nature of gossip itself, and they emphasize the role of network change in difficult relating.

Stephanie S. Rollie offers an original and exciting analysis of the ways in which similar network change results from divorce and in particular how noncustodial—and therefore nonresidential—parents conduct and maintain their visitations with their children. It is a particular difficulty for these parents that their relationships are conducted in a triangulated way, where another parent, from whom they are now divorced, exercises the major care and control of the children. Because this leads the nonresidential parents to be somewhat anxious that the relationship with the children is in jeopardy, their relational maintenance strategies are adversely affected. The author carefully contrasts these particular kinds of maintenance strategies with those that have been previously studied in the case of romantic relationships and marriages, and finds that there are significant and notable differences.

Renee Lyons, Lynn Langille, and Steve Duck explore the difficulties of relational maintenance that are consequent on the acquisition of long-term disability or chronic illness. It is too often assumed that chronic illness is an individual affliction, and so these authors point to the relational consequences both for the individual concerned and for partners, friends, and other social targets, including coworkers. Not only do disability and chronic illness render people less socially accessible to others but they also have consequences for the person's own perception of his or her value as a relater in addition to the restrictions that are placed on relational abilities and performances. Furthermore, outsiders very often find it difficult to know what to expect of people with disability or chronic illness and sometimes project their own social embarrassment onto the interactions that they then have with the person, making it awkward for everyone.

In the final chapter, the editors draw together several strands from the preceding chapters and emphasize the nature of triangulation for the performance of relating. In essence, we conclude that the key elements of difficulty in relating to other people are a composite of reference to social norms, expectations, comparison with other forms of relating, and the standards for relating as competent and normative social entities in a complex social environment about which outsiders have a tendency to make judgments.

The book as a whole thus introduces a number of new ways of conceiving the complexities of relating and encourages researchers to add these factors into their future conceptualization of the management of relationships. Although our focus here is on difficulties in relating, there are broader issues about relating in general that are opened up by these considerations.

—*D. Charles Kirkpatrick, Steve Duck, and Megan K. Foley*

REFERENCES

Cupach, W. R., & Spitzberg, B. H. (Eds.). (1994). *The dark side of interpersonal communication*. Hillsdale, NJ: Lawrence Erlbaum Associates.

Duck, S. W., & Wood, J. T. (Eds.). (1995). *Confronting relationship challenges*. Thousand Oaks, CA: Sage.

Fritz Harden, J., & Omdahl, B. (Eds.). (2006). *Problematic relationships in the workplace*. Bern & New York: Peter Lang.

Montgomery, B. M. (1988). Quality communication in personal relationships. In S. W. Duck (Ed.), *Handbook of personal relationships* (pp. 343–362). Chichester, UK: Wiley.

Spitzberg, B. H., & Cupach, W. R. (Eds.). (1998). *The dark side of close relationships*. Mahwah, NJ: Lawrence Erlbaum Associates.

About the Authors

Graham Allan is Professor of Social Relations at Keele University in the United Kingdom. He is particularly interested in the sociology of the family, friendship and informal relations. His recent publications include *The Sociology of the Family: A Reader* (Blackwell, 1999); *Families, Households and Society* (Palgrave, 2001, with Graham Crow); *Social Relations and the Life Course* (Palgrave, 2003, with Gill Jones); *Social Networks and Social Exclusion* (Ashgate, 2004, with Chris Phillipson and David Morgan), and *The State of Affairs* (Lawrence Erlbaum Associates, 2004, with Jean Duncombe, Kaeren Harrison, & Dennis Marsden).

Scott D. Bradshaw is Director of the Center for Research and Evaluation and Associate Professor in the Department of Psychology at Elizabeth City State University in North Carolina. He earned his Ph.D. in social psychology at Virginia Commonwealth University. His research has focused on the effects of shyness on individuals' social networks and group interactions. He also has an interest in the application of research to address social problems and shape public policy.

Steve Duck is a Professor of Communication Studies and the Daniel and Amy Starch Research Chair at the University of Iowa. He is the founding editor of the *Journal of Social and Personal Relationships* and the editor or author of 42 books on personal relationships. In addition, he founded the International Network on Personal Relationships (now merged into the International Association for Relationship Research) and two series of international conferences on relationships.

Megan K. Foley is a Presidential Graduate Fellow in Communication Studies at the University of Iowa. Her research focuses on the interrelationship of the communicative act, agency, and structure. She is exploring this interest in the context of family discourse and intimate partner violence in particular.

Eric K. Foster received a master's degree in literature and in business and a doctorate in social psychology from Temple University. He is Study Director at Temple's Institute for Survey Research, which conducts social, educational, and epidemiological studies. He is also Adjunct Assistant Professor of Marketing at the Wharton School of Business at the University of Pennsylvania. He has developed and published his own statistical software, currently used in both commercial and academic organizations.

Christian Gerstner is a Ph.D. student at Keele University in the United Kingdom. He is particularly interested in the sociology of money and online research methodology. His Ph.D. thesis is "Online Social Research: Methodology, Ethics and the Law."

D. Charles Kirkpatrick is a doctoral candidate at The University of Iowa. His teaching interests include interpersonal and group communication as well as communication theory. His research focuses on maintenance of close relationships through computer-mediated systems and long-distance relating using both quantitative and qualitative methods.

Lynn Langille is the Research Consultant at the Atlantic Health Promotion Research Centre (AHPRC) at Dalhousie University in Halifax, Nova Scotia, Canada. Her academic background is in anthropology and sociology, and she has taught in these disciplines at universities in eastern Canada. At AHPRC, she provides advice on research design, proposal writing, sources of funding, qualitative data analysis, and report writing. She has been a part of the Relationship Issues research group for more than 10 years. Other research interests include food security, healthy rural communities, and the impacts of social determinants on health.

Michael J. Lovaglia is Professor and Chair of the Department of Sociology at the University of Iowa. His research investigates power, status, and identity and how those social processes can be applied to problems of educational achievement, leadership, and the abuse of power.

Jeffrey W. Lucas is Assistant Professor of Sociology at the University of Maryland–College Park. His primary research interest is the experimental analysis of theories of basic social processes. Recent works include "Theory Testing, Generalization, and the Problem of External Validity" (*Sociological Theory*, 21(3), 236–253) and "Status Processes and the Institutionalization of Women as Leaders" (*American Sociological Review*, 68(3), 464–480).

Renee Lyons is Director and Professor of the Atlantic Health Promotion Research Centre (AHPRC) at Dalhousie University in Halifax, Nova Scotia, Canada, with appointments in the School of Health and Human Performance and the Department of Psychology. She holds a Canada Research Chair in Health Promotion. She is currently principal investigator for health research projects totaling over 13 million dollars, all involving national and international collaborative partnerships with a special focus on health issues in Atlantic Canada. The July, 2002, edition of *Canadian Living Magazine* featured her as one of 10 Medical Megastars in Canada, acknowledging the important role that health promotion research (and the research of AHPRC) plays in the health of Canadians.

Mary Claire Morr Serewicz is Assistant Professor of Human Communication Studies at the University of Denver. Her research interests include in-law relationships, privacy in family relationships, and transitions in romantic relationships. In 2003, she received the dissertation award from the Interpersonal Communication Division of the International Communication Association for her Ph.D. dissertation at Arizona State University. Her recent work has appeared in *Communication Monographs* and *Communication Research*.

Elizabeth L. Paul is Associate Professor and Chair of Psychology and an affiliate of the Women's and Gender Studies Program at The College of New Jersey in Ewing, New Jersey. She received her Ph.D. in personality psychology at Boston University. Her research focuses on youths' risky sexual experiences and how gender delimits personal relationship development and experience. She has also examined relational challenges of late adolescence and young adulthood as they impact and are impacted by the college transition. Recently, her work on hookups, youths' spontaneous and anonymous sexual experiences, was featured in *Newsweek* and on the *Today Show*. She is currently writing a book on youth sexuality and is an active advocate of community-based research. In addition, she directs the Trenton Youth Community-based Research Corps.

Stephanie S. Rollie is Assistant Professor in the Department of Communication at Miami University in Ohio. She earned her Ph.D. and M.A. in the Communication Studies Department at the University of Iowa. Her research interests include nonresidential parent-child relationships, absence, relationship maintenance, relationship dissolution and divorce, and identity issues, and she has recently published a chapter in the *Handbook of Divorce and Relationship Dissolution* (Lawrence Erlbaum Associates, 2005). She was also the 2005 winner of the Central States Communication Association's Cooper Award for excellence in teaching.

Ralph L. Rosnow is Thaddeus Bolton Professor Emeritus at Temple University, where he served as a faculty member in the Psychology Department from 1967 to 2001. He has also taught at Boston University and Harvard University. He is the author or coauthor of more than two dozen books and many journal articles and chapters. His most recent books are (with Robert Rosenthal) *People Studying People* (W. H. Freeman, 1997); *Beginning Behavioral Research* (5th ed., Prentice Hall, 2005); (with Rosenthal & Donald B. Rubin) *Contrasts and Effect Sizes in Behavioral Research* (Cambridge University Press, 2000); and (with Mimi Rosnow) *Writing Papers in Psychology* (7th ed., Thomson Wadsworth, 2005).

Erin M. Sahlstein is Assistant Professor of Communication Studies at the University of Richmond in Virginia. Her research interests are in communication, distance, and technology, primarily within dating and marital relationships. She is currently shifting her research focus to military marriages and families, as well as the interactions between long-distance partners and their social networks.

Chapter 1

Difficulty In Relating: Some Conceptual Problems With "Problematic Relationships" and Difficulties With "Difficult People"

Steve Duck
D. Charles Kirkpatrick
Megan K. Foley
University of Iowa

We have all met "difficult people" and we tend to see them as just that—people with a disposition to be difficult. However, at different times in life, it is possible that almost anyone can be attributed with that label. Also it is all too easy to think of some people or behavior as inherently awkward or intentionally obnoxious, but the fact that almost anyone can be seen as difficult by someone or other might give us pause. Furthermore, most of us can recognize that when we are in a good mood, even difficult behavior in others can be tolerated and is not inherently offensive. Also, that crazy, stupid driver who just carved us up might turn out on closer inspection to be our boss or the local church leader, whose behavior is then greeted with a friendly, if resigned, permissive wave.

Perhaps, then, "obnoxiousness" and "difficulty" are after all externally attributed assessments rather than inherent characteristics. If so, then we should take a closer look at how a person's behavior comes to be labeled as "difficult" by someone else. We should also ask what it is that differentiates real shortcomings from perceived difficulties and what characteristic features tend to create agreement about the classification of behavior as difficult. Although there may be real behaviors that are most often perceived simply as inadequacy, limitation, inability, or even incompetence by most of us, there may be behaviors whose repeated performance leads to general agreement that someone deserves to be characterized as "a difficult person."

1

For such matters to be addressed, there must be some sort of criteria for classification that ratify or challenge the simple judgment by one person of another as difficult, some quasi-objective criterion or set of criteria by reference to which "difficulty" could be established. In some cases, a person can be construed as awkward or difficult in context but not necessarily a difficult person as a whole. For example, two people may experience difficulties because of tensions between the two persons' roles, as in whether to perceive one's mother-in-law as a friend or as just a designated part of the family (Morr Serewicz, chap. 6, this volume), or from jealousy arising from unfavorable comparisons of self and other, as in arguments over which family member receives the largest inheritance (Allan & Gerstner, chap. 5, this volume), or from an unexpected change in the core identity of one of them as a result of a stroke (Lyons, Langille & Duck, chap. 11, this volume). In other cases, a person may be seen as (or may intend to be) difficult in a specific role only for a specific length of time. For example, people in organizations can decide to withdraw effort and deliberately follow a path of minimalist activity for the organization (Vardi & Weitz, 2004), or they may go on strike or obey rules to the letter even when (and indeed because) this slows down performance of the task, or simply set out to sabotage the productivity and performance of others during an industrial dispute. Although such ideas evolved from organizational contexts, similar processes may also develop in other forms of social and personal relationships. The "silent treatment" is an example of a kind of withdrawal of effort that can occur in a nonorganizational relationship, and it may be adopted to achieve a particular goal for a limited length of time. It does not necessarily result in the person being seen as wholly difficult, just difficult at the moment and perhaps for cause.

This leads us to question of the extent to which judgments about difficulty are context dependent. Is there any intrinsically difficult characteristic or mechanism inherent in the person, or is difficulty a form of social construction? At least it is clear that such judgments *may* be context dependent. A person who is difficult at work may be quite pleasant in a bridge group. Also, the task-oriented nature of work and long periods of enforced proximity might engender conflict regardless of the individual characteristics of coworkers. Such points invite us to explore not the character of the condemned other but rather the relationship between person and other. It is not that a person is absolutely "difficult" but that they are difficult relative to circumstances and to the judges making the call.

We tend toward the view that while someone may make the attribution of another person as a "difficult person," it would most often be wiser to say that people generate difficulty between or among themselves. Furthermore, the phenomenon of the "difficult person" is actually a reference to social norms and standards for judgment within a given society, and this level of analysis also needs weaving into the discussion. This, of course, does not mean that it is never the case that one person consistently creates difficulties with others. If this is what it means to be a "difficult person," we should nevertheless recognize that the label describes more than just inherent qualities and does so in the context of a range of other variables.

Unfortunately (perhaps), difficulty is not the fault of the person alone, but often a result of interaction between the characteristics of the person, the interaction partner, the context, and/or or social norms for relating. In attributing difficulty, therefore, it is clear that some form of complex *social* process is involved rather than a purely personal description of an idiosyncratic style, as is normally supposed. At most, the idiosyncratic style is being judged against a social standard rather than against some natural law, and hence such judgments can both vary across time within a culture and differ between cultures at a given time. Katriel (1986) has already demonstrated this point in her discussion of "dugri" styles of behavior in Israel, which appear normatively assertive in Israel, but are regarded as difficult, brusque, and even rude in other cultures. Once it is understood that attribution of "difficulty" has a large social element, then a number of its nuances must be considered.

Let us first assume the validity of the position that we do *not* accept, namely that difficulty is a personal quality. Then let us explore that notion in order to pick apart some of the problems with the idea. The first point is that, as Davis and Schmidt (1977) indicated, many characteristics that appear to be individual are in fact inherently social. Whereas "melancholic," "depressive," or "neurotic" are essentially individual characteristics, there are some apparently individual characteristics that are ambiguous in referent. For instance, such characteristics as "paranoid," "introverted," and "lonely" are only speciously individual. In fact, the terms make implicit reference to sociality in that a person could not be described with any of these labels were not sociality first assumed, as the implied threatening presence, willful rejection of, or aversion to other people is built into these terms. Even more important, examples for the present purposes are provided by characteristics such as "niceness" or "obnoxiousness," which are assessable only in terms of sociality and the effects of an individual's behavior on other persons (Davis & Schmidt, 1977).

In face of such an important point, the discussion of "difficult persons" or "obnoxiousness" or even "problematic behavior" assumes a different compass. The analysis therefore turns to the distinction between characteristics that are truly personal attributes, and those that are more properly ascribed to *Person* × *Situation* effects, *Person* × *Person* effects—the various social constituents of difficulty and unpleasantness.

PERSONAL FEATURES

When people attribute personal characteristics to another individual, it often seems as if they are describing a general and entirely objective reality. This conveniently overlooks the filter of the self-serving bias and the various ways in which people perceive the world in ways consistent with their own predispositions. This body of scholarship shows that it is naïve of us to assume that personal perceptions of other people and their behavior are simply objective reports.

Early research on impression formation (Warr & Knapper, 1968) indicated the significant ways in which psychological features of a perceiver might "distort" perception of truth about others. For example, there is often a closer correspondence between one person's attributions about several different targets than between different others' attributions about the same target. Prejudiced people overperceive a target's likelihood of being a member of a despised racial group, and paranoids tend to mistrust even the most benign others as a matter of course. These well-substantiated findings clearly indicate that the perception of other people's attributes is partly a function of the person doing the perceiving rather than only a matter of the actual characteristics of the person being perceived (Warr & Knapper, 1968). The research also began to unpick the complex ways in which perception of certain features is associated with a tendency to make specified perceptual errors about other characteristics. For example, prejudiced persons tend to overestimate the number of Jews in an array of photographs (Warr & Knapper, 1968). Thus, although such research sets out to establish how we judge that individuals *have* various characteristics, the research actually tends to demonstrate that these judgments are also a result of perceptual errors of various kinds.

An independent explosion of research on attribution (and, somewhat characteristically, of attribution "errors") identified ways in which perceivers tended to perceive their own behavior in terms of contextual or situational features and others' behavior in terms of inherent and underlying psychological characteristics (Heider, 1958; Jones, Kanouse, et al., 1972; Ross, 1977). Such research has been immensely rich and complex, but the key feature for our argument here is simple. Perceivers were once again assumed to be naïve and error-prone in such a way as to distort their perception of the "true" characteristics of others and of the "true" balance between personality and situational effects on human activity. In truth, such research encapsulates quite neatly several assumptions of everyday life where it is presumed that the underlying true characteristics of Others are *realities* that can be detected.

Feeding into such persistent common and academic styles of analysis is the assumption that people have a steady, persistent personality; that is, the belief that humans' behavior can be explained by reference to perduring characteristics. These characteristics are conceived to be an *inherent* organization of cognition, habits, and attitudes that not only describe habitual styles of behavior but actually in some sense (which differs across different theoretical positions) drives, causes, facilitates, or precipitates behavior (and cognition or affect) and does so reliably and relatively immutably over time (Watson 2000). Given the prevailing tendency to see human behavior as the *result* of personality inherent to individuals (rather than seeing the attributions or descriptions of personality as a result of behavioral consistencies detected by a perceiver), it is natural enough for us to want to find a persistent personality explanation for "difficulty" or "obnoxiousness." On such a presumption, difficult people are *inherently* incapable of interacting well with others, do not fit into teams, are uncongenial, conflictual, and uncooperative, and are personally responsible for unsuccessful outcomes in social life.

As noted earlier, however, Davis and Schmidt (1977) add some sophistication to the foregoing basic view. Not only are some "personal" attributions effectively social, but they establish a type of person (such as "difficult person" or "obnoxious person" or even "nice person") as a social object. At best, they are social types that acknowledge and are responsive to the presence and judgment of third parties. Whether physically or metaphorically, bodies and selves are just like other physical and social entities in that they can intrude into the physical and social spaces of others. Such intrusion can be positive, negative, or unmarked. For example, a person may brush against another's personal space in ways that are intimate and are seen as either exciting (when desired), intrusive (when it is sexual harassment), or excused (when the infraction occurs in a confined space such as an elevator and is judged to be unintentional). The judgments made about the behavior are modified by knowledge of these circumstances or other relevant elements of the situation. We judge others in the context of social norms for intrusion into spaces deemed "personal." The categorical labels, or social types, that appear to refer to the individual characteristics of a person are in fact what we refer to when making such attributions.

Furthermore, Davis and Schmidt (1977) introduce the conception of micro-deviance that draws attention to the associated interactional behaviors of people classified into abnormal or deviant social psychological types. Those persons who are intrusive in either an excessively offensive (obnoxious) or excessively positive (extreme niceness) way tend to be typified as micro-deviant, which is to say that their behavior is not regarded as deviant in the gross sense of delinquency or reprobation, but rather as falling outside the boundaries of social comfort. Thus, we become uncomfortable in the presence of excessively nice or obnoxious persons without classifying them as outcasts or social deviants in the same way that thieves, batterers, pedophiles, or murderers are deviants (see Duck & VanderVoort, 2002). The features of micro-deviance are to be found in interactional characteristics rather than in motivation, attitudes to society, or in criminal intent—in short, they are found in relative social judgments rather than in the "true" characters of the person so described. Obnoxious people just appear not to know how to behave well, but do not manifest inherently antisocial intent.

Davis and Schmidt (1977) characterize both the nice and the obnoxious, then, as rule breakers whose projected selves impose undesired face implications on partners in interaction. The person described as obnoxious imposes an unwanted self in the other person either by being hypercritical or by forcing the person to feel slighted—disrespected, ignored, or undervalued, for example—or extorts an undesired sense of self from that person—forcing the person to behave in a way that is servile or instrumental, imposing requirements to do unwarranted favors or services, for example (see Lovaglia & Lucas, chap. 4, this volume). People classified as obnoxious also typically ignore group ethos and warnings that group ethos has been violated (e.g., not just talking during movies, but then ignoring requests to be quiet). Such behaviors lead to a typification of the person as obnoxious and, once the label is assigned, credits for good behavior do little to wash off the label. After a person has been categorized as obnoxious, the category sticks indelibly in the mind of the perceiver or at least is easily revived and reapplied.

Against such an analysis, the idea that people *are* or *are not* obnoxious becomes paradoxically a matter of dispute. The label itself depends not simply on behavior but with reference to some social rule or norm, some perceiver's assessment of the behavior, and their relation. This process also presupposes a personal judgment about the importance of that relation. Although we can recognize that certain behavioral characteristics, once defined, are more or less irrevocably associated with obnoxiousness or difficulty (such behavioral characteristics as arrogance, hostility, and irritability, e.g., are more or less equivalent to difficulty). As such, the associations are not merely semantic but cultural. Uncooperativeness may be regarded as a virtue in cultures or circumstances where menial subservience or consensual conviviality has no value; arrogance may not be altogether bad if the culture appreciates a sense of command and self-confident independence (as, e.g., in CEOs, military commanders, or captains of starships).

Reference only to an individual's personal characteristics is thus an insufficient guide to the classification of his or her "difficulty." Not only do any "real" personality characteristics have no absolute value but their relation to situations and behaviors in context must be evaluated in ways supplementary to absolute descriptions. Although certain behaviors do, in a given culture, tend to be ascribed negative evaluations, their mere occurrence is not sufficient to render a typification of a person as a specific sort of individual. Even such systematic and intentional behaviors as withdrawal of effort (Vardi & Weitz 2004), working to the rules, industrial sabotage, and bloody-minded resistance to authority (all of which we assume to have the key feature of intentionality that would merit an attribution to personality; Heider, 1958) must be gauged against a standard of social appropriateness that presupposes cooperation and willing collaboration with the demands of situational structure and authority.

One basis for inference and attribution therefore is the notion of social appropriateness. Social appropriateness is an example of the effects of social norms on categorization judgments made about social behavior. Just as we find certain behavior appropriate for children, but not for adults, so there are certain kinds of activity that we tolerate even when they break the norms (e.g., joking or teasing in serious places). Other activities are regarded as entirely outside the norms and therefore unsuitable for social performance, rendering their perpetrators negatively labeled or even punished (e.g., having tantrums in a business meeting or showing contempt of a judge in a courtroom). Although individuals differ in their ability to recognize the power of social norms, and there are also different levels of skill in ability at enacting them, some people may be less willing than others to abide by the norms that they do recognize. Thus, it is not entirely clear whether difficulties in relationships result from skill deficits rather than from purposeful norm violation.

PERSON × SITUATION/NORM INTERACTION

An extension of the previously presented argument can be derived from the claims by Lucien Seve (1969) that "personality" is necessarily derived from social relations that transform the real. In other words, social relations are the basis for real-life processes in which personalities develop; personalities do not originate only from within the individual or exert control over behavior in ways un-influenced by social contact. Without social relations, individual personalities do not exist, says Seve, and without social relations the transformed selves that evolve in individuals cannot be created or sustained (Burkitt 1991).

Such an analysis urges us to focus on the interaction of the person with the rules and norms that apply to social situations because these are essentially an embodiment of the (presumed) presence of other people and they represent a person's awareness of the essentially social nature of individual behavior and thought. The behavior of individuals cannot be characterized or understood without a previous consideration of the normative social frameworks within which any behavior is conducted, judged, and held morally accountable. Therefore, whenever someone judges another as difficult, that judgment is made *relative to norms for social practices* that are jointly held and commonly understood. Individual behavior cannot be judged without assuming that a person interacts within a context of social norms almost every time a choice is made about the behavior to perform (Duck, 1990; Shotter, 1992).

The interaction of a person with the social rules occurs in many situations and forms. All of us are, at some level, aware of the fact that there are rules governing our behavior, and there are also many situations where we come directly into contact with these rules and their consequences. Goffman (1959) carried out extensive analyses of social norms enacted in the obvious or implied presence of others, and Brown and Levinson (1978) have noted the more localized effects of the rules of politeness on the conduct of specific interactions and sequences of speech. They show that we are all aware of the fact that other people may observe—and will likely judge—our behavior. Accordingly, we shape our public performances in ways that broadly conform to those social expectations, and we fear the moral whipping of being gossiped about (Bergmann 1993).

This general principle represents a simple fact: that we prefer to carry out our public performances in ways that will not generate negative assessments by other people. That is, when guided by the expectation of normative perception, we prefer to behave in ways that are not regarded as "difficult." The very nature of social life is guided by the assumption that people will largely behave in ways that are "appropriate" (Duck & Vandervoort, 2002). However, it is not always the case that norms offer predominant guides for behavior. One of the issues this chapter addresses is precisely the question of when people choose to be guided by norms instead of by their own personal proclivities if the latter will lead to them being rated as difficult, obnoxious, or inappropriate. Of course there are occasions when people are less concerned with normative perception than with personal needs (e.g., Lyons et al., chap. 11, this volume describe the fact that some teenagers saw their mother's breast cancer as a big personal inconvenience, and Sahlstein, chap. 7, this volume, reports that long-distance relaters often neglect their proximal friendships when their long-distance partners are in town). However, we will now consider the case where norms are the major guiding force of behavior.

Norms and Inappropriateness

Duck and Vandervoort (2002) indicate that the broad differentiation of relationships into appropriate and inappropriate can be further categorized according to whether the relationship is unconventional, disapproved, or forbidden. Clearly, there are different levels of tolerance for kinds of relationships that are not normative. Some of these are widely tolerated (e.g., affairs—Kipnis, 1998—or relationships between people of widely different ages, say a 70-year-old man marrying a 30-year-old woman: odd but ultimately acceptable), and some are regarded as beyond the pale (e.g., affairs between a physician and patient, or pedophilia). Thus, a multiyear difference in age between romantic partners constitutes an unusual feature of a relationship that has no absolute value: It is tolerated in some cases (man 70 years old, woman 30 years old) and not in others with an equivalent age difference (man 50 years old; girl 10 years old).

Persons would not be labeled as difficult simply because they carried out relational behavior that is not normative, but all the same it is likely that nonnormative behavior is more likely to lead to a label of "difficulty" than is normatively guided behavior, particularly if it occurs frequently or characterizes *most* of a person's relationships.

There are also different latitudes of acceptance for relationship behaviors by people of different levels of power. As was originally noted by Hollander (1958), greater latitude is allowed to people in power, and they are permitted by their age, power, or genius to behave in ways that violate social norms, a situation that he describes as due to "idiosyncrasy credit." Powerful people can therefore act in ways which unpowerful people may not adopt or for which they would be labeled as "difficult," when a powerful person will not be so labeled. A CEO flouting the company dress code will get away with it where an underling will not.

Although Hollander's observation was originally focused on formal power and leadership status, it is clear that in relationships, such permissiveness also comes from sources other than formal status. Idiosyncrasy credits can be derived from such factors as physical attractiveness, education, age, race, ethnicity, sex, and even newness on the job, where tolerance for error may be somewhat greater in earlier days than later ones.

Norms obviously can be related to broad categories of allowable performance or can be localized to specific conduct of particular interactions, with failure in either case rendering the performer liable to a negative judgment. Brown and Levinson (1978) discussed norms of politeness and noted the ways in which individuals in interaction consider one another's positive face wants (the need to be recognized and appreciated) and the other's negative face wants (the need not to be constrained or imposed on or burdened in an interaction). For example, the phrase "I am sorry to bother you but I wonder if you would be kind enough to ..." begins by addressing negative face wants and rapidly moves on to positive face wants.

The analysis by Brown and Levinson concerning polite conduct of interaction is itself presumptive of some larger grounding features of social life concerning the existence of roles, the pervasiveness of hierarchy, and the importance to the individual of the reaffirmation of self. However, its major contribution is to note that participants in interaction are expected to consider not only their own needs and face wants but also those of the partner. Given that we assume this burden in social interaction and presume that the partner does too, assessments of difficulty are premised in assumptions of failure to observe norms of politeness as well as those of any other larger contextual features, such as workplace ethics.

In the workplace, tasks have to get done irrespective of personal feelings, though of course those feelings can affect not only how but when things get done. In the workplace, interactions are not simply limited to tasks but can be informal, sociable, friendly, and "atmospheric." Someone at work can be seen as an obnoxious person socially but as an excellent colleague at the job and vice versa. Most bosses on television are portrayed this way: difficult, demanding, and obnoxious but nevertheless loyal and supportive of their junior colleagues, including the star of the show who is routinely backed and trusted in eccentric work decisions and rule-breaking despite the boss vehemently objecting at first to the choices made.

Likewise, people at work can be dependent on an obnoxious colleague for productivity or other resources, and so simple reactions and normal social sanctioning may simply not work. Indeed, dynamics of work are not necessarily as simple as they appear. The dynamics of such normative reality are not necessarily self-evident, as they contextualize assessment of power or politeness. Hepburn and Crepin (1984) carried out work on prison guards that indicated that there are complex interdependencies in workplace situations that do not reflect official status. For example, guards are dependent on prisoners for personal safety and also for the reputation that the guards have with their superiors (whether they are seen as competent or incompetent in their performance of the job, for example) as a result of the ways in which prisoners respond to their instructions. A guard who is obnoxious and overreliant on formal power soon finds that informal power and the unstated interdependencies of day-to-day activity are at least as important as any formal power may be.

Therefore, difficulty in relationships is not something that automatically leads to rejection or to unwillingness to work with someone: Its effects must be felt in the performance or quality of the relationship rather than its mere existence. The consequences of difficulty can be both social and task related, but these are two independent registers of difficulty that are not equivalent in effects.

PERSON × PERSON INTERACTION

It is commonly believed that some people simply do not go together and, like chalk and cheese, never will be compatible. Their relationship will always be difficult, especially if external constraints force them toward some common goal—for example, a goal necessitated by working in the same place. Likewise, some relationships appear to be difficult in themselves. It is widely assumed that sibling relationships are difficult (Nicholson, 1998), for example. Some sociobiologists have argued that this is partly a functional difficulty that serves to decrease the incidence of incest (Shepher, 1971; Wolf, 1995).

A contextualized view of relating necessarily simplifies life and gives the fluctuating and inconsistent actions of all of us an apparent consistency that our experience actually belies from moment to moment. People, even "other people," are simply not universally consistent or unproblematically uniform in all interactions. While we do not suggest that there are *no* observable consistencies or monotones in life or other people, we do contend that these flatlines are overstated, and that personality or other personally descriptive terms can be too elastic, when they do not rigidly encompass all of a person's behaviors. A general label, such as "extrovert," simply tells us about the predominance of certain styles of behavior as compared to other behaviors that can also be observed in the self-same person. It does not claim to suggest that all of a person's behavior is always extroverted in every way and indisputably. Hence, difficulty involves an interactive and performative element, where those predominant consistencies of one person rub up against the predominant consistencies of another person is such a way as to make difficulty a result of those two persons' interaction. Jarring and incompatible styles and even a mere (lack of) meshing of persons' interactions can produce difficulty. As Winch (1958) noted nearly 50 years ago, some styles of behavior tend to be incompatible with one another. For example, we could reasonably and intuitively expect that two dominant people would run into difficulties until they had worked out how each could dominate some facets of the joint experiences in ways that allowed the other to control other parts. Likewise, interaction partners may experience *role jarring* (Murstein, 1977), where the performance of relational roles can be carried out by two relational partners in ways that show themselves incompatible, even when the two persons agree on the nature of the roles that each is performing. For example, a husband and the wife need to have relatively interlocked ideas about the ways in which "a husband" and "a wife" should divide their shared labor, or else strife and discord can result.

Although couched in psychological trait terminology, such observations actually stress the *performative* consequences of roles and hence are importantly behavioral, communicative, and processual. In emphasizing these three elements of such abstract concepts as roles and the "difficulty" that arises between roles, our analysis has moved us from the inherency of difficulty to its relativity—or more precisely to its basis in the performance of relating, in the application of social norms rather than in people themselves.

Norms, then, represent a constant ground against which the figure of individual behavior is judged as appropriate or not and hence as difficult or not. Without such grounding norms, the difficulty of socially relevant behaviors cannot be determined. The behavior requires contextualization to be judged, and implicit in our social assessments is that very fact.

Such a point helps explain how different uses of the term *difficulty* can deploy different degrees of social construction, ranging from the level at which two persons can evoke undesirable behavior in one another, right through to the attempt to explain obnoxiousness as not individually, but situationally produced (e.g., cases where competition and aggressiveness are evoked by the requirements and norms of the workplace, rather than by individual preference and desire).

Social networks are integral to the other areas we have delineated. Claiming someone is difficult involves a network of people or culture(s) influencing personal constructs of difficulty. For example, I'm at work. I encounter Wally for the first time. Wally seems gruff. I encounter him for a second time; he comes off as terse. I may go to others in the office and ask, "Is Wally always stand-offish?" The reply may be, "Oh, Wally. He's a real problem. Don't even try to work with him." At that point, Wally gets labeled as "difficult" by me. The result is wholly different if the person in my network says, "Wally's having a bad time this week. He's really a good guy."

Consensus by many Others suggests that something generalizable about a person's behavior is not fitting. Perhaps that is what we mean by "difficult person." However, in order to reach that conclusion we have to consider that criteria for assessing someone as difficult are not personal, but based on context, roles, the perceptual styles of observers, and finally on agreements between several different people about a perceived consistency of performance across situations and persons. Difficulty clearly results when behavior evokes an undesired and inappropriately negative face in the observer, when it is possible to typify the person creating the difficulty and when some moral sanctioning is implied in the label.

What we have in "difficult people," then, is the force of social constraint exercised over individual impulses and preferences. Thus "difficult people" are really exemplary instances of the interaction of the individual and the social, the unfettered individual, and the compulsions of society. The essence of difficulty in relating is therefore better understood as strongly contextualized rather than as an inherent quality of persons or relationships.

ACKNOWLEDGMENT

We are grateful to Brendan Young for his insightful reading of this chapter and for his helpful suggestions and examples.

REFERENCES

Bergmann, J. R. (1993). *Discreet indiscretions: The social organization of gossip.* New York: Aldine de Gruyter.

Brown, P., & Levinson, S. C. (1978). Universals in language usage: Politeness phenomena. In E. E. Goody (Ed.), *Questions and politeness* (pp. 56–289). Cambridge, UK: Cambridge University Press.

Burkitt, I. (1991). *Social selves: Theories of the social formation of personality.* London: Sage.

Davis, M. S., & Schmidt, C. J. (1977). The obnoxious and the nice: Some sociological consequences of two psychological types. *Sociometry, 40*(3), 201–213.

Duck, S. W. (1990). Relationships as unfinished business: Out of the frying pan and into the 1990s. *Journal of Social and Personal Relationships, 7,* 5–29.

Duck, S. W., & VanderVoort, L. A. (2002). Scarlet letters and whited sepulchres: the social marking of relationships as "inappropriate." In R. Goodwin & D. Cramer (Eds.), *Inappropriate relationships: The unconventional, the disapproved, and the forbidden* (pp. 3–24). Mahwah, NJ: Lawrence Erlbaum Associates.

Goffman, E. (1959). *Behaviour in public places*. Harmondsworth, UK: Penguin.

Heider, F. (1958). *The psychology of interpersonal relations*. New York: Wiley.

Hepburn, J. R., & Crepin, A. E. (1984). Relationship strategies in a coercive institution: A study of dependence among prison guards. *Journal of Social and Personal Relationships, 1*, 139–157.

Hollander, E. P. (1958). Conformity, status and idiosyncrasy credit. *Psychological Review, 65*, 117–127.

Jones, E. E., Kanouse, D. E., et al. (1972). *Attribution: Perceiving the causes of behavior*. New York: General Learning Press.

Katriel, T. (1986). *Talking straight: "Dugri" speech in Israeli Sabra culture*. Cambridge, UK: Cambridge University Press.

Kipnis, L. (1998). Adultery. *Critical Inquiry, 24*, 289–327.

Murstein, B. I. (1977). The stimulus-value-role (SVR) theory of dyadic relationships. In S. W. Duck (Ed.), *Theory and practice in interpersonal attraction* (pp. 105–107). London: Academic Press.

Nicholson, J. H. (1998). Sibling alliances: Joining forces in the family. *Communication Studies*. Iowa City: University of Iowa.

Ross, L. (1977). The intuitive psychologist and his shortcomings: Distortions in the attribution process. *Advances in Experimental Social Psychology, 10*, 173–220.

Seve, L. (1969). *Marxism and theory of the personality*. Hemel Hempstead, UK: Harvester.

Shepher, J. (1971). Mate selection among second generation kibbutz adolescents and adults: Incest avoidance and negative imprinting. *Archives of Sexual Behavior, 1*(4), 12–23.

Shotter, J. (1992). What is a "personal" relationship? A rhetorical-responsive account of "unfinished business." In J. H. Harvey, T. L. Orbuch, & A. Weber (Eds.), *Attributions, accounts and close relationships* (pp. 19–39). New York: Springer-Verlag.

Vardi, Y., & Weitz, E. (2004). *Misbehavior in organizations: Theory, research and management*. Mahwah, NJ: Lawrence Erlbaum Associates.

Warr, P. B., & Knapper, C. (1968). *The perception of people and events*. Chichester, UK: Wiley.

Watson, D. (2000). *Mood and temperament*. New York: Guilford.

Winch, R. F. (1958). *Mate selection: A study in complementary needs*. New York: Harper & Row.

Wolf, A. P. (1995). *Sexual attraction and childhood association: A Chinese brief for Edward Westermarck*. Stanford, CA: Stanford University Press.

Chapter 2

Shyness and Difficult Relationships: Formation Is Just the Beginning

Scott D. Bradshaw
Elizabeth City State University

> I ain't too good at conversation, girl,
> So you might not know exactly how I feel,
> But if I could, I'd bring you to the mountaintop, girl,
> And build you a house made out of stainless steel.
> But it's like I'm stuck inside a painting
> That's hanging in the Louvre,
> My throat starts to tickle and my nose itches
> But I know that I can't move.
> > *Don't Fall Apart on Me Tonight*
> > —Bob Dylan

Therein lies the dilemma for shy persons. In order to form, develop, and maintain a relationship, they must engage in an open conversation with their relationship partner so as to reveal their feelings, desires, and interests. Relationships are realized and enacted in the process of conversation (Duck & Pond, 1989). The shy person is aware of this need, but is also keenly aware of the potential costs inherent in revealing feelings, desires, and interests and so the shy person is "stuck." It therefore seems appropriate to include a chapter on shyness in a book on difficult relationships, because for shy persons, all relationships are difficult.

Of course, relationships involve more than one person. If the shy person is stuck and not discussing feelings or desires, it is more difficult for the partner to do so. The opportunity to communicate about one's self is an important provision we gain from relationships (Weiss, 1974). If that opportunity is not provided, dissatisfaction with the relationship is a likely outcome which may lead the relationship partner to feel at risk of emotionally "falling apart."

This chapter will review and discuss research on shyness at different stages and in different types of relationships. However, as research has focused on social and romantic relationships, so too will our discussion.

WHAT IS A DIFFICULT RELATIONSHIP?

The fact that we are talking about difficult relationships implies that we believe there are easy relationships. If we view easy and difficult relationships as being different ends of a continuum, then perhaps we could derive a working definition of a "difficult" relationship by first conceiving of an idealized, "easy" relationship. In this conceptualization, the distinction between easy and difficult relationships would be a difference in quantity (as the number of difficulties increases, the more likely the relationship is to be considered by at least one partner as a difficult one). It is also possible that the distinction between easy and difficult is a qualitative one, wherein there is some characteristic or set of characteristics that separate the two. The question of which conceptualization is correct is an empirical one. The working definitions of easy and difficult relationships discussed below assume that the difference is one of quantity. The possibility that the difference is one of quality is discussed later in the chapter.

It should be realized that any such definitions are, at least in part, culturally defined. Montgomery (1988) discussed how our social ideology shapes our definitions of easy or good relationships and leads us to conduct research to test the assumptions derived from our social ideology. According to Montgomery, in Western culture, modern researchers have typically assumed that the more communication between partners the better. Communication, in turn, is assumed to lead to increased intimacy, which allows the partners to be in control of their relationship. Increased levels of intimacy and control, like communication, are assumed to be positive goals. Researchers, then, have focused their efforts on largely confirming these assumptions. The idealized easy relationship discussed next follows in this tradition by being based on those assumptions and supported by the research largely conducted to test them.

In our idealized easy relationship, before the meeting, the two future relationship partners would be mentally healthy, happy, outgoing people without any severe personal problems or difficulties (Kenrick, Groth, Trost, & Sadalla, 1993). The relationship partners would come together and quickly determine through open discussion, with little concern about any emotional risk or anxiety, their common interests, attraction, and desires for the relationship (e.g., Bowers, Metts, & Duncanson, 1985; Byrne, Clore, & Smeaton, 1986; Caspi & Herbener, 1990). Conflicts would be openly discussed, changes made where possible or desired, and the relationship would strengthen. Any conflicts that later arose in the relationship would be dealt with in the same manner. If the relationship partners felt the need or desire for change in the relationship, they would openly discuss those desires, either strengthening or dissolving the relationship, and the changes would occur at a mutually agreed on pace for each person (Noller & Feeney, 2002). The partners would get exactly what they wanted from the relationship, with all relationship-related behaviors directed toward the mutual benefit of both partners. Partners would naturally take the feelings, desires, and needs of the other relationship partner into account. Each relationship partner would have a social network that would provide a source for social support and other resources adaptive for relationships (Sprecher, Felmlee, Orbuch, & Willetts, 2002). The relationships with other social network members would be managed so that challenges to the relationship would be minimized and, in sum, the contributions from other relationships in the social network would be positive. Outside pressures or conflicts, such as work-related stressors, would be managed through discussion between the relationship partners.

If that is an idealized easy relationship, then a paradigmatic difficult relationship would be marked by a lack of those various qualities. Relationship partners' ratings of relationship difficulties would vary depending on the type and number of qualities the relationship lacked, as well as by how strongly they deviated from the ideal. For example, a person who never remembers anniversaries or other special dates would not be taking the feelings, desires, and needs of the relationship partner into account. This would be perceived by one of the partners as creating a certain amount of difficulty in the relationship. However, a physically abusive spouse would also be lacking the same quality, but would be creating a much more difficult relationship. How much difficulty does shyness create in a relationship? While there are certainly characteristics and behaviors that create more difficulty in relationships than does shyness, the reviewed research will show that shyness does create difficulty and that difficulty will affect all stages of the relationship, extending far beyond simply the formative stage of the relationship.

SHYNESS DEFINED

Shyness is defined as a dispositional tendency to experience feelings of anxiety and to exhibit behavioral inhibition in social situations (Cheek & Melchior, 1990). These effects are most pronounced in new or unfamiliar situations with strangers, but can arise in any situation where one perceives that one is being evaluated and social acceptance is a concern (Leary & Buckley, 2000). Moreover, shy persons tend to view all social interactions as inherently evaluative and tend to expect the results of those evaluations to be negative (Goldfried, Padawar, & Robbins, 1984). Casual relationships typically involve new acquaintances where the shy person is uncertain of the appropriate behaviors to create a positive impression in the relationship partner. By engaging in only the appropriate behaviors, the shy person can avoid self-disclosure and the negative evaluation that is expected to follow. Close relationships, on the other hand, require levels of intimacy and self-disclosure that can leave the shy person feeling extremely vulnerable and at risk of being negatively evaluated. The shy person's attempts to cope with the anxiety felt in these situations results in the behaviors associated with shyness. These coping behaviors, how they are displayed in various types of situations and in different types of relationships at different stages in those relationships, will be discussed in this chapter. Many of these coping behaviors result in behaviors that are contrary to those described in the idealized easy relationship.

While shyness will create difficulty for the person attempting to form, develop, and maintain relationships, it will also create difficulty for the other person in the relationship. The potential romantic relationship partner may be unable to find the level of self-disclosure from the shy person to either satisfy their relationship expectations or to create the level of intimacy he or she desires. Further, the shy person may not actively facilitate the self-disclosure of the potential romantic relationship partner. These problems may be exacerbated when both relationship partners are shy.

It is important to remember throughout this chapter as we discuss "shy persons" and the "effects of shyness" on behavior, that we are using these phrases or terms as shorthand to simplify the discussion of what are very complex behaviors and interrelationships among a variety of different variables. Persons who may be described as shy will differ in the degree or extent of their shyness and, as a result, the degree or extent of the effects on their behavior and relationships will also differ. Further, while the same kinds of situations will typically generate anxiety for all persons categorized as shy, the specific details or aspects of those situations (e.g., size of the group, familiarity with the partner, topic discussed, face-to-face vs. telephone, etc.) that maximize the anxiety generated will differ among persons. Research has largely examined differences between shy and not-shy persons, rather than examining differences between those described as shy. As research on shyness moves from reporting simple correlations to studying effects in complex personal relationships, these differences become more important.

I will now review and discuss research on shyness at different stages of various types of relationships. First, I will consider the shy person as an individual before entering into a new relationship, and then examine the formation stage of both social and work-oriented relationships. This will be represented by research on first-meeting dyads and laboratory-created work groups. Discussion will then turn to research examining long-term and ongoing relationships. As each stage is discussed, we will consider how the behaviors associated with the shy person at that stage makes the relationship difficult for the shy person and their relationship partner. Finally, we will attempt to find common threads between the difficulties in relationships created by shyness and difficulties in other difficult relationships. While shyness has been extensively studied, the connection between shyness and difficult relationships has not been. In some cases, further research will be necessary in order to fully determine the connection between shyness and difficult relationships. These opportunities for additional research will be noted.

SHYNESS: THE INDIVIDUAL

Relationships would likely be much easier if all of us were self-actualized; however, few of us are (Maslow, 1954). In any relationship, personal or emotional issues can affect the nature of the relationship, can threaten its long-term stability, and can lead to the relationship being defined as a difficult one. In the case of shyness, there are a number of associated behaviors, personality traits, and characteristics that can create difficulties in relationships. Shyness is correlated with low self-esteem, higher levels of depression, and higher levels of loneliness (Gough & Thorne, 1986). In fact, the pattern of attributions shown by shy persons in social situations is very similar to that of depressed persons (Johnson, Petzel, & Johnson, 1991). Shy people, as compared to not-shy people, also display a wide-ranging tendency to rate characteristics of themselves and others more negatively (Cheek & Melchior, 1990).

For the shy person, social anxiety is the biggest obstacle to establishing a relationship: the other associated characteristics simply amplify that difficulty. Given that people tend to be attracted to positive, happy, outgoing others, these characteristics would appear to put the shy person at a great disadvantage. For example, Burgoon and Koper (1984) had shy persons interact for 9 minutes with a friend and 9 minutes with a stranger. The verbal and nonverbal behaviors of the shy persons were largely the same between the two interactions. However, the strangers interpreted the behaviors as negative and hostile, whereas the friends did not. Essentially, the shy persons' fears that others will perceive them negatively appear to be realistic ones. Further, unlike the mentally healthy partners in the idealized easy relationship, the shy member(s) of the relationship will import other challenges. How does all of this affect the shy person during the first interactions with a new acquaintance? The majority of research on shyness has focused on this particular question.

SHYNESS: RELATIONSHIP FORMATION

In considering the anxiety that shy persons tend to experience when entering, or preparing to enter, social situations, one is reminded of the old joke about the man going to the physician complaining of pain when he holds his arm in a certain position. The physician advises,

"Stop holding your arm in that position." Why doesn't the shy person simply stop entering social situations? Researchers have repeatedly made a distinction between the inhibited behavior shown in social interactions by shy persons and the desire to engage in social interactions. For example, Cheek and Buss (1981), in developing their Shyness scale, established sociability as a separate construct and went on to find that the negative effects of shyness were greatest for those high in both shyness and sociability. While research has not been consistent in supporting this interaction between shyness and sociability (e.g., Arkin & Grove, 1990), shyness has been often conceptualized as an approach-avoidance conflict (e.g., Arkin, Lake, & Baumgardner, 1986; Cheek & Melchior, 1990; Schlenker & Leary, 1982). For example, research on shyness and adult attachment styles has found that shyness is correlated with both the "Fearful" attachment style—anxiety regarding and hesitancy in entering relationships—and the "Preoccupied" attachment style—marked by striving for the acceptance of others—but not correlated with the "Dismissing" attachment style—marked by a complete avoidance of relationships (Bartholomew & Horowitz, 1991; Duggan & Brennan, 1994).

How do shy persons cope with their anxiety when entering new social situations? Research has typically examined this question by placing shy persons in situations with strangers, often in get-acquainted dyads and sometimes in task-oriented groups. Not-shy persons, when placed in such situations, tend to engage in a process of positive self-presentation and attempt to maximize the positive impression they create in the other person. Shy persons, on the other hand, tend to adopt a strategy of protective self-presentation (Arkin et al., 1986). Instead of attempting to maximize the positive impression they create in the other person, the shy persons attempt to prevent a negative impression of the self from being formed. While this pattern of behavior will minimize the potential cost of a negative impression, it also tends to minimize the likelihood of gaining any potential benefits of a positive impression. This pattern of self-presentation will have specific effects in different relationship situations. The two discussed here are social relationships and task-oriented relationships.

Social Relationships

In first-meeting, get-acquainted situations, shy people, as compared to the not-shy, tend to interact minimally, appear nervous (to observers and their interaction partners), confine the majority of their talk to nonpersonal questions, acknowledgments ("uh-huh"), and confirmations ("I think so, too"), report more discomfort and anxiety, evaluate their own performance negatively, and tend to be evaluated negatively by their interaction partners (Cheek & Buss, 1981; Garcia, Stinson, Ickes, Bissonnette, & Briggs, 1991; Leary, Knight, & Johnson, 1987;

Pilkonis, 1977). These effects are most pronounced for persons with higher levels of shyness. While shy persons interact minimally, it is important to realize that they are anything but passive. Part of what makes relationship formation difficult for shy persons is that they are attempting to interact, but are frustrated in their attempts, in part because they tend to doubt their social abilities and expect their efforts to fail (DePaulo, Kenny, Hoover, Webb, & Oliver, 1987).

For example, Garcia et al. (1991) examined the effects of shyness and physical attractiveness on opposite-sex dyadic interactions among new acquaintances. They found that high-shy men initiated just as many mutual gazes with their interaction partners as did the not-shy men, but the gazes were significantly shorter in duration. The high-shy men were initiating gazes, but, when the women started to return the gaze, they looked away.

Another example of frustration created by shyness in these dyadic interactions, both for the shy person and the relationship partner, was found in a study by Manning and Ray (1993). They examined conversational patterns of high-shy and low/not-shy participants in dyadic interactions. High-shy participants, who were strangers to one another, were paired and asked to engage in a conversation so as to get to know one another. The majority of the shy participants' behavior was consistent with previous research, with many silences and little actual conversation as compared to the low-shy participants.

Surprisingly, Manning and Ray found a small group of shy participants for which this pattern did not hold. In these dyads, the interaction was, at first, typical of shy participants until a particular topic, which differed by dyad, was touched on. In one example described by the researchers, two participants happened on a shared interest in the nursing program. It appeared that one was a nursing major while the other was trying to get into the program. At this point the participants began an "enthusiastic" discussion of the nursing program that Manning and Ray described as being more than simply "normal": "Both participants displayed an *exaggerated* commitment to the topic, over and above the expected requirements for casual talk between strangers. It is as if too much personal identity can be detected" (Manning & Ray, 1993, p. 187, emphasis in original).

The authors referred to these topics as "favored topics." The enthusiastic conversation, however, occurred only when the participants were discussing the favored topic. When the conversation changed to some other topic, the conversation once again became awkward and consistent with the typical pattern of shy participants. As with the situation described in Garcia et al. (1991), one can imagine the frustration in the situation for both the shy participants and the interaction partners.

Unlike the idealized easy relationship, the initial meeting between potential relationship partners is hardly an open and free discussion. It is easy to imagine from these results how shyness makes relationship formation difficult for the shy person, especially a person who is severely shy. They make repeated attempts to foster a conversation, as seen in Garcia et al. (1991), using strategies which should be effective, but the results are not as desired. When they do happen into a conversation that is fully engaging, as seen in Manning and Ray (1993), it only lasts for a short period of time and only on a particular topic. They seem unable to continue the interaction and to generalize successfully to other topics or over time. The extent of these effects, as discussed previously, will differ depending on the shyness level of the individual.

For the interaction partner, the difficulty in establishing a relationship is also clear. In the case of a not-shy partner, behaviors that usually result in a full and engaged interaction lead to little response from their shy partner. While the shy partner may reciprocate the behaviors, the reciprocation tends to be less than would be expected or would be considered socially appropriate. Self-disclosure, which is key to the development of a relationship, is largely absent. This is not surprising when one considers that the shy partner expects the disclosure of personal information to result in a negative evaluation. It is difficult to get to know someone who will not provide personal information. Even more frustrating, the shy person may suddenly begin to engage in an enthusiastic conversation when some specific topic is discussed, which may be seen as overly enthusiastic and inappropriate. This more fully engaged interaction, however, is relatively temporary. In the case of a shy partner, the interaction never gets off the ground. It would seem unlikely that these relationships would develop beyond the initial interaction unless there was something that led the potential relationship partners to remain together, such as mutual physical attraction, mutual friends, perhaps a shared favored topic, or shared tasks (classmates, coworkers). It is to one such factor, task–oriented relationships, that I next turn.

Task-Oriented Relationships

Businesses and other organizations increasingly rely on task- and decision-making groups. Central to the effectiveness of these groups is the sharing and discussion of task-related information (Forsyth, 1998). Given the tendency for shy persons to inhibit their behavior in social situations, one would expect shy persons to have difficulty in such groups and, potentially, to adversely affect the performance of those groups. Research has generally confirmed those expectations.

Camacho and Paulus (1995) examined the effects of shyness on four-person, interacting brainstorming groups composed of all not-shy members, all shy members, and mixed groups with two members of each type. They found that shy members experienced more nervousness and anxiety while interacting in the group, and, as a result, groups with all shy members generated significantly fewer ideas than groups will all not-shy members. Other research has replicated these findings in brainstorming groups where the group members generated their ideas separately (Bradshaw, Stasson, & Alexander, 1999). Camacho and Paulus (1995) also found that the behavior of the shy members affected the not-shy members. In the mixed groups, the not-shy members reduced their performance to match the performance of shy members, resulting in the mixed brainstorming groups generating significantly fewer ideas than the not-shy groups. The mixed-group members' feelings regarding their group's reduced performance was not assessed.

Zimbardo and Linsenmeier (1983) similarly examined the performance, behaviors, and perceptions of four-person decision-making groups, physically separated, who communicated via intercom or computer-based "chat." The shy participants talked significantly less, expressed fewer emotions, offered fewer solutions, and, when they did offer solutions, did so less assertively. The other group members were also less likely to view the shy members as leaders. Groups composed entirely of shy members made less effective decisions.

It appears from these studies that the difficulties experienced by shy people in task-oriented groups are essentially the same as those in social relationships. While the cited studies have not generally considered perceptions of specific group members, it would seem likely that the reduced participation of the shy group members would generate similar negative evaluations to those found in the dyadic, social relationship interactions. One important difference between task-oriented groups and social relationships concerns the effects of shy members on group performance. Unlike social relationships, task-oriented relationships have an expressed goal for which it is possible to determine success or failure. The previously cited research found that shy members adversely affected the performance of the groups of which they were part; however, neither study examined how the outcome of group performance affected the group members. Group satisfaction and cohesion can suffer in response to poor group performance. The attributions that group members make for their group's performance are especially important in determining members' later behavior and the relationships within the group. The relationship between shyness and attributions for group performance was examined by Bradshaw and Stasson (1998).

Bradshaw and Stasson (1998) presented small groups (3–6 persons) with a decision-making task. After the groups interacted on the task for 10 minutes, the groups were given false success or failure feedback and were asked to make an attribution for their group's performance and answer a series of questions about themselves and their group. Not-shy members tended to make group-serving attributions, attributing the cause of success to qualities of the group and their interactions and attributing failure to aspects of the situation. The shy members, on the other hand, minimized their personal responsibility for both group success and failure. This attribution seems reasonable considering the shy members' self-reported reduced participation in the group discussion. However, the shy members did not attribute the cause of success to the other group members, as the not-shy members had done; rather, they attributed the cause of group success equally to the group members and to the situation. The most striking difference was for attributions for failure. The shy members attributed the cause of group failure not to the situation, or to themselves (for their reduced participation), but to the other group members themselves.

The shy and not-shy members also differed in their perceptions of their own and their group's performance. Shy members, as compared to the not-shy members, rated their own contribution to the group as less important than the contributions of the other group members, reported more dissatisfaction with their performance and the performance of their group, were more likely to report withholding ideas and comments from the group, and identified less with their group's decision. Group success tends to create positive affect for group members. While this pattern was found for not-shy group members, the shy members' affect was not influenced by either the success or failure feedback.

Bradshaw and Stasson (1998) characterized the shy members as isolated within the group: taking part in the group activities, but not adopting the group identity as the other members did. While the research did not consider how group members perceived the other individuals in their groups, one could easily imagine how the attitudes and behaviors of the shy members could create difficulty for the other group members. Given the tendency for persons to make less egoistic attributions when those attributions will be made public (Miller & Schlenker, 1985), it is unlikely that the attribution concerning the causes of group success or failure would be made public by the shy member; however, the lack of positive affect after group success would be noticed. If the shy member has less of a sense of group cohesion than the not-shy members, then one would expect this pattern of behavior to affect long-term occupational success.

The not-shy group members are confronted with a member who does not fully participate in the group, yet they must work with the shy member in order to be successful. In terms of the idealized easy relationship, the fellow group member needs to contribute to the group product or the member is not working in a manner which benefits the group. As noted by Zimbardo and Linsenmeier (1983), inequity of group contributions over time could have severe consequences for group cohesion and performance, and affect both the low and high contributors. This pattern of behavior may change as the group develops; however, research has not examined how the behavior of shy group members changes over time.

The issue of change over time is one that confronts almost all of the research discussed to this point. They have all examined small groups or dyads, be they task-oriented or social, together only for the duration of a laboratory experiment. How do these initial effects of shyness play themselves out over time? A number of longer term and longitudinal studies have attempted to answer this question.

Long-Term Consequences

Change is a constant. This also means that the demands and stressors of change are also constants. How we cope with change goes a long way in determining the events of our lives and the long-term success of our relationships. Each person has unique characteristics and traits and some of these will help manage and cope with changes, while others will hinder this process. One of the resources that we call on to help us manage and cope with change is our relationships. Given the pattern of behavior described to this point for the shy person, if the pattern continues, one would expect shy persons to have a difficult time coping with changes and fewer resources in the form of relationships to help in the process. Research has generally supported this expectation.

The shy person's cautious pattern of interacting, protective self-presentation, described in both the dyadic interactions and the decision-making groups, is not limited to initial interactions in a lab setting. Langston and Cantor (1989) studied how this cautious interaction style affected students adapting to college over a 3-year period. Initial measures were completed by 147 participants during the fall and spring semesters of their first year. These measures assessed both academic and social domains, and included measures of satisfaction, perceived stress, and GPA (grade point average). A smaller sample of the students completed a similar measure during the spring semester of their second year. Also during the second year, 67 of the participants were interviewed for a total of 2 hours to determine their satisfaction with college, their goals, and their strategies for dealing with the typical problems and challenges they faced in their lives. Finally, a telephone interview was completed with all of the participants during the second semester of their third year which focused on life satisfaction, academic outcomes, and psychological and physical health outcomes.

Participants, during their first semester of their first year in college, were presented with a questionnaire containing a listing of different life tasks that the participants would need to perform during their time in college. These tasks were categorized as either achievement oriented (e.g., getting good grades) or interpersonal (e.g., making friends). Participants rated the life tasks on a variety of dimensions, including importance to them, their perceived ability to successfully perform the task, how much time and effort they expected to spend on the task, and how much stress the task would likely create for them. A cluster analysis of these data revealed a group of students high in social anxiety who expressed more negative evaluations on the interpersonal-related life tasks. The researchers found that the students who were identified with high levels of social anxiety performed just as well as the other students on measures of academic performance. However, the socially anxious students over the 3 years in college reported more anxiety and nervousness, lower social satisfaction, and more health problems, such as sleep disturbances and nausea.

Because the main focus of the study was to determine how students coped with the transition into and changes throughout college, the researchers interviewed the students to determine the strategies the students used for dealing with those changes. There was a tendency for the socially anxious participants to report using a protective, avoidant manner (e.g., hoping problems would go away) as opposed to a direct manner involving talking about and attempting to confront the problem. These socially anxious participants also were more likely to report that their family dynamics discouraged the open discussion of feelings and beliefs. One of the aspects of our idealized easy relationship was that the relationship members openly discussed and dealt with change adaptively. It would appear that the management of change is another area where shyness creates difficulty in a relationship. The researchers did not specifically assess the quality of the participants' relationships, but one can imagine there would be difficulties in the shy/socially anxious participants' relationships.

Asendorpf and Wilpers (1998; see also Asendorpf, 2002) also examined the adaptation of students to college in an effort to understand the effects of personality on relationships and relationship formation. Approximately 132 students participated over their first 18 months at a Berlin university. The students completed a measure of general personality as well as measures of shyness and sociability every 6 months during the study term. Relationship measures were completed at the same time and included assessments of the number of personally important persons in their social network, how often they interacted with these persons, the amount of conflict, and the amount of support they perceived as available from this social network. In addition, the students indicated whether or not they were falling in love with member(s) of their social network. The shy students' social networks increased at a significantly slower rate than did the not-shy students. The researchers noted that it took the shy students 15 months to achieve the same increase in their social networks as the not-shy students had after 3 months. The shy students also reported interacting less with members of their social network and reported less available support from opposite-sex members of the social network. Given these results, it is not surprising that the shy students were significantly less likely to report falling in love during the 18 months of the study. There were no shyness-related differences in the amount of conflict the students reported in their relationships. The researchers did not examine the perceptions of members of the students' social networks. How the difficult person in a difficult relationship is viewed by the relationship partner would be an important area to examine in future research on both shyness and other types or causes of difficult relationships.

These studies have found evidence of the difficulties created by shyness in coping with change, including having a smaller social network and less available social support. These studies have dealt with change only during the first few years of college. Several studies have considered the effects of shyness over the life span.

Caspi, Elder, and Bem (1988) reanalyzed data from the Berkeley Guidance Study, which followed a group of approximately 182 children born in 1928 and 1929 to examine the effect of shyness on life-course patterns. Shyness was assessed at three main points during the study. Initial assessments of shyness were made based on interviews with the mothers of the children between the ages of 8 and 10 (years 1936–1938). These ratings of shyness were then compared to teacher ratings of shyness between the ages of 10 and 12, and adult self-reports of shyness gathered from interviews at approximately age 30 (year 1960) and 40 (years 1968–1971). The researchers found strong correlations between the three assessments of shyness, which clearly shows the stability of this individual difference.

The researchers also looked at the effects of shyness on the timing of various life events. Caspi et al. suggest that experiencing life events, like marriage or childbirth, out-of-sync with the norms for one's particular society or culture would reduce the amount of social support available for those transitions (e.g., adjustment problems for older students returning to college). Because of the reduced social support, if there are differences in the timing of life events due to shyness, then this could be another source of difficulty in relationships. Further, one could also imagine problems created simply by perceiving one's self as different, or less capable, than others (e.g., "The people I graduated with have been promoted and have families. What's wrong with me?").

Men who as children were rated as shy married and entered stable careers on average 3 years later than those rated as not-shy. These effects for shyness were found even when taking various other demographic and socioeconomic variables into account. Because of the delayed entry into stable careers, the shy children also had lower occupational achievement (e.g., lower status occupations at the same age) and lower job stability.

For women, shyness was also found to be a stable individual difference; however, there were no differences related to shyness with regard to the age of first marriage. The authors suggested this might be due to traditional sex roles, including the obligation for men to take the lead in romantic relationship behaviors, which predominated in the 1940s and 1950s. The effects of traditional sex roles could also be seen in the assessment of occupational status where the majority of women did not pursue, or were not allowed to pursue, careers in the same way that was expected of men. Women who as children were rated as shy worked significantly less than did those rated as not-shy (6.25 years of work vs. 9.41 years between the ages of 18 and 40) and were more likely to quit work on marriage or childbirth. Essentially, the shy women were significantly more likely to conform to the social norms of the day.

Kerr, Lambert, and Bem (1996) conducted a conceptual replication of Caspi et al. (1988) using a Swedish sample of 90 girls and 122 boys that have been followed from birth in the years 1955 to 1958. Participants were assessed yearly until age 16, with follow-ups conducted at age 25 and 35. Childhood shyness was assessed using ratings by their mothers each year between the ages of 8 and 10. Shyness was again assessed at age 35 using Buss' measure of shyness (Buss, 1980).

Consistent with the findings of Caspi et al. (1988), ratings of childhood shyness predicted self-reported shyness in adulthood. During the follow-up, done at age 35, participants completed a measure of shyness and provided information on their own education, employment, income, and family. Shy women, as compared to not-shy women, evidenced significantly lower levels of education. For example, while 44% of the not-shy women earned college degrees, none of the shy women did. This difference was not caused by the timing of marriage or childbirth, as these were not related to shyness level, nor was it related to the socioeconomic status of the women's family. This difference in education was not found for shy men; however, shy men married, on average, 4 years later than did not-shy men.

Researchers are continuing to follow this sample, and Moller and Stattin (2001) have utilized it to examine the effects of adolescent relationships, both with parents and peers, on satisfaction with romantic partner relationships at an average age of 37. As with Kerr et al. (1996), shyness was assessed from ratings by the children's mothers; however, Moller and Stattin (2001) used ratings conducted between ages 14 and 16. During interviews, the mothers were asked whether their children were "often shy with other teenagers" and responded using a 5-point scale from "never" to "always." In addition to this somewhat limited assessment of shyness, the children, at age 15, completed a 65-item measure that assessed their concerns regarding heterosexual relationships. While some of the items addressed specific components of sexual relationships (e.g., unwanted pregnancy), others appeared to be more generally related to shyness (e.g., feeling nervous around the opposite sex, concerns that others would make fun of them). How were these measures related to satisfaction with romantic partner relationships at mid-life? Adolescents rated shy by their mothers between ages 14 and 16 were less satisfied with their romantic partner relationships in adulthood. Additionally, girls, but not boys, who reported more concerns about heterosexual relationships at age 15 were also less satisfied with their adult relationships.

Is the reduced relationship satisfaction reported by shy persons related to the out-of-sync life transitions, frustrations with reduced levels of career success, or to other variables not assessed? It is also possible for this to simply be an artifact caused by the tendency for shy persons to rate a variety of things more negatively than others (Cheek & Melchior, 1990). Unfortunately, as noted previously, research has not focused specifically on the question of shyness and difficult relationships. The cited longitudinal and life-span studies identify the problems related to shyness, but they largely, except for Langston and

Cantor (1989), do not establish how shyness causes or contributes to those problems.

The pattern of protective self-presentation described to this point for shy persons suggests that they are unlikely to openly discuss the problems and challenges created by change, particularly if discussing those problems and challenges would reveal a weakness to the other person, and that could certainly be a main contributor to the problems identified. However, the cited research has not looked more directly at the nature and dynamics of ongoing relationships involving one or more shy persons. It is to this line of research that we next turn.

SHYNESS: ONGOING RELATIONSHIPS

The vast majority of the research on shyness has considered its effects during the formation stage of relationships and groups with relatively little focus on its effects in stable relationships. This is related, at least in part, to the belief that the effects of shyness largely disappear once the person is in a stable relationship. The evidence reviewed demonstrates that this is not the case, and, further, it appears to be based on an oversimplification of the nature of relationships.

While a relationship may be stable, in that it has been in existence for some time, the relationship itself is always changing. The changes can come from outside forces, such as changes in job status; changes within the relationship, such as the addition of children; or from within the person, such as age-related biological changes as evidenced by the recent spate of products aimed at addressing erectile dysfunction. Any one of these changes could alter the relationship between the partners and, in dealing with those changes, create a risk of embarrassment or loss of status for a relationship member (Leary & Buckley, 2000). It is the process of how the relationship partners respond to and cope with these changes which will determine the continuation of the relationship. It is also where shyness can have its most direct effects on relationship difficulty.

How does shyness influence the processes of responding to and coping with change in existing relationships? Unfortunately, this will have to be the subject of further study because the research is largely silent on this question. We will examine the shyness research that pertains to stable, or at least ongoing, relationships: friendship ratings, utilization of the social network for coping, and sexual relationships.

Friendship Ratings

Jones and Carpenter (1986) conducted a series of studies examining shyness in the context of ongoing relationships. Specifically, the studies examined relationships between shyness and relationship satisfaction, social support, and shyness in friendships. Consistent with the other research discussed in this chapter, the shy participants reported less relationship satisfaction and higher levels of loneliness across four different types of relationships: romantic, platonic friendship, family, and community.

In another study, Jones and Carpenter (1986) presented shy participants with a list of 20 qualities of being a friend and asked them to list for each quality whether they had a same-sex friend, opposite-sex friend, or both same-sex and opposite-sex friends who displayed or provided that quality for them. Not surprisingly, shy participants were more likely to report not having friends that satisfied particular dimensions. Most typically, the authors noted that the unsatisfied dimensions related to intimacy and esteem needs. Somewhat counter to the findings that shyness has stronger effects in opposite-sex romantic interactions, shy participants were more likely to report having opposite-sex friends who met the various dimensions than same-sex friends. Further, in several studies, shy persons were rated by members of their social networks, including family members and friends. Like research with strangers, the shy persons were rated more negatively by members of their social networks than were not-shy persons.

Shy participants were also found to have smaller social networks and to report receiving less social support from their networks. It is not clear from the research whether this reflects their ineffectiveness at widening the group or because of satisfaction with a smaller number of more intense relationships. However, given the higher levels of loneliness also reported by the shy participants, it appears somewhat likely that the smaller social networks were not by choice. Interestingly, while the shy participants' social networks were smaller, they had a higher percentage of friends whom they had known for more than five years. This would suggest that while shyness creates difficulty in relationships, it is not the type or degree of difficulty that prevents the shy person from maintaining at least some long-term relationships.

Shyness, in contrast to creating difficulty in a relationship, may also present certain benefits or positive qualities, as pointed out in research by Gough and Thorne (1986). Shyness is typically conceptualized from a deficit-model perspective (e.g., What does the shy person lack or do poorly?) rather than from a diversity-model perspective (e.g., What does the shy person do differently?). As noted by Gough and Thorne (1986), while it is possible to define shyness in negative terms with adjectives like anxious, awkward, and silent, it can also be defined in more positive terms with adjectives like modest, tactful, and sensitive. Using the Adjective Checklist, the researchers created measures of shyness that represented the typical negative conceptualization of shyness, a positive conceptualization of shyness, or a balanced conceptualization and then had others who differed in relationship to the shy person (strangers, peers, spouses) rate the shy person using those scales. The stronger the existing relationship, the more positive the shy person was rated. The most positive ratings were made by the spouses or romantic relationship partners, whereas the most negative ratings were made by strangers who interacted with the shy person only in an interview situation. These results are largely consistent with those of Burgoon and Koper (1984) discussed earlier. Unfortunately, the researchers did not examine issues related to relationship satisfaction or behavioral patterns within the relationship.

This study does raise an interesting question regarding difficult relationships. Perhaps there is a certain degree of tension created between the benefits of a particular relationship (the positive characteristics of shyness) and the difficulties or costs presented by that relationship (the negative characteristics of shyness). If there were only benefits, then the relationship would be ideal. If there were only costs, then there would be no relationship. The positive characteristics of shyness Gough and Thorne (1986) described may be what actually allow the difficult relationships to exist; otherwise, the shy persons might not be in relationships at all. From this perspective, the distinction between easy and difficult relationships would be qualitative, rather than the quantitative. This possibility is discussed further in the section on common threads between shyness and difficult relationships in general.

Shyness, Friends, and Coping

Shy persons in relationships are still shy persons. Social situations, particularly with strangers, will continue to produce anxiety and inhibition. How do they cope with this anxiety?

Sheppard and Arkin (1990) have suggested that shy persons may regulate their environments in ways to create situations which reduce their anxiety and inhibition to allow them to interact more fully. One way to do this would be to limit interactions to one's existing social network. For example, Arkin and Grove (1990) had college students complete measures of shyness and sociability and then, later in the semester, complete a survey concerning the person with whom they ate lunch the day before. The reported behaviors of the shy participants was not related to their level of sociability. Shy participants tended to have known their lunch partner for a significantly longer time than had not-shy participants. Further, the shy participants were more likely to have planned the lunch date in advance, as opposed to it being the result of a spontaneous, spur of the moment, meeting. Likely as a result, there were no significant differences between the shy and not-shy participants on how stressful or anxiety-provoking they perceived the interaction to be. While their feelings of anxiety were reduced, the shy persons still rated the interactions as less effective, less enjoyable, and less successful than did the not-shy persons. Unfortunately, the researchers did not assess the perceptions of the lunch partners. While these meetings may be intended for the mutual enjoyment and benefit of both relationship partners, which would be true in our idealized, easy relationship, one could easily imagine a situation where the shy relationship partners pressured the other to satisfy their own need or desire (e.g., "Please come to lunch with me again tomorrow; I don't like to eat alone."). In this way, a behavior, such as eating lunch together, which on the surface appears to be a positive component of the relationship, could actually be leading to the relationship being conceptualized by the partner as difficult.

In the hypothesized situation above, the shy person is using a member of the social network to help cope with social anxiety and making this process a part of the relationship itself. This has been referred to by Bradshaw (1998) as the Social Surrogate hypothesis. Bradshaw (1998), building on Hobfoll's (Hobfoll & Stokes, 1988) theory of the processes and mechanics of social support, hypothesized that shy persons would utilize relationship partners and other members of their social networks (the social surrogates) to engage in or facilitate social interactions they find anxiety-provoking. The provided assistance could vary from simply being present during the interaction (e.g., going with the shy person while they talk to a professor), to actively facilitating interactions (e.g., shy person stays with the social surrogate throughout a party only interacting with others through the surrogate), to engaging in interactions in the place of the shy person (e.g., making a phone call for the shy person). In two studies, Bradshaw (1998) found that shy persons, as opposed to those not-shy, were more likely to report recruiting other persons to accompany them into anxiety-provoking social situations, allowing or utilizing the social surrogate to directly facilitate social interactions, and avoiding entering specific social situations if the social surrogate was not available. Further, reports of recruiting the social surrogate for a particular situation were related to the amount of anxiety provoked by the situation. Recruiting was also influenced by the social appropriateness of bringing another person into the situation (e.g., job interviews are certainly anxiety-provoking, but not an appropriate situation to which to bring a friend).

Bradshaw, Williams, Linton, Parker, and Rosemond (1999) used an Internet-based questionnaire to further explore how shy persons utilized social surrogates. Participants, 178 women and 90 men, completed a questionnaire via a link on the American Psychological Society Web site. The study was described as examining how shy persons coped with their shyness. Among other questions, participants were asked whether they had a friend who could accompany them to social gatherings and how often they recruited the friend to accompany them into anxiety-provoking social situations. In a series of open-ended questions, participants were asked why they recruited other persons, how the person helped, when they did not recruit, why, and how their behavior changed when the other person was with them. Pairs of independent raters read and categorized the open-ended responses.

The most common reasons cited for recruiting were companionship (37%; e.g., "that way I know I will know somebody there") and anxiety reduction (24%; e.g., "because I feel unsecure (sic) alone"). Approximately 20% cited either active support ("to bail me out in case I don't know what to say") or motivation ("because I know they'll egg me on to do what I really want to do") from the surrogate. The responses reveal shyness as a quality that has a dynamic effect on relationships by shaping not only the behavior of the shy person, but also the nature of the interactions with the other person.

It can be easy to imagine where this kind of behavior would place strain on a relationship and begin to make a relationship "difficult." This was anticipated by three participants in comments made in the Internet survey in response to the question: "When you do not recruit, why do you not recruit?"

- "Generally because I know that the other person has his/her own concerns, and I feel like I am bothering him/her."
- "Because I don't want to make the person do something they would rather not."
- "Shame—I don't want to appear needy or helpless or immature."

Research has not examined how the person in the role of social surrogate feels about playing that role, including whether or not it is seen as making the relationship difficult. Is this an activity that creates resentment for the relationship partner or is this an attractive quality of the relationship because it allows the partner to satisfy a need to provide nurturance (Weiss, 1974)? Research has also not examined, more broadly, how shy persons perceive the effects of their shyness on their relationships. For example, are there systematic differences between shy persons and their relationship partners in the extent to which shyness is perceived as a source of difficulty in their relationship?

Shyness and Sexual Relationships

Sexual relations are a key determinant of satisfaction with romantic relationships, both short-term and long-term. Given the anxiety reported by not-shy couples when discussing their sexual relationships, it is surprising to note that relatively little research has examined the effects of shyness on sexual attitudes and behaviors. Not surprisingly, however, the few studies there are suggest that shyness has negative effects. Kerr (1995), in other follow-up research with the longitudinal Swedish sample, found that childhood shyness predicted reduced sexual adjustment for men. No such effects were reported for women. On a somewhat positive note, Pollack (2001) found that heterosexual social anxiety, a situation-specific form of shyness, was not related to sexual aggression. Leary and Dobbins (1983), on the other hand, did find effects for heterosocial anxiety. While the research revealed no differences in terms of sexual attitudes and knowledge, persons high in heterosexual anxiety, as compared to those low in heterosexual anxiety, reported fewer sexual experiences, and more apprehension concerning sexual contact. While no effects were found for men, high heterosexually anxious women were more likely to use condoms as compared to low heterosexually anxious women who were more likely to report using birth control pills. It is unclear whether this correlation was somehow caused by the women's anxiety or simply the result of differing expectations regarding the likelihood of needing birth control.

In perhaps the only published study examining adult shyness and sex, Bruch and Hynes (1987) examined shyness and college women's attitudes and behaviors related to contraceptive use. Shyness was related to communication difficulties concerning contraceptive use both for initial and recent sexual contacts. Shy women were also more likely to use less effective contraceptive methods, such as withdrawal, during their initial sexual contact.

Cowden and Bradshaw (2001) examined the relationships between shyness and the Attitudes Related to Sexual Concerns Scale (Koch & Cowden, 1990), which measures concerns related to a variety of sexual and sexual relationship behaviors, such as sexual discussions with a partner and masturbation. The study utilized two diverse samples: a Washington, D.C., area community college (n = 241) and a historically Black state university in North Carolina (n = 124). Shyness was found to be related to a variety of sexual concerns including poor body image, anxiety about the relationship commitment of their partners, communication about sexual issues, increased performance anxiety, guilt, and reduced sexual self-understanding. For example, shy persons reported more anxiety about discussing their negative feelings about their sexual relationship with their partner and were more likely to agree that there would be aspects about their sexual relationship that they could not talk about with their partner. These effects were present even when controlling for religiosity and sex and were largely consistent across the two samples differing in age, race, and relationship status. It is not hard to imagine how shy persons' failure to discuss their dissatisfaction or concerns about their sexual relationships with their partners would lead to reduced overall relationship satisfaction and the conceptualization of the relationship as a difficult one.

SHYNESS AND DIFFICULT RELATIONSHIPS IN SUMMARY

It is clear from the reviewed research that shyness creates difficulty in relationships for both the shy person and the relationship partner, and these difficulties extend beyond the formative stage of the relationships. The effects are made the most stark if we compare the idealized easy relationship with the image of relationships involving shy persons created by the research reviewed.

In contrast to the idealized easy relationship where the two future relational partners enter the relationship mentally healthy, shy persons have higher levels of depression and lower levels of self-esteem. Instead of openly discussing common interests and desires during initial meetings, shy persons tend to interact minimally and to avoid revealing personal information or disagreeing with the other relationship partners. Instead of addressing conflicts directly, shy persons tend to avoid coping with the conflicts. Any communication that would threaten the status of the shy person in the relationship and result in potential embarrassment, such as a desire for change in the relationship, tends to be avoided. In the idealized, easy relationship, all relationship-related behaviors would be directed toward the mutual benefit of both partners. Research on the use of social surrogates suggests that, in at least some situations, the shy person may put coping with social anxiety over the needs of the relationship partner. In contrast to the easy relationship where both partners have extensive social networks that provide a source of social support and other resources adaptive for relationships, shy persons, not by choice, have significantly smaller social networks that provide less social support. The behaviors of shy persons also adversely affect their career achievement, which can create outside stress on long-term relationships, especially romantic ones.

There are some ways, however, in which the characteristics and behaviors of shy persons are very much like those of partners in the easy relationships. A key component of the idealized, easy relationship is that partners naturally take the feelings, desires, and needs of the other relationship partner into account. Shy persons are almost chronically concerned about being negatively evaluated by their relationship partners. In order to avoid this, the shy person has to be continually monitoring the feelings, desires, and needs of the partner. While these behaviors may create problems for the shy person in the relationship, and, indeed, adversely affect the relationship, they are also very attractive to other people. For example, cross-cultural research by Buss (1989) found that both women and men ranked the qualities of kindness and understanding as most important for a potential mate. This was seen in the research by Gough and Thorne (1986) on the positive aspects of shyness, where spouses used adjectives like modest, tactful, and sensitive to describe the shy person. Similarly, while shy persons had significantly smaller social networks, they tended to have known the members of their social network for longer periods of time (Jones & Carpenter, 1986). It would appear that while shyness creates difficulty, and, in fact, may cause a relationship to be conceptualized as a difficult one, it also has advantages that help maintain the relationship. This may be where the research on shyness can best inform the larger issue of difficult relationships.

SHYNESS AND DIFFICULT RELATIONSHIPS: COMMON THREADS

A common suggestion for those in a relationship is to "be themselves." Unfortunately, shy people typically believe that if they are "themselves," then they will be rejected by the other person. It is this fear of negative evaluation that produces a pattern of behaviors that leads to difficulties in relationships. Specifically, the shy person is overly concerned with monitoring the feelings, interests, and desires of the other person, so as to not say or do something the other would not like. Because it is hard to tell what another person wants, particularly with a new acquaintance, the shy person often says or does very little to avoid saying or doing the wrong thing. This pattern of reduced communication and withholding of information continues as the relationship develops, and it leads to numerous problems, including delayed relationship development, difficulty in coping with change or conflict, and reduced relationship satisfaction. What are the implications of this information for understanding more generally what makes relationships difficult?

It almost goes without saying that communication is important in relationships. If communication is reduced in a relationship, regardless of the reason, then there will be difficulties created. One would expect to find communication playing a major role in difficult relationships. In some relationships the reduced communication will be a causal factor, as with shyness, while in others it will be central to coping with the actual cause of the difficult relationship, as with something like substance abuse.

This analysis, though, seems incomplete. There are always difficulties in relationships, and we do not define every relationship as a difficult one. There has to be more to it. Using shyness as a starting point, I would suggest the following two common threads for what makes some relationships difficult.

First, shyness is a personality trait. By definition, it will tend to affect the person's behavior across both time and place. Unlike some other problems in a relationship that can be easily solved, the problems created by personality traits will continually recur. Many of the other relationships described as difficult also feature some fixed, unchanging, characteristic of one or both relationship partners or the situation itself. Examples of these fixed characteristics include age differences (May/December romance), intercultural relationships, status differences, long distance relationships, and chronic illness. The difficulties created by these fixed characteristics will continually affect the relationship and routinely lead to conflict (e.g., "We talked about that last month!" "Every holiday it's the same thing." "You never want to go somewhere to meet new people!"). It is likely that for the relationship partners, this creates a sense of the relationship as troubled and a feeling that no progress is being made.

Why do persons remain in these difficult relationships? All other things being equal, one would expect persons to leave such relationships for less difficult ones. In some situations, of course, the person does not have a realistic choice to leave the relationship (e.g., work relationship, family member). When the person does have the choice to leave, there must be something that draws them to the relationship that makes the difficulty tolerable.

The second suggested common thread is that, in many instances, the source of the difficulty in the relationship is also the source of attraction in the relationship. This can be seen in the research on the positive aspects of shyness described by Gough and Thorne (1986). While the fear of negative evaluation causes the shy person to limit communication, it also leads the shy person to focus on the needs, desires, and feelings of the other person. The resulting behaviors directed toward the relationship partner are described by the partners as attractive ones (sensitive, tactful, modest). In other words, the behaviors used by shy persons to cope with their anxiety are attractive to the relationship partner. This can be seen in a variety of other difficult relationships such as the previously cited May/December romance (e.g., "You're older and not like the people my age") or in relationships with a substance abuser (e.g., "He's so dangerous"). Further research will be necessary to determine whether these suggested common threads are correct.

CONCLUDING COMMENTS

Like the characters in the song at the beginning of this chapter, researchers may themselves feel "stuck" and at risk of emotionally "falling apart" when considering the limits of what we understand regarding difficult relationships. Despite the many decades of research on shyness, there have been many more questions generated concerning shyness and difficult relationships from this review of the research than have been answered. Why do some partners overcome the obstacles to relationship formation presented by shyness and form relationships? How do these relationships change over time? Does shyness represent a constant difficulty in these relationships, or does it only arise in certain situations? Are the perceptions of the difficulties created by shyness the same for both partners? How does shyness influence the processes of responding to and coping with change in existing relationships? These questions can be answered, along with broader questions concerning difficult relationships of all sorts, if we make several changes in how we pursue the research.

First, we need to broaden the scope of the research to consider the other relationship partner. The partner is not passive, but an active participant in all aspects of the relationship from formation through maintenance to dissolution. We must understand both individuals before we can understand the relationship between them. Second, in order to understand the relationship, we need to narrow the scope of the research to focus on the details of the relationship and study the dynamics of the interactions between the relationship partners. There has been much research examining the dynamics of specific interactions between shy persons and partners in first-meeting dyads, such as Garcia et al. (1991) described in this chapter, but little such research examining partners in ongoing relationships or as they confront real-world situations. Relationships are enacted in these interactions, and we must study these interactions in order to understand the relationships. We need more detail than is provided by a simple rating of relationship satisfaction. Finally, we need to examine how these relationships change over time. Relationships are not static, but our typical approaches to studying them (correlational studies, lab experiments with college students) have been.

In sum, research which followed new acquaintances over the course of a year, maintained a broad scope and considered both partners as active participants, and regularly assessed the dynamics of their interactions during that year would be an especially fruitful way to answer the many questions raised in this chapter. Answers to those questions, while they are specific to shyness and difficult relationships, will provide invaluable insight into all relationships.

ACKNOWLEDGMENT

REFERENCES

Arkin, R. M., & Grove, T. (1990). Shyness, sociability and patterns of everyday affiliation. *Journal of Social and Personal Relationships, 7*, 273–281.

Arkin, R. M., Lake, E. A., & Baumgardner, A. H. (1986). Shyness and self-presentation. In W. H. Jones, J. M. Cheek, & S. R. Briggs (Eds.), *Shyness: Perspectives on research and treatment* (pp. 189–204). New York: Plenum Press.

Asendorpf, J. B. (2002). Personality effects on personal relationships over the life span. In A. L. Vangelisti & H. T. Reis (Eds.), *Stability and change in relationships: Advances in personal relationships* (pp. 35–56). New York: Cambridge University Press.

Asendorpf, J. B., & Wilpers, S. (1998). Personality effects on social relationships. *Journal of Personality and Social Psychology, 74*(6), 1531–1544.

Bartholomew, K., & Horowitz, L. M. (1991). Attachment styles among young adults: A test of a four-category model. *Journal of Personality and Social Psychology, 61*(2), 226–244.

Bowers, J. W., Metts, S. M., & Duncanson, W. T. (1985). Emotion and interpersonal communication. In M. L. Knapp & G. R. Miller (Eds.), *Handbook of interpersonal communication.* Beverly Hills, CA: Sage.

Bradshaw, S. D. (1998). I'll go if you will: Do shy persons utilize social surrogates? *Journal of Social and Personal Relationships, 15*(5), 651–669.

Bradshaw, S. D., & Stasson, M. F. (1998). Attributions of shy and not-shy group members for collective group performance. *Small Group Performance, 29*(3), 283–307.

Bradshaw, S. D., Stasson, M. F., & Alexander, D. (1999). Shyness and group brainstorming: Effects on productivity and perceptions of performance. *North American Journal of Psychology, 1*(2), 267–276.

Bradshaw, S. D., Williams, C., Linton, M., Parker, K., & Rosemond, J. (1999, November). *Shy persons and their use of social surrogates: Results of an internet-*

based questionnaire. Poster presented at the 22nd annual meeting of the Society of Southeastern Social Psychologists, Richmond, Virginia.

Bruch, M. A., & Hynes, M. J. (1987). Heterosocial anxiety and contraceptive behavior. *Journal of Research in Personality, 21*(3), 343–360.

Burgoon, J. K., & Koper, R. J. (1984). Nonverbal and relational communication associated with reticence. *Human Communication Research, 10*(4), 601–626.

Buss, A. H. (1980). *Self-consciousness and social anxiety*. San Francisco: Freeman.

Buss, D. M. (1989). Sex differences in human mate preferences: Evolutionary hypotheses tested in 37 cultures. *Behavioral and Brain Sciences, 12*, 1–14.

Byrne, D., Clore, G. L., & Smeaton, G. (1986). The attraction hypothesis: Do similar attitudes affect anything? *Journal of Personality and Social Psychology, 51*, 1167–1170.

Camacho, L. M., & Paulus, P. B. (1995). The role of social anxiousness in group brainstorming. *Journal of Personality and Social Psychology, 68*, 1071–1080.

Caspi, A., Elder, G. H., Jr., & Bem, D. J. (1988). Moving away from the world: Life-course patterns of shy children. *Developmental Psychology, 24*(6), 824–831.

Caspi, A., & Herbener, E. S. (1990). Continuity and change: Assortative marriage and the consistency of personality in adulthood. *Journal of Personality and Social Psychology, 58*, 250–258.

Cheek, J., & Buss, A. (1981). Shyness and sociability. *Journal of Personality and Social Psychology, 41*, 330–339.

Cheek, J., & Melchior, L. (1990). Shyness, self-esteem, and self-consciousness. In H. Leitenberg (Ed.), *Handbook of social and evaluation anxiety* (pp. 47–84). New York: Plenum Press.

Cowden, C. R., & Bradshaw, S. D. (March, 2001). *Sexual concern, religiosity, and shyness*. Paper presented at the 72nd annual meeting of the Eastern Psychological Association, Washington, DC.

DePaulo, B. M., Kenny, D. A., Hoover, C., Webb, W., & Oliver, P. V. (1987). Accuracy of person perception: Do people know what kinds of impressions they convey? *Journal of Personality and Social Psychology, 52*, 303–315.

Duck, S., & Pond, K. (1989). Friends, Romans, countrymen, lend me your retrospections: Rhetoric and reality in personal relationships. In C. Hendrick (Ed.), *Close relationships: Review of Personality and Social Psychology*, Vol. 10 (pp. 17–38). Newbury Park,, CA: Sage.

Duggan, E. S., & Brennan, K. A. (1994). Social avoidance and its relation to Bartholomew's adult attachment typology. *Journal of Social and Personality Relationships, 11*, 147–153.

Forsyth, D. R. (1998). *Group dynamics* (3rd ed.). New York: Wadsworth.

Garcia, S., Stinson, L., Ickes, W., Bissonnette, V., & Briggs, S. (1991). Shyness and physical attractiveness in mixed-sex dyads. *Journal of Personality and Social Psychology, 61*, 35–49.

Goldfried, M. R., Padawar, W., & Robbins, C. (1984). Social anxiety and the semantic structure of heterosocial interactions. *Journal of Abnormal Psychology, 93*, 87–97.

Gough, H. G., & Thorne, A. (1986). Positive, negative, and balanced shyness: Self-definitions and the reactions of others. In W. H. Jones, J. M. Cheek, & S. R. Briggs (Eds.), *Shyness: Perspectives on research and treatment* (pp. 205–226). New York: Plenum.

Hobfoll, S. E., & Stokes, J. P. (1988). The processes and mechanics of social support. In S. Duck (Ed.), *Handbook of personal relationships: Theory, research, and interventions* (pp. 497–518). New York: Wiley.

Johnson, J. M., Petzel, T. P., & Johnson, J. E. (1991). Attributions of shy persons in affiliation and achievement situations. *Journal of Psychology, 125*, 51–58.

Jones, W. H., & Carpenter, B. N. (1986). Shyness, social behavior, and relationships. In W. H. Jones, J. M. Cheek, & S. R. Briggs (Eds.), *Shyness: Perspectives on research and treatment* (pp. 227–238). New York: Plenum.

Kenrick, D. T., Groth, G. E., Trost, M. R., & Sadalla, E. K. (1993). Integrating evolutionary and social exchange perspectives on relationships: Effects of gender, self-appraisal, and involvement level on mate selection criteria. *Journal of Personality and Social Psychology, 64*, 951–969.

Kerr, M. A. (1995). Adult outcomes of childhood shyness in a Swedish longitudinal sample. *Dissertation Abstracts International, 55*(11-B), 5096.

Kerr, M., Lambert, W. W., & Bem, D. J. (1996). Life course sequelae of childhood shyness in Sweden: Comparison with the United States. *Developmental Psychology, 32*(6), 1100–1105.

Koch, P. B., & Cowden, C. R. (1990). *Development of a measurement of attitudes related to sexual concerns.* Unpublished manuscript.

Langston, C. A., & Cantor, N. (1989). Social anxiety and social constraint: When making friends is hard. *Journal of Personality and Social Psychology, 56*(4), 649–661.

Leary, M. R., & Buckley, K. E. (2000). Shyness and the pursuit of social acceptance. In W. R. Crozier (Ed.), *Shyness: Development, consolidation, and change* (pp. 139–153). New York: Routledge.

Leary, M. R., & Dobbins, S. E. (1983). Social anxiety, sexual behavior, and contraceptive use. *Journal of Personality and Social Psychology, 45*(6), 1347–1354.

Leary, M. R., Knight, P. D., & Johnson, K. A. (1987). Social anxiety and dyadic conversation: A verbal response analysis. *Journal of Social and Clinical Psychology, 5*, 34–50.

Manning, P., & Ray, G. (1993). Shyness, self-confidence, and social interaction. *Social Psychology Quarterly, 56*, 178–192.

Maslow, A. H. (1954). *Motivation and personality.* New York: Harper.

Miller, R. S., & Schlenker, B. R. (1985). Egotism in group members: Public and private attributions of responsibility for group performance. *Social Psychology Quarterly, 48*, 85–89.

Moller, K., & Stattin, H. (2001). Are close relationships in adolescence linked with partner relationships in midlife? A longitudinal, prospective study. *International Journal of Behavioral Development, 25*(1), 69–77.

Montgomery, B. M. (1988). Quality communication in personal relationships. In S. W. Duck (Ed.), *Handbook of personal relationships: Theory, research, and interventions* (pp. 343–359). New York: Wiley.

Noller, P., & Feeney, J. A. (2002). Communication, relationship concerns, and satisfaction in early marriage. In A. L. Vangelisti & H. T. Reis (Eds.), *Stability and change in relationships: Advances in personal relationships* (pp. 129–155). New York: Cambridge University Press.

Pilkonis, P. A. (1977). The behavioral consequences of shyness. *Journal of Personality, 45*, 596–611.

Pollack, S. J. (2001). Sexual anxiety and heterosexual anxiety as it relates to sexual aggression in college men. *Dissertation Abstracts International, 61*(11-B), 6146.

Schlenker, B. R., & Leary, M. R. (1982). Social anxiety and self-presentation: A conceptualization and model. *Psychological Bulletin, 92*, 641–669.

Sheppard, J. A., & Arkin, R. M. (1990). Shyness and self-presentation. In W. R. Crozier (Ed.), *Shyness and embarrassment: Perspectives from social psychology* (pp. 286–314). New York: Cambridge University Press.

Sprecher, S., Felmlee, D., Orbuch, T. L., & Willetts, M. C. (2002). Social networks and change in personal relationships. In A. L. Vangelisti & H. T. Reis (Eds.), *Stability and change in relationships: Advances in personal relationships* (pp. 257–284). New York: Cambridge University Press.

Weiss, R. S. (1974). The provisions of social relationships. In Z. Rubin (Ed.), *Doing unto others: Joining, molding, conforming, helping, loving* (pp. 17–26). Englewood Cliffs, NJ: Prentice Hall.

Zimbardo, P., & Linsenmeier, J. (1983). *The influence of personal, social, and system factors on team problem solving* (Tech. Rep. No. Z-83-01). Stanford, CA: Stanford University, Office of Naval Research.

Chapter 3

Locating "Difficulty": A Multi-site Model of Intimate Terrorism

Megan K. Foley
University of Iowa

Writing a chapter on the difficulty of intimate partner violence is a different task from writing chapters on other kinds of relational difficulty. Other authors face the task of pinpointing exactly what is difficult about shyness (Bradshaw, chap. 2, this volume) or gossip (Foster & Rosnow, chap. 9, this volume), for example. However, there is no question about what is difficult about intimate partner violence—in fact, the word *difficulty* hardly begins to acknowledge the gravity of the problem. Each year, 200,000 people in the United States are assaulted by intimate partners; 2,000 of those assaults are fatal (Barnett, Miller-Perrin, & Perrin, 1997). These fatalities typically result from intimate terrorism, the most severe form of intimate partner violence, motivated by one (typically male) partner's desire for control over the other (typically female) partner (Johnson, 2001). Johnson (2001) distinguishes intimate terrorism from three other types of violence: (a) common couple violence, which is less severe and occurs in noncontrolling relationships; (b) violent resistance, in which abused partners defend themselves against their abusers; and (c) mutual violent control, in which both partners attempt to control the other through physical aggression. This chapter will focus specifically on intimate terrorism, "the most extreme and dangerous kind of intimate partner violence" (Wood, 2004, p. 557). Because the problem of intimate terrorism is all too clear, this chapter will concentrate on locating, rather than identifying, difficulty in intimate terrorism.

The desire to locate the source of difficulty is part of a larger concern in the intimate partner violence literature. The goal of abuse prevention and intervention fuels research on intimate partner violence. Most authors discuss potential practical applications of their work (e.g., Wood, 2004); some even explicitly use their research to develop intervention strategies (e.g., Merritt-Gray & Wuest, 2001). To stop intimate partner violence, researchers aim to pinpoint the site from which the difficulty comes. This recurring question has been framed in a number of different ways: for example, (a) how do victimized partners make sense of their relationships? (Riessman, 1992; Wood, 2000), (b) what are the characteristics of people who abuse their partners? (Christopher & Lloyd, 2000), (c) what behaviors typify violent relationships? (Feldman & Ridley, 2000; Sabourin & Stamp, 1995), and (d) what sociocultural factors contribute to abuse? (Mihalic & Elliott, 1997; Meyers, 1997). All of these different efforts have the same underlying goal to create social change by first locating the causes and sources of intimate partner violence.

To locate the difficulty of intimate partner violence, and intimate terrorism more specifically, I first chart the primary places where people have situated difficulty in intimate partner violence scholarship: (a) the abused partner, (b) the abusive partner, (c) relational interaction, and (d) societal discourses. At each site, scholars, activists, and participants in violent relationships struggle with contradictions. Abused partners are active participants in violent episodes, but cannot be held accountable for them. Abusive partners cannot be excused for violence, yet they act within the bounds of patriarchal discourses that condone their aggression. Both abusive and abused partners participate in relational interaction patterns that lead to violence, yet despite their mutual participation, they are not equals. Societal discourses of patriarchy make intimate terrorism a social rather than a personal problem, but those discourses exist only insofar as they are materially embodied in the practices of individual agents. Toward the end of the chapter, I will turn to a dialogic theory of organizational emergence (Taylor, 1995; Taylor, Cooren, Giroux, & Robichaud, 1996; Taylor & Van Every, 2000) that helps navigate these contradictions. This theory offers an account of the relationship between social actors, social action, and social structure, showing how these different sites of intimate partner violence research might productively supplement one another.

THE ABUSED PARTNER AS THE SITE OF DIFFICULTY

Assertions that the abused partner is responsible for intimate terrorism point to just one social actor as the site of difficulty. Male abusers often describe their female partners as provoking them (Gilligan, 2003). In Wood's (2004) interviews, violent men justified abuse by claiming that their partners disrespected them as men or attacked them verbally. Consonantly, women sometimes describe themselves as initiating or provoking violent episodes with their partners (Olson & Lloyd, in press). However, abused women have also reported that they "walk on

eggshells" to avoid any situation that might lead to their partner's violence (Hoff, 1993, p. 46). Wood (2001) explains this apparent contradiction: Women's beliefs that they can control or contain abuse by not
provoking their partners support the idea that they are to blame for
their abuse. That is, women tread lightly to avoid abuse and assume
that if they are abused, it is because they failed to tread lightly enough.
The common denominator is the assumption that victims are to blame
for abuse. It is common for both abusive and abused relationship partners to pin the blame for violence on the "difficult" victim.

However, scholars and activists have made significant progress since
the late 1970s and 1980s toward shifting the responsibility for intimate
terrorism away from the abused partner (Gilfus, 1999). They accomplished this goal, in part, by reframing abused women as victims
(Gilfus, 1999). In an autoethnographic account of intimate partner violence, one scholar explains, "the label 'victim' (at least temporarily)
turned my life around. I began to really believe that what my husband
had done was not because of *my* inadequacies, but because of *his*"
(Olson, 2004, p. 24). Naming the abused partner "victim" holds the abusive partner socially and legally accountable for the violence. It is for
this reason that Lawless (2001) suggests that accounts of victimization
are necessary for abused women to successfully prosecute their abusers.
Likewise, Kanuha (1996) explains that the receipt of help in women's
shelters often depends on a perception of the abused as helpless and
blameless. Positioning the abused partner as a blameless victim mobi-
lizes support. Christopher and Lloyd (2000) note, "The analysis of female victims of intimate violence has come a long way from the early
assertions that battered wives are 'masochistic'" (p. 333).

While the construction of abused partners as blameless victims mobi-
lizes much-needed support, it also suggests that abused partners have
no agency (Lamb, 1999). In demonstrating the abused partners' need
for help, it ignores how they can and do help themselves. Wood and
Roche (2001) assert that the victim label implies an understanding of the
abused woman as deficient—traumatized at best, pathological at worst.
Similarly, Lamb (1999) argues that discourses about abused women
produce an understanding of victims as long-suffering, pathologized,
and passive. Furthermore, Merritt-Gray and Wuest (2001) argue that
helping professionals who treat abused women as victims undermine
their efforts to break from violent relationships: "Helpers who fail to
heed the voices of survivors negate their experience" (p. 411).
McDermott and Garofalo (2004) demonstrate that interventions intended to empower victims often "contain the seeds of disempowerment" (p. 1245). They point to several practices (e.g., mandatory
arrests and "no-drop" prosecutions of abusers) in which victim advo-
cates work against the will of victims, presuming that victims are powerless and unable to act in their own best interests.

In response to these criticisms, scholarship has increasingly focused
on the ability of abused partners to resist and recover from violence.

Lloyd and Emery (2000) illustrate this turn: "We would like to emphasize the incredible strengths displayed by women who have experienced
physical or sexual battering" (p. 518). In the last 15 years, scholars have
reformulated the agency of abused women, labeling them "survivors"
rather than "victims." In these formulations, survivorship stands for
the agency of abused women (a) to construct meaning from their experience of violence (Hoff, 1993; Lempert, 1996; Riessman, 1996) and (b)
to counter the violence perpetrated against them by, for example, fight-
ing back or leaving the relationship (Hoff, 1993; Lamb, 1999). While
scholars aim to reframe abused women as active agents, many proceed
carefully, aware that assigning the abused partner some degree of control over intimate terrorism might easily lead to blaming the victim.
Lempert (1996) captures this tension well: "It disempowers abused
women to continuously cast them as powerless, passive victims of violence. The men are not always totally responsible and the women are
not always totally innocent. Yet it is also problematic to assign equal
blame" (p. 284). Blame, responsibility, and agency must be disentangled
in order to understand abused women. That is, scholars of intimate terrorism are faced with the challenge of creating an image of abused
partners who are active in, but not personally accountable for, the
violence perpetrated against them.

THE ABUSIVE PARTNER AS THE SITE OF DIFFICULTY

While the agency of the abused is often debated, male abusers are generally described as hyperagentive: strong, controlling, and powerful
(Gerber, 1991). Lloyd and Emery (2000) show that abusive men's control is a key dynamic in intimate aggression, which manifests itself as
dominating arguments, expressing possessiveness and ownership of
the abused woman, keeping the abused woman in the relationship, and
otherwise controlling her behavior. Relative to men who do not perpetrate violence against intimate partners, aggressive male partners are
more controlling and demanding in conversation (Coan, Gottman,
Babcock, & Jacobson, 1997; Jacobson et al., 1994). Men who are violent toward intimate partners tend to value asserting their rights and
tend to be more authoritarian than men who do not engage in violence
(Rogers, Castleton, & Lloyd, 1996). Overwhelmingly, empirical research demonstrates that intimate terrorism occurs within larger communication patterns of domination and control.

However, abusive and abused partners' own accounts of violence
provide an alternative interpretation: while they acknowledge that violence is a means of *gaining* control, they often describe the abusers as
losing control in episodes of violence. For example, Wood's (2004) infor-
mants justified their violence by claiming that a man has a right to control his woman. At the same time, they dissociated themselves from the
violence, questioning whether the violent act was "really [them]" and

suggesting that they did not intend to be violent, "it just happened" (p. 565). Similarly, women who describe being dominated and controlled by violent partners dissociate that violence from their abusers, claiming "that wasn't the real him" (Wood, 2000, p. 1). In these cases, abusers avoid constructions of themselves as difficult. Lloyd and Emery (2000) argue that accepting abusers' lack of control is problematic because it excuses them for their actions. Researchers often interpret abusive men's accounts of violence as excuses, attempts to pin "difficulty"—and responsibility—elsewhere (Dutton & Golant, 1995; Scott & Lyman, 1968; Stets, 1988). However, Wood (2004) argues that there is value in seriously considering the ostensible excuses of abusers: "Researchers and clinicians may not agree with violent men's perceptions, but understanding violent men's views of themselves and their actions is a necessary starting point for efforts at intervention and rehabilitation" (p. 558). Certainly, simply accepting abuser's accounts would dangerously preclude them from responsibility for violence. However, understanding what violence means to the people who commit it may help change their attitudes and behavior.

Several scholars agree that perpetrators make sense of intimate terrorism based on norms of patriarchal masculinity. Wood's (2004) examination of abusive men's accounts of their own violence reveals that their violence against women partners was, at least in part, a compensatory reaction to feeling they were not regarded as "real men" in their relationships and in society at large. Boyd (2002) argues that male abusers identify with and enact dominant cultural norms of male superiority in the extreme, suggesting that abusers' behavior is not deviant, but instead hypernormative. Ferraro (1996) argues that analyzing intimate terrorism as a problem of individual men covers over societal norms of male dominance.

A tension exists here. Scholars and activists who emphasize abusers' power and control over their partners risk scapegoating individuals who act within, rather than against social norms. However, those who focus on the social nature of intimate terrorism risk excusing those individuals for their abusive behavior. The "difficulty" of intimate terrorism operates at both social and personal levels. This calls for a model that recognizes abusive partners as accountable agents, but not sole authors, of the violence they commit.

RELATIONAL INTERACTION AS THE SITE OF DIFFICULTY

Scholars have pointed to a number of interaction patterns that distinguish abusive from nonabusive relationships. First, communication skill deficits typify relationships in which violence occurs. Both partners in violent relationships tend to lack skills in coping with conflict productively, demonstrating more unilateral and reciprocal verbal aggression and less mutual discussion, feeling expression, and compromising than nonviolent couples (Feldman & Ridley, 2000). Abusive and abused partners exhibit negative communication behavior that aggravates conflict and catalyzes physical violence, without concurrent positive communication behaviors to deescalate it (Feldman & Ridley, 2000). Abusive and abused partners also lack communication skills in everyday conversation; for example, vagueness, interruption, and expressions of negativity distinguish their talk from that of nonviolent couples (Sabourin & Stamp, 1995). These nonconflict behaviors may also catalyze violence: Coan et al. (1997) suggest that violent men respond to their partners' low-level negative affect—such as sadness—with high-intensity, aggressive expressions of negative affect. Overall, violent men are more likely than nonviolent men to attribute hostile intent to their partner's behavior (Dugan, Umberson, & Anderson, 2001).

While abusive and abused partners reciprocate and escalate negativity, this additive cycle is organized into patterns of demand and withdrawal. One partner seeks a behavioral change in the other, and the other partner avoids change by withdrawing from the relationship (Berns, Jacobson, & Gottman, 1999). Anderson, Umberson, and Elliott's (2004) review of demand-withdraw patterns in violent relationships reveals contradictory empirical findings: Studies have found patterns of husband-demand and wife-withdrawal (Babcock, Waltz, Jacobson, & Gottman, 1993), wife-demand and husband-withdrawal (Sagrestano, Heavey, & Christensen, 1999), and ones in which both partners use demand and withdrawal strategies (Holtzworth-Munroe, Smutzler, & Stuart, 1998). Both demand and withdrawal strategies—attempts to change the other or refusal to change oneself—are attempts to gain power in violent relationships (Christopher & Lloyd, 2000). Although it is unclear whether abusive and abused partners play symmetrical or asymmetrical roles in escalating violence, it is clear that both actively struggle for control in violent relationships.

Furthermore, some scholars argue that women are just as likely to commit intimate partner violence as men (e.g., O'Leary, 2000; Straus, 1999). Although it may be true that both men and women are physically aggressive in intimate relationships, the consequences and context of women's aggression suggest that women cannot be understood as "equally violent." Women's violence is generally less severe than men's, and is most commonly used in self-defense (Johnson, 2001). Men and women's violent acts have different meaning and impact. Similarly, men and women's communicative acts are positioned differently in the interaction that precipitates violent episodes. Acknowledging that abused partners participate in destructive interaction patterns is not to say that they are complicit with, or responsible for, violent episodes. Lloyd and Emery (2000) rightly assert that this would be tantamount to victim blame: "There are multiple ways to ensure that the victim is at least partially to blame, ... [including] emphasizing that physical violence is nothing more than a transactional pattern of interaction" (p. 508). Empirical research does suggest that abused and abusive partners' interaction patterns lead to acts of physical aggression, but the analysis cannot end there. Men's privileged position in society affords them more discursive resources (e.g., the ability to legitimize controlling their partners) and material resources (e.g., the ability to exert economic control over partners) in heterosexual relationships (Hoff, 1993). Lempert (1996) explains that while abused women actively participate in violent relationships, their agency is limited "within the structural conditions of violence" (p. 271).

SOCIETAL DISCOURSE AS THE SITE OF DIFFICULTY

Intimate terrorism operates by drawing on and covering over the social discourses that structure and legitimize it. Patriarchal notions of masculinity, discussed earlier, represent only one thread in a complex weave of discourses that perpetuate violence by asserting male dominance. Often, dominant discourses of love encourage women to stay in violent relationships. Aggression can occur in the context of relational satisfaction (O'Leary et al., 1989), and approximately one quarter of people who have been abused by their partners interpret the violent act as a sign of love (Cate, Henton, Koval, Christopher, & Lloyd, 1982). Such interpretations enable intimate terrorism by making it appear normal and natural; they construct a world in which violence appears reasonable. Wood (2001) shows how abused women make sense of intimate violence with fairy-tale and dark romance narratives that legitimize female subordination to men.

While narratives of love frame the meaning of violence for abusive and abused partners, violent episodes also present "inexplicable, unanticipated experiences that are outside the script for intimate relationships" (Lloyd & Emery, 2000). This mutually supporting but contradictory relationship between narratives of love and violence must function covertly. Kelly (1990) suggests that abused partners are often hesitant to interpret assaults as abuse because other women's experiences with intimate terrorism remain largely hidden and unnamed. Lloyd and Emery (2000) point to a number of social discourses that cover over this relationship. For example, the purported equality between the sexes masks gendered power differences implied by romantic narratives. Additionally, framing gendered violence as the acts of strangers renders the intimate, relational nature of aggression invisible. Intimate terrorism both relies on and masks over the patriarchal discourses that legitimate it.

These patriarchal discourses do not exist as abstract forms or structures; they exist only insofar as they are constructed through social action (Lloyd & Emery, 2000). The intergenerational transmission of violence, a cycle in which men who witness or experience abuse as children are more likely to victimize their female partners, demonstrates how social action ongoingly reproduces the legitimacy of aggression.

Social action not only reinforces dominant ideologies but can also challenge them. Couples' framing of initial violent episodes had a significant impact on whether violence continued in their relationship. Couples for whom violent acts recurred framed violence as normal and natural (e.g., denying that the act was "violence"), while couples who did not exhibit further violence framed the initial violent act as deviant and dangerous (e.g., bringing in law enforcement). Riessman (1992) illustrates how a woman accounts for a decision to divorce due to marital rape, strategically resisting and supporting dominant cultural ideologies of sexuality and marriage. Demonstrating how women break free from abusive relationships by defining themselves as abused and reclaiming independent identities, Merritt-Gray and Wuest (2001) explain that it is necessary to account for "both subjective experience and the reciprocal influence of social structure" (p. 400). In both cases, it is the social act of accounting that points and responds to discourses of male dominance. Here, patriarchal ideologies lead to particular social acts, which then produce and reproduce those ideologies.

Sugarman and Frankel's (1996) meta-analysis suggests a need for an alternative to this circular relationship between patriarchal norms and acts of intimate terrorism. They show that individuals' subscription to patriarchal beliefs does not increase their likelihood of assaulting or being assaulted by their partners. While violent men are more likely to condone violence, their overall acceptance of patriarchal ideologies cannot be meaningfully distinguished from men who do not abuse. Furthermore, relative to nonassaulted women, assaulted women held more negative attitudes toward prescribed gender behaviors. Both of these findings suggest that individuals' patriarchal beliefs do not beget violence in their relationships. However, Sugarman and Frankel did find that relative to nonassaulted female partners, assaulted women's self-descriptions conform more fully to cultural definitions of gender-appropriate attributes, and that abusive men's self-descriptions conformed to neither characteristically masculine nor feminine traits. This suggests that individuals' attitudes about gendered ideologies have less impact than their embodied practice of those ideologies. Although individuals may subscribe to patriarchal beliefs, it is only when they claim those beliefs as part of their identity that violence occurs (Sugarman & Frankel, 1996). In other words, patriarchal ideology gains material force through embodiment. Locating the "difficulty" of intimate terrorism in societal discourses is to locate difficulty in the practices of individual agents who constitute—or challenge—those discourses.

However, this is not to say that intimate terrorism is a problem of particular individuals. Framing intimate terrorism as a purely personal problem downplays the need for community support through helping organizations, such as women's shelters (Gilfus, 1999). Masking the social nature of intimate terrorism also serves to silence women who feel that they will be stigmatized and revictimized if they seek help (Eisikovits, 1996). Failure to recognize the social antecedents and con-

sequents of partner abuse is a failure to recognize the material constraints that the actions of individuals impose on others. Lempert
(1996) explains that "violence and the threat of violence are gendered social acts that establish and maintain the control of men over women" (p.
269). While intimate terrorism is an extreme and marginal gender performance (Boyd, 2002), Marcus and Fischer (1986) challenge us "to
bring the insights gained on the periphery back to the center to raise
havoc with our settled ways of thinking and conceptualization" (p.
138). While it is certainly true that many people subscribe to gendered
discourses like patriarchal masculinity or heteronormative romance
without becoming abusers or victims, the prevalence of these discourses
and their potential to enable violence might give us pause (Wood, 2001,
2004). While individual agents perform gender ideologies into existence, those discourses exist at a societal level, rendering intimate terrorism a problem worthy of collective attention and action.

A SYSTEMIC MODEL OF DIFFICULTY IN INTIMATE TERRORISM

Locating the difficulty of intimate terrorism is sometimes seen as a
matter of determining a single origin, but I argue that this approach is
too reductive. Rather, this difficulty emerges at interrelated individual,
relational, and societal sites. While it is problematic to assign responsibility for violence to abused partners, they nevertheless are agentive
participants in relational interaction. Abusive partners are responsible
for their violent acts, yet should not be held accountable for patriarchal
societal discourses that engender violence. Abusive and abused partners
do not have equal control over violence, although both partners take
part in relational interaction patterns that precede violent episodes.
While the embodied practices of individuals constitute societal ideologies, recognition of intimate terrorism as a public rather than a solely
private issue requires an understanding of collective social discourse.

Taylor and his colleagues (Taylor, 1995; Taylor et al., 1996; Taylor &
Van Every, 2000) have presented a theory of organizational emergence
that provides an explanation for these seeming contradictions in violent
relationships. This theory of organizing accounts for both fluid construction and fixed structures, and it places conversation (the saying) in
dialogue with text (the said) (Taylor et al., 1996). That is, this theory accounts for the systemic nature of interaction without ignoring
structural relations of power.

Coorientation: Difficulty in People

Taylor and Van Every (2000) describe conversation as a process of coorientation, whereby communicators recursively supplement each
other's acts. This draws attention to the fact that communicative ac-

tion has no force without response: "The constituting of agency necessarily requires the recruitment of an object" (p. 161). While Taylor and
Van Every (2000) suggest that every conversation necessarily involves
taking the other as an object, Sabourin and Stamp (1995) show that objectification of partners in violent relationships is markedly different
from that in nonviolent relationships. Their study shows that whereas
nonviolent couples tended to collaborate when discussing routine topics ranging from money to child care, abusive and abused partners tend
to oppose each other. Relatedly, nonviolent couples resolved conflicts in
mutually satisfactory ways, whereas abusive and abused partners described conflicts as a zero-sum game in which only one partner could
win. Furthermore, nonviolent couples' conversations focused on the
content of the task at hand. In contrast, couples characterized by violence focused on each other in conversation, often complaining about
their relationship. Taken together, these differences show that individuals in nonviolent relationships act *toward* their partners, whereas individuals act *on and against* their partners in violent relationships.

Moreover, although both partners act as subject and object in most
relationships, in violent relationships, aggressors resist their partners'
attempts to take them as objects. Relative to men who do not perpetrate
violence against intimate partners, aggressive male partners are more
likely to reject their partners' attempts to influence them and are unlikely to admit that their own behavior is harmful (Coan et al., 1997; Jacobson et al., 1994). Although there is some debate about who demands
and who withdraws in everyday interaction, Feldman and Ridley (2000)
specify that *conflicts* in violent relationships are often characterized by
the abusive partner's demanding and nagging and the abused partner's
withdrawal. Strikingly, abuse is often triggered by the abused partner's
rejection or possible abandonment of the abusive partner (Goldner,
1999). The aggressors of violence treat their partners as objects and
refuse to be taken as objects themselves.

Yet even as they attempt to unilaterally assert control over their partners, perpetrators of violence grant their victims power. Because action
has no power without response (Taylor & Van Every, 2000), aggressors'
power is dependent on their victims. Male perpetrators of intimate terrorism assert that their partner legitimized the abuse by staying in the
relationship—that their partner's acceptance of one abusive act sanctions further abuse (Wood, 2004). However, admitting their partner's
power to legitimize abuse also grants them the power to invalidate it.
Eisikovits (1996) demonstrates that the abused partner's response to
episodes of violence, not the violent act itself, determines the impact of
that abuse on the abused partner and the relationship. The contingency
of the abuser's power on the victim's response explains why abusive
partners are often highly dependent and enmeshed in their intimate relationships (Jacobson & Gottman, 1998). Dutton (1995) attributes
these patterns of dependency to abuser's "deep-seated feeling of power-
lessness" (p. 121). Exercise of power over another requires response; an
individual cannot be an aggressor without a victim. Taylor and Van

Every (2000) explain that because the subject requires the object's response, all interaction is necessarily "diagentive" (p. 89).

Although a diagentive perspective acknowledges that meaning and action are constructed by partners jointly, it draws a clear distinction between joint activity and equality. In other words, it explains how "abused [partners] are active, although not co-acting equals" (Lempert, 1996, p. 270). Taylor and Van Every (2000) distinguish between the "agent/source" and the "agent/recipient" (p. 89). The aggressor of intimate terrorism possesses agency defined as "that which acts" (p. 161). In responding to the aggressor, the victim gains agency, but *only through the validation of the aggressor's agency over her or his own*. As a vehicle, or medium, for the aggressor's agency, "[the victim] becomes [the aggressor's] agent, both acting and acting *for*" (Taylor & Van Every, 2000, p. 50). This analysis is corroborated by Merritt-Gray and Wuest (2001), who found that victims' identities and sources of self-esteem are deeply enmeshed with their participation in violent relationships. Abused partners' agency and sense of self come to depend on their violent partners; victims do retain some rewards by remaining in dangerous relationships. Through the theorization of hierarchy in conversation, Taylor and his colleagues (Taylor, 1995; Taylor et al., 1996; Taylor & Van Every, 2000) provide a model that accounts for the mutual yet unequal relationship between abusers and their partners. In other words, co-construction is structured even at its most fluid level.

Double Translation: Difficulty in Relational Interaction

Conversation builds its own structure from the ground up: Social acts "become part of the circumstances for some future interaction" (Taylor & Van Every, 2000, p. 39). Relative to nonviolent couples, partners in violent relationships exhibit more negative reciprocity in verbal interaction that tends to escalate over time (Cordova, Jacobson, Gottman, Rushe, & Cox, 1993). Abusers' physically violent acts also tend to become more severe over time (Hoff, 1993). Both female victims' (Hoff, 1993) and male abusers' (Wood, 2004) accounts suggest that this is due to an expectation of violence established in earlier interaction: After the first violent act, more violence was seen as inevitable and even acceptable. In relationships characterized by ongoing abuse, violence becomes ritualized, "[losing] its event-like quality" (Eisikovits, 1996, p. 468). Therefore, specific social acts and social structure exist in double translation, forming a self-organizing loop (Taylor, 1995; Taylor et al., 1996).

Thus, conversation (social action) is translated into text (social structure). In this first translation, text (and hence structure) are products of conversation: "Conversation is the site of organizational emergence; text, its surface" (Taylor & Van Every, 2000, p. 37). Textualization is accomplished by creating narratives about interaction. Abused partners often render their experiences with violence in narrative form in order to make sense of them. For example, Riessman (1992) describes one abused wife's story: "Narrative retelling enables her to transform her consciousness: to name the abuse, to interpret it as oppression, to reexperience her anger, and to make the transition from victim to survivor" (p. 232). Of course, these narratives are not always emancipatory; they often reframe violent episodes as nonabusive and thus enable abuse to continue (Wood, 2001). In both cases, social actors organize their interaction into meaningful texts that impact subsequent action.

In the subsequent translation, those stories are repositioned as springboards for action, generic templates that both serve as resources for and constrain social action, "translating the generic into the specific, by cloaking the spare structural in the dressy figurative" (Taylor & Van Every, 2000, p. 42). This cloaking is accomplished by embedding a descriptive representation of the text within a larger prescriptive modal statement. That is, when actors cite a text, they implicitly or explicitly state what should be done about it. The concept of double translation can be seen in the intergenerational cycle of violence, the tendency for people who experienced violence as children to be abusive in their intimate relationships as adults (Mihalic & Elliott, 1997). The performance of past violence becomes a model for future conversation.

Communicators always translate conversations from texts, even if only to reject those texts. For example, Mihalic and Elliott (1997) note that victims of abuse can stop the intergenerational cycle of violence by acknowledging the abuse and refusing to repeat it. Victims of intimate terrorism use reports of abuse to solicit help from their social networks and community organizations (Eisikovits, 1996). Narratives of abuse can also help victims successfully prosecute their abusers (Lawless, 2001). In short, narratives that may perpetuate violence within intimate relationships can also open up spaces to counteract that violence. It is this circular relationship between social interaction and social structure that "enables human interaction to transcend itself (future possibility), yet also constrains it (effect of the past)" (Taylor & Van Every, 2000, p. 161). That is, it allows for resistance within oppressive systems of meaning, even as those systems are being reproduced.

Distanciation: Difficulty in Societal Discourse

In distanciation, a text is increasingly abstracted from specific instances of conversation and takes on a seemingly objective status. In other words, the text appears "real." A text is "both naturalized and socialized: it is made an object like any other and legitimated socially" (Taylor & Van Every, 2000, p. 45). In relationships characterized by violence, interaction patterns are concretized, or turned into objects, through repetition: "A pattern of coercive efforts can gradually develop, creating a rigid pattern of negative, polarized interaction" (Holtzworth–Munroe et al., 1998, p. 732). The text can be understood as an a priori form. Taylor and Van Every (2000) conceptualize the term *a priori* in a specialized way: "not as given or presumed, but found" (p. 72). Once found, things appear as though they were given in the first place. Once texts render social relations recognizable and meaningful, those meanings then appear to be natural or necessary. As discussed earlier, discourses of patriarchal masculinity and heteronormative romance narratives are examples of the texts that abusive and abused partners use to make sense of violence. For those who accept these patriarchal narratives, violence then appears like the normal and natural order of things.

When individual agents use social discourses, or texts, their acts represent collective intentionality: the individual is "speaking for himself, as someone with personal ambitions, but he also aims to speak for the organization of which he is merely a part" (Taylor & Van Emery, 2000, p. 232). In intimate terrorism, aggressors and victims never encounter patriarchal ideology directly; they bring relatively fixed, yet abstract norms to bear on the relationship through their enactment of it. In other words, gendered social norms have impact and are reproduced only insofar as they are embodied by individuals. While individual actors do become the agents of abstracted structure, Taylor and Van Every (2000) paint a more complex picture of the actor:

> Narrative actors lead a double life. They are at one and the same time specific psychological actors, in a specific sociological situation, and yet also generic actors in an abstract narrative situation where intentionality is no longer to be thought of as that of a psychological subject but rather an obligatory function in a genre of narrative origin—a necessary motive force in a predetermined pattern of events. (p. 43)

Thus, the patriarchal discourses that enable violence would not persist without individuals' enactment of them. As incidents of a behavior proliferate, past behavior is institutionalized and serves as the warrant for future behavior. Even when resisting a particular discourse, social actors must point to it and thus confirm its status as a social object (albeit a problematic, even amoral one). Pointing to the necessary relationship between individual action and societal discourses, the theory deftly sidesteps the traps of either scapegoating the individual for societal or relational problems or excusing the aggressor in order to blame a faceless society. While perpetrators of intimate terrorism can be understood as operating within hegemonic discourses or relational constraints, this does not absolve them of responsibility. Taylor's theorization of both conversation and text leads to a rejection of binaries throughout his theory of organizational emergence, providing a dialogic model of agency for intimate terrorism.

RELATING DIFFICULTIES

In this chapter, I set out to locate the "difficulty" of intimate terrorism by examining the sites from which it emerges. I reviewed four places that scholars, activists, and participants point to as sources of difficulty: the abused partner, the abusive partner, relational interaction, and societal discourses. None could adequately account for difficulty alone; instead, difficulty emerged from each site and at the intersections between these sites. A victim is blamed for abuse because she stays with a violent man, but she cannot leave because the few emotional and material resources she has left depend on that relationship. Whose problem is this? Hers? His? Theirs? Ours? Rather than searching for an origin, a single thread that unravels the problem, scholars and other social actors constitute these origins by making strategic cuts into the intricate weave of intimate terrorism. A complete formulation of this weave must relate individual actors, their interaction, and the societal norms it embodies. The processes of coorientation, double translation, and distanciation draw such relationships between these sites.

What is the value of mapping the relations between sites of difficulty in intimate terrorism? Beyond identifying the sites at which difficulty emerges, this model traces the ongoing process of supplementation between those sites. That is, each site of difficulty from which intimate terrorism emerges supplements—both adds to and displaces—the last site. Formulations of the aggressor's accountability point to patriarchal discourses, which point to the interaction that constructs them, which points to the participation of the victim, which requires a reformulation of the aggressor's accountability. Although I arbitrarily begin and end the loop there, this process of supplementation does not originate at any particular site. No instantiation of difficulty can stand without the others. By showing the need to understand the individual, relational, and societal constituents of intimate terrorism as a whole, this model provides a framework that encourages dialogue among scholars who approach intimate terrorism from different sites.

REFERENCES

Anderson, K. L., Umberson, D., & Elliott, S. (2004). Violence and abuse in families. In A. Vangelisti (Ed.), *Handbook of family communication* (pp. 629–645). Mahwah, NJ: Lawrence Erlbaum Associates.

Babcock, J. C., Waltz, J., Jacobson, N. S., & Gottman, J. M. (1993). Power and violence: The relation between communication patterns, power discrepancies, and domestic violence. *Journal of Consulting and Clinical Psychology, 61*, 40–50.

Barnett, O. W., Miller-Perrin, C. L., & Perrin, R. D. (1997). *Family violence across the lifespan*. Thousand Oaks, CA: Sage.

Berns, S. B., Jacobson, N. S., & Gottman, J. M. (1999). Demand-withdraw interaction patterns between different types of batterers and their spouses. *Journal of Marital and Family Therapy, 25*, 337–348.

Boyd, N. (2002). *Beast within: Why men are violent.* Vancouver, BC: Groundwood Greystone Books.

Cate, R. M., Henton, J. M., Koval, J. E., Christopher, F. S., & Lloyd, S. A. (1982). Premarital abuse: A social psychological perspective. *Journal of Family Issues, 3*, 79–90.

Christopher, F. S., & Lloyd, S. (2000). Physical and sexual aggression in relationships. In C. Hendrick & S. Hendrick (Eds.), *Close relationships: A sourcebook* (pp. 330–343). Thousand Oaks, CA: Sage.

Coan, J., Gottman, J., Babcock, J., & Jacobson, N. (1997). Battering and the male rejection of influence from women. *Aggressive Behavior, 23*, 375–388.

Cordova, J. V., Jacobson, N. S., Gottman, J. M., Rushe, R., & Cox, G. (1993). Negative reciprocity and communication in couples with a violent husband. *Journal of Abnormal Psychology, 102*, 559–564.

Dugan, S., Umberson, D., & Anderson, K. L. (2001). The batterer's view of the self and others in domestic violence. *Sociological Inquiry, 71*, 221–240.

Dutton, D. G. (1995). A scale for measuring propensity for abusiveness. *Journal of Family Violence, 10*, 203–221.

Dutton, D. G., & Golant, S. K. (1995). *The batterer: A psychological profile.* New York: Basic Books.

Eisikovits, Z. (1996). The aftermath of wife beating: Strategies of bounding violent events. *Journal of Interpersonal Violence, 11*, 459–474.

Feldman, C., & Ridley, C. (2000). The role of conflict-based communication responses and outcomes in male domestic violence toward female partners. *Journal of Social and Personal Relationships, 17*, 552–573.

Ferraro, K. J. (1996). The dance of dependency: A genealogy of domestic violence discourse. *Hypatia, 11*, 77–91.

Gerber, G. L. (1991). Gender stereotypes and power: Perceptions of the roles in violent marriages. *Sex Roles, 24*, 439–459.

Gilfus, M. E. (1999). The price of the ticket: A survivor-centered appraisal of trauma theory. *Violence against Women, 5*, 1238–1257.

Gilligan, J. (2003). Shame, guilt, and violence. *Social Research, 70*, 1149–1181.

Goldner, V. (1999). Morality and multiplicity: Perspectives on the treatment of violence in intimate life. *Journal of Marital and Family Therapy, 25*, 325–336.

Hoff, L. (1993). Women in violent relationships: Why they stayed. In L. Hoff (Ed.), *Battered women as survivors* (pp. 32–55). London: Routledge.

Holtzworth-Munroe, A., Smutzler, N., & Stuart, G. L. (1998). Demand and withdraw communication among couples experiencing husband violence. *Journal of Consulting and Clinical Psychology, 66*, 731–743.

Jacobson, N. S., & Gottman, J. M. (1998). *When men batter women.* New York: Simon & Schuster.

Jacobson, N. S., Gottman, J. M., Waltz, J., Rushe, R., Babcock, J., & Holzworth-Monroe, A. (1994). Affect, verbal content, and psychophysiology in arguments of couples with a violent husband. *Journal of Consulting and Clinical Psychology, 62*, 982–988.

Johnson, M. P. (2001). Conflict and control: Symmetry and asymmetry in domestic violence. In A. Booth, A. Crouter, & M. Clements (Eds.), *Couples in conflict* (pp. 95–104). Mahwah, NJ: Lawrence Erlbaum Associates.

Kanuha, V. (1996). Domestic violence, racism, and the Battered Women's Movement in the United States. In J. L. Edleson & Z. C. Eisikovits (Eds.), *Future in-*

terventions with battered women and their families (pp. 34–50). Thousand Oaks, CA: Sage.

Kelly, L. (1990). How women define their experiences of violence. In K. Yllo & M. Bograd (Eds.), *Feminist perspectives on wife abuse* (pp. 114–132). Newbury Park, CA: Sage.

Lamb, S. (1999). Constructing the victim. In S. Lamb (Ed.), *New versions of victims: Feminists struggle with the concept* (pp. 108–138). New York: New York University Press.

Lawless, E. J. (2001). *Women escaping violence: Empowerment through narrative.* Columbia: University of Missouri Press.

Lempert, L. (1996). Women's strategies for survival: Developing agency in abusive relationships. *Journal of Family Violence, 11,* 269–289.

Lloyd, S., & Emery, B. (2000). The context and dynamics of intimate aggression against women. *Journal of Social and Personal Relationships, 17,* 503–521.

Marcus, G., & Fischer, M. M. J. (1986). *Anthropology as cultural critique: An experimental moment in the human sciences.* Chicago: University of Chicago Press.

McDermott, M. J., & Garofalo, J. (2004). When advocacy for domestic violence victims backfires: Types and sources of victim disempowerment. *Violence against Women, 10,* 1245–1266.

Merritt-Gray, M., & Wuest, J. (2001). Counteracting abuse and breaking free: The process of leaving revealed through women's voices. *Journal of Care for Women International, 16,* 399–412.

Meyers, M. (1997). *News coverage of violence against women: Engendering blame.* Thousand Oaks, CA: Sage.

Mihalic, S., & Elliott, D. (1997). A social learning theory model of marital violence. *Journal of Family Violence, 12,* 21–47.

O'Leary, K. (2000). Are women really more aggressive than men in intimate relationships? Comment on Archer (2000). *Psychological Bulletin, 126,* 685–689.

O'Leary, K. D., Barling, J., Arias, I., Rosenbaum, A., Malone, J., & Tyree, A. (1989). Prevalence and stability of physical aggression between spouses: A longitudinal analysis. *Journal of Consulting and Clinical Psychology, 57,* 263–268.

Olson, L. N. (2004). The role of voice in the (re)construction of a battered woman's identity: An autoethnography of one woman's experiences of abuse. *Women's Studies in Communication, 27,* 1–23.

Olson, L. N., & Lloyd, S. A. (in press). "It depends on what you mean by starting": An exploration of how women define initiation of aggression and their motives for behaving aggressively. *Sex Roles.*

Reissman, B. (1992). Making sense of marital violence: One woman's narrative. In G. Rosenwald & R. Ochberg (Eds.), *Storied lives* (pp. 231–249). New Haven, CT: Yale University Press.

Rogers, L. E., Castleton, A., & Lloyd, S. A. (1996). Relational control and physical aggression in satisfying marital relationships. In D. D. Cahn & S. A. Lloyd (Eds.), *Family violence from a communication perspective* (pp. 218–239). Thousand Oaks, CA: Sage.

Sabourin, T., & Stamp, G. (1995). Communication and the experience of dialectical tensions in family life: An examination of abusive and nonabusive families. *Communication Monographs, 62,* 213–242.

Sagrestano, L. M., Heavey, C. L., & Christensen, A. (1999). Perceived power and physical violence in marital conflict. *Journal of Social Issues, 55,* 65–79.

Scott, M., & Lyman, S. (1968). Accounts. *American Sociological Review, 33,* 46–62.

Stets, J. E. (1988). *Domestic violence and control.* New York: Springer.

Straus, M. A. (1999). The controversy over domestic violence by women: A methodological, theoretical, and sociology of science analysis. In X. B. Arriaga & S. Oskamp (Eds.), *Violence in intimate relationships* (pp. 17–44). Thousand Oaks, CA: Sage.

Sugarman, D., & Frankel, S. (1996). Patriarchal ideology and wife-assault: A meta-analytic review. *Journal of Family Violence, 11,* 11–40.

Taylor, J. R. (1995). Shifting from a heteronomous to an autonomous world-view of organizational communication: Communication theory on the cusp. *Communication Theory, 5,* 1–35.

Taylor, J. R., Cooren, F., Giroux, N., & Robichaud, D. (1996). The communicational basis of organization: Between the conversation and the text. *Communication Theory, 6,* 1–39.

Taylor, J. R., & Van Every, E. J. (2000). *The emergent organization: Communication as its site and surface.* Mahwah, NJ: Lawrence Erlbaum Associates.

Wood, G. G., & Roche, S. E. (2001). Situations and representations: Feminist practice with survivors of violence. *Families in Society: The Journal of Contemporary Human Services, 82,* 583–591.

Wood, J. T. (2000). "That wasn't the real him": Women's dissociation of violence from the men who enact it. *Qualitative Research in Review, 1,* 1–7.

Wood, J. T. (2001). The normalization of violence in heterosexual romantic relationships: Women's narratives of love and violence. *Journal of Social and Personal Relationships, 18,* 239–261.

Wood, J. T. (2004). Monsters and victims: Male felons' accounts of intimate partner violence. *Journal of Social and Personal Relationships, 21,* 555–576.

Chapter 4

Leadership as the Management of Power in Relationships at Work

Michael J. Lovaglia
University of Iowa
Jeffrey W. Lucas
University of Maryland–College Park

In everyday thinking, leadership is often conceived in terms of the formal power that leaders have to command the behavior of their followers. In sociology, the term has been given more differentiated consideration and in the relationship literature too, there are complexities beyond this everyday analysis. For example, the power to control others makes relationships difficult between leaders and followers. New leaders are cautioned against trying to be friends with their subordinates and advised that it is better for a leader to be respected than liked (Cohen, 2000). Individuals recently promoted to a supervisory position have difficulty because they can no longer interact as equals with coworkers. The problem is especially difficult for women and minority group members because their authority is more likely to be resisted (Ridgeway, 2001). They may be required to make greater use of their formal power, resulting in negative reactions from followers and even more difficult relationships with them.

Other aspects of a leader's power, status, and relationships may, therefore, be more important than formal structural power when it comes to managing difficult relationships with coworkers and, surprisingly, to more effectively achieve group goals. The term *informal power* is used in the literature on relationships to indicate the kind of influence that develops in a relationship when, for example, one person likes another. While such influence falls outside our narrow definition of power as a structural capacity to reward or punish, its use as an antidote to problems created by power use is discussed later. The influence generated by sentiments such as liking has been shown to combine with other kinds of status characteristics (Shelly & Webster, 1997).

Weber (1920/1968) noted that social hierarchies have several dimensions—of which formal power is only one. Status based on informal prestige and honor rather than formal power is another dimension, one capable of mitigating some of the problems created by unequal structural power. When a leader is held in sufficiently high regard in terms of informal prestige and honor, then workers will follow her lead without the spur of formal power use. We propose that the attainment and use of high status may allow leaders to manage formal power in ways that maintain relationships and effectively accomplish goals.

SOCIAL POWER AT WORK

Power is a basic concept used in both the natural and social sciences to understand our experience; as such, it has a variety of meanings (Wrong, 1979). In its broadest sense, it can mean the capacity to accomplish anything. Weber (1920/1968) defined the social nature of *power* as the ability to carry out one's will despite others' resistance. Rather than "power to" accomplish a goal, Weber emphasized an individual's "power over" others. His definition still influences much social research. More recently, Elliott and Smith (2004) define social power at work as "authority and control over others in the workplace" (p. 365). *Authority* is power that has been legitimated or institutionalized and is local in scope. Managers have the authority to require workers to dress appropriately in the office but have no authority to regulate their attire at home. Most working definitions used by current social researchers are consonant with Weber's definition that includes resistance as a necessary aspect of power use. Control over others implies resistance because it requires that absent the power they would not have behaved in the desired way.

Social power that counts is more than individual ability. Rather, it emanates from an individual's position in society. Hobbes (1881) noted that no individual is so able that he or she can resist an attack by several others working together. Yet a general in command of an army controls thousands of individuals. When that general leaves the military, however, his or her power stays with the position to be used by the next general to occupy the position.

Recent research in sociology defines power narrowly to separate it from other related concepts and to facilitate research.[1] We define power as emanating from a social position, whether formal or informal, that allows one individual to reward or punish another. Power is similarly conceived in political science as the ability to take resources from one group or individual and give them to another (Hermann et al., 2004). In our narrow definition, power is relational; it exists in any relationship where one individual has power over another or several others (Emerson 1962). Power can develop in relationships without formal authority. For example, suppose that a client will buy from only one salesperson in a company and from no one else. The salesperson has acquired power over a third person—her supervisor—to the extent that the supervisor values that client's business. The salesperson may be in a position to demand privileges that the supervisor denies to other salespeople. A supervisor, then, can have formal authority over a top salesperson but be unable to exercise it because the salesperson has informal or relational power over the supervisor.

Power is a fundamental aspect of social interaction. Suppose, for example, that a lonely man asks a popular woman out on a date. The woman, confident that she will have a number of alternative invitations, has the power to dictate the couple's activities. If the man refuses, she will go out with someone else while the man will have more difficulty finding a companion. Waller and Hill (1951) proposed the Principle of Least Interest, which states that the individual in a relationship who has the least interest in continuing it has the most control over it. For example, the person most in love in a romantic relationship has the least power. When one member of a couple is madly in love and the other relatively indifferent, it is the one who cares less that can direct the couple's activities. In Emerson's (1962) theory, the more dependent a person is on a relationship, the less power they have in it. He proposed that power develops in relationships when one person becomes dependent on the other. The more a person values a relationship and the less she is able to obtain comparable rewards from alternate relationships, the more power the relationship partner will have. For example, when a person falls in love she becomes dependent on the other person in the relationship, increasing her partner's power over her.

The relational problems associated with power use are well researched. While attaining a position of power may be satisfying (Lovaglia & Houser, 1996), being in a low-power position induces negative emotions. Willer, Lovaglia, and Markovsky (1997) created a working environment in which participants acted as buyers for a manufacturing concern negotiating in a network of buyers and suppliers. Some positions in the network had power over others when buyers bid for scarce supplies or when several suppliers competed for a buyer's business. Participants randomly assigned to a high-power position reported feeling more happy and satisfied than did those assigned to a low-power position. Those assigned low-power positions reported feeling more angry and resentful than did those assigned to high-power positions.

Unequal power is also hard on relationships because power use creates resistance. Lawler and Yoon (1993, 1996, 1998) found that continuing exchange relationships such as those commonly found in the workplace build commitment. The relationship between two individuals grows stronger as they negotiate the exchange of goods and services over time. However, Lawler and Yoon also found that commitment to the relationship grows only to the extent that exchanges are equal. Relationships characterized by unequal power inhibit the establishment of commitment.

Research in organizations shows the benefits of restraint in the use of power. That is, work groups function best when those with power are not using it. Leaders are least likely to need to use their power when others in the organization believe that the power is deserved. Brass and Burkhardt (1993) found that when power is legitimate—that is, authorized or perceived to be earned—those with power do not need to use any specific tactics to show that they are powerful. When power is not legitimate, however, the situation is different. Rodriguez-Bailon, Moya, and Yzerbyt (2000) found that when power is seen as illegitimate, those with power feel threatened by the fact that their positions may be disputed. As a result, these individuals begin to engage in processes allowing them to justify their privileged positions. They do this in part by paying more attention to negative characteristics of other group members. Yukl, Kim, and Falbe (1996) found that superiors who were liked, respected, and admired used power less and yet had more influence over their subordinates than did less respected managers.

The power of a leader is likely to be seen as illegitimate when group members question the competence of the leader. In these cases, leaders become more likely to use their power. The leader might convince subordinates of her or his power, but a further result in most cases will be even lower perceptions of the leader's competence. Bruins and De Gilder (1999), for example, found that managers who used more power, compared to those who used less power, were evaluated as less likable, less cooperative, and lower on managerial qualities. Moreover, they found that power use was considered significantly less legitimate when subordinates considered the superior less competent.

In sum, recent research suggests that effective leaders use power least because power use creates difficulties for ongoing relationships. To be effective, however, leaders must do more than maintain positive relationships; they must also manage and motivate subordinates. How can workers be managed and motivated without a leader who uses power?

STATUS IN WORK GROUPS AND SOCIETY

We use the term *status* to refer to an individual's rank in the prestige hierarchy of a group. When a coworker is held in high regard, when she is esteemed and honored by people who work with her, she has high status. It is a good thing to have and many people work hard to attain it. As a motivator, the prospect of increased status is as effective as the prospect of higher pay and even power. For example, executives on the job market will often choose a vice presidency at a smaller company over a middle-manager position at a larger company that pays more and controls more people (Frank 1985). Thus, a formal position such as vice president comes with a degree of authorized power but is also a status characteristic, bringing with it prestige and expectations for the competence of the person in it.

Status, as conceived in status characteristics and expectation states theories, is a property of task groups (Berger, Fisek, Norman, & Zelditch, 1977). When social equals get together in a group to solve some problem, a status hierarchy usually forms quickly. The theories propose that group members seek information on which to base expectations for how much each group member is likely to contribute to the group. Those expectations for members' contributions to group goals then determine their relative status. That is, status hierarchies emerge because of a group's focus on a collective task. To the extent that social groups have members focused on a collective goal, status hierarchies would be predicted to emerge in them as well. Creation and maintenance of status hierarchies in social groups as opposed to task groups have been little studied and could be a fruitful topic of research for those interested in difficult relationships because status competition seems to occur in social situations as well. The unspoken and sometimes unconscious expectations that engender status distinctions might produce difficulties for relationships when relationship partners hold differing expectations for each other's social position.

To investigate the value that workers place on status, Greenberg (1988) conducted a field experiment in which workers at an insurance agency temporarily performed their jobs in the offices of higher-status or lower-status coworkers. He found that those placed in the offices of higher-status coworkers worked harder and felt overpaid compared to those in lower-status offices who worked less and felt underpaid. Not only are workers motivated by the esteem and honor of high status, but they also value proximity to others of high status as well as the symbolic perquisites that accompany status.

Competition for status can also cause problems, although usually not as serious as those produced by the struggle for power (which can lead to violence and even war). When people compete for the symbols of status—prime parking places or corner offices, for example—rather than for status itself, the result sometimes provides insight into our human quirks. A colleague of ours is both a sociologist and a lawyer. He tells the story of a prestigious Chicago law firm that remodeled its offices in the top floors of a tall office building. Law offices have a clear status hierarchy with partners on top, associates in the middle, and paralegals at the bottom. Partners had their large offices on the upper floor while paralegals were crammed into cubicles in the center of the lower floor. For a few weeks, while the lower floor was being remodeled, paralegals were moved to the upper floor while partners moved out to temporary offices elsewhere. Coming to work that Monday morning, some paralegals were delighted to find that they shared a spacious corner office with a gorgeous view of Lake Michigan. Excited by their good fortune, they told their friends and word spread. Others, however, found this blow against the status order difficult to accept. When the paralegals arrived at their corner office the following Monday, they found that their floor-to-ceiling windows had been boarded over with plywood. The windows remained covered until the paralegals moved back to their windowless cubicles on the lower floor. Thus, status competition such as that between lawyers and paralegals can itself motivate arbitrary power use that makes relationships at work more difficult.

The competition for status itself, for the esteem and honor of those with whom one works, usually has positive effects on workplace relationships and productivity. An individual's status is composed of the expectations of coworkers for that individual's contributions to the group (Berger et al., 1977). If we asked members of a work group to rank each other in terms of their contributions and value to the group's success, then those members ranked high would have the highest status. The connection between status and group productivity is easy to see. Group members compete to contribute the most to the group's success. Lucas and Lovaglia (1998) randomly created status differences between group members and then assigned high-status members to leadership positions. They found that although assignments were random, group members evaluated high-status members as more competent and harder working than low-status members. Leadership accompanied by status, then, carries with it expectations for competence.[2] Further, increased status might increase competence as well. Lucas (1999) assigned high-performing workers to high-status leadership positions in groups. He found that these workers, compared to high performers not given high-status leadership assignments, worked harder and were more committed to the group. Also, when individuals believe that they have high status within a group, they become more likely to carry out activities explicitly for the benefit of the group (Tyler & Blader, 2002).

The rewards for high status are substantial and cumulative over the course of a career. When working with others on group tasks, high-status members are advantaged in four important ways (Berger et al., 1977). First, they are given more opportunities to perform. For example, when working in a group, high-status members are more likely to be asked for their advice on how the group should proceed. Second, high-status members also perform more. For example, they more often contribute their ideas and advice about how best to complete a group task. Third, high-status members receive higher evaluations for their performances. Their contributions will be viewed as more important and effective than those of low-status members. Fourth, high-status members have greater influence over group decisions than do other group members. That is, other group members will more likely follow the advice of high-status members than the advice of low-status members.

These four outcomes of high status—opportunity, performance, positive evaluation, and influence—yield profound long-term advantages for those who enjoy high status. When an individual receives a higher performance evaluation because of her status, it implies that she is evaluated more highly than a coworker *for the same level of performance*. That is, when the choice is between two equally competent and productive workers, the worker with higher status will receive the promotion. Moreover, because high-status workers have more opportunities to perform and perform more, they can more easily demonstrate their competence and productivity, thus ensuring their continued higher status. The status order of a group, then, becomes relatively stable and is self-fulfilling. Quite unlike power, there is a large degree of consensus in a stable status hierarchy over who should be high status and who should be low. That is, even low-status members of a group generally agree that high-status members are more competent and contribute more to the group's success.

Other aspects of the status process, how individuals attain and maintain their status, are less benign. Status differences based on sex and race contribute to some of our most difficult relationships. Status results from the *expectations* of group members for each others' competent performance and valuable contributions to group success. While actual performance and contributions affect expectations, other factors alter expectations as well. The process of attaining and maintaining social status is important not only at the level of the work group but in the larger society as well. Human beings are remarkably status conscious and we become adept at reading the sometimes subtle cues that indicate where a person fits in the status hierarchy. When individuals come together to form a work group, they automatically (often unconsciously) read these cues and quickly establish a status hierarchy (Berger et al., 1977). Thus, individuals' social status in society at large is imported into work groups meeting for the first time, a process called *status generalization* (Webster & Foschi, 1988).

The main *status characteristics* that those in the United States use to form expectations about coworkers' competence and contributions are sex/gender, race, age, physical appearance, education, and occupation (Webster & Foschi, 1988). For example, when a work group forms, those members who are male and White will assume higher status than members who are female and non-White. As the group works together over time, the demonstrated competence and contributions of individuals can alter their relative status. But recall the self-fulfilling nature of the status process. Once formed, status hierarchies are remarkably stable. Women and minorities, for example, will have lower status in their groups than they would otherwise have based on their competence and contributions. In contrast, White men have higher status than is justified by their performance. A brilliant suggestion made by a woman can be dismissed by coworkers, or attributed to a man who then gets the credit. Productivity suffers when the valuable contributions of some group members are systematically devalued while the mistakes of other are rewarded.

Our individual working lives are conducted in a broader social context. We bring society with us to work every day. How we relate to people and the techniques that allow us to succeed at work vary depending on our position in society. That is, a person's sex, race or ethnicity, education, and socioeconomic status complicate relationships at work, changing the way that people relate to each other. Ways of relating that prove effective for White male managers may create resistance in co-workers when applied by a white woman or by a Black man. Elliott and Smith (2004) surveyed workers and found that not only do women and minorities have less access to positions of power than do White men, but that the level of inequality increases at higher levels of power. The result is a glass ceiling effect with few women and minorities in top leadership positions.

The organization of work, then, is as blatantly unfair as society in general. Although many work hard to mitigate that unfairness, effective intervention requires an accurate picture of relationships at work. It may also be true that working in groups is fundamentally unfair. People work in groups to accomplish goals that no individual could achieve working alone. When a task is so complex that it requires the specialized contributions of more than a few individuals, someone has the job of organizing the work of others. That is, someone is in charge, telling other people what to do. While this may be necessary to coordinate work on complex tasks effectively, nonetheless, someone is giving an order and someone else takes it.

Relationships of unequal power characterize work in organizations, and are necessary to accomplish complex tasks. The goal of an effective leader is to manage unequal power relationships in ways that minimize the problems caused by them. Understanding status processes can help us manage relationships made difficult by structural power differences.

STATUS ATTAINMENT AND THE MAINTENANCE OF POSITIVE RELATIONSHIPS

Status research has found that the effects of various status characteristics combine in predictable ways to determine an individual's status (Berger, Norman, Balkwell, & Smith, 1992). In most work settings, each individual has several status characteristics that group members use to form expectations for that individual's contributions to the group. These aggregated expectations then determine the group's status hierarchy.

The discovery that the effects of different status characteristics combine is noteworthy because it is to some extent counterintuitive. It was commonly believed that being a woman or a minority prevented significant achievement for most individuals because their low status on one characteristic would dominate the expectations that others held for their ability to contribute. For example, when a Black executive in a hotel lobby is mistaken for a bellhop and asked by a White guest to carry his suitcase, or when a young female executive with an MBA is asked to serve coffee rather sit at the conference table for an important meeting, it seems plausible that personal achievement, education, and occupation do little to overcome discrimination. Instead, however, research has shown that no single status characteristic overrides the others (Berger et al., 1992). Moreover, several low-status characteristics produce only slightly lower expectations than does a single low-status characteristic, but adding one high-status characteristic to several low-status characteristics will have a large effect on expectations. The unjust relegation to lower status of a Black woman, for example, is alleviated to a large degree when she attains higher education.

The theory also proposes that some characteristics have a greater impact on an individual's status than do others (Berger et al., 1977). Diffuse characteristics such as sex and race affect expectations in a wide variety of settings but have limited impact. People may expect women and minorities to be less competent in a wide variety of situations, but other characteristics may carry more weight. Specific characteristics that are directly relevant to group success have the greatest impact. If, for example, a group has a difficult legal problem to solve and the one lawyer in the group is a woman, she will have more influence than a male group member will. Past performances also affect expectations for future contributions (Berger et al., 1977). A reputation for success, while harder for a low-status person to acquire than for a high-status person, will raise expectations for that individual's contributions and eventually her status.

Notice that individuals have relatively little control over some characteristics that determine their status, such as sex and race, but more control over others such as education and occupation. The increasing control that individuals have over their physical appearance has interesting implications. Because physical beauty confers status advantages (Webster & Driskell, 1983), the current popularity of cosmetic surgery likely reflects more than vanity resulting from an increasingly self-centered society. Rather, as work becomes more important to many people, more of them may discover that increasing their physical attractiveness and delaying the appearance of aging can extend their effectiveness at work.

The benefits of high status give people good reason to consider cosmetic surgery and also explain why they might want to keep the procedure secret. One reason that status hierarchies are stable is that people resist their alteration. When a low-status worker makes an unexpectedly valuable contribution, it will be viewed with suspicion. Its value will be questioned as will her motivation. Rather than a status-worthy contribution to the group, it will be viewed as an illegitimate bid for a position to which she is unentitled (Ridgeway & Berger, 1986, 1988). Because beauty is a characteristic that brings status, an individual who appears more attractive will have more influence and generally more positive interactions with coworkers. An individual, however, who is perceived to have gone to great lengths to become more attractive may be viewed with suspicion as someone making an illegitimate attempt to enhance status.

Status research explains the difficulty that women and minorities have when they attain leadership positions. When a White man attains a leadership position, coworkers assume that some degree of merit was involved in the promotion. The new leader fairly easily reestablishes relationships with peers who are now subordinates. In contrast, coworkers hold quite different assumptions about a newly promoted woman. She may be accused of using unfair advantage to achieve her position. Affirmative action is commonly the reason attributed to the promotion of minorities to management positions. Because the promotion of women and minorities is assumed to be illegitimate, relationships between the new leader and subordinates remain strained. Even when workers think as highly of a female leader as they do a male leader, they consider their group to be less effective when led by a woman (Lucas & Lovaglia, 1998). Moreover, Lucas (2003) found that women had less influence than otherwise similar men did, even when women were assigned to leadership positions based on their demonstrated ability.

Using Group Motivation to Maintain Relationships

Ridgeway (1982) discovered a way for low-status leaders to enhance their status and repair the relationships strained by their status attainment. Low-status group members can attain higher status by presenting themselves as individuals who are more motivated to contribute to the group. In designing her research, Ridgeway theorized that high status involves more than group members' expectations about an individual's competence. For those competence expectations to translate into higher prestige, group members also have to expect that an individual will use her competence to help the group succeed. Therefore, low-status individuals who show themselves to be not only competent but also group-motivated (rather than selfishly motivated) will attain higher status in the group.

Ridgeway (1982) also proposed that people assume that high-status group members will use their competence to help the group. That is why they are high status. In contrast, people assume that low-status members are selfishly motivated rather than group motivated. That is one reason why the contributions of women and minorities meet such resistance from other group members. Not only might presenting oneself as group motivated increase the influence and prestige of a low-status group member, but it also might lessen the resistance faced by women and minorities who become leaders.

Ridgeway designed an experiment to test her theory. In it, group members worked with a man or a woman who presented himself or herself as either group motivated or selfishly motivated. A group-motivated person might stress the importance of working together as a group and cooperating. Whereas selfishly motivated persons might say they were primarily interested in earning a bonus. The results were as predicted and striking. When the man and woman presented themselves as self-motivated, the man had much more influence over group decisions than did the woman. That difference disappeared, however, when the man and woman presented themselves as group motivated. Presenting himself as group-motivated increased the man's influence only slightly. In contrast, women gained substantial influence by presenting themselves as group-motivated. The result was that men and women who presented themselves as group-motivated had almost equally high influence. Women leaders, then, who present themselves as group-motivated, are likely to have as much or more influence over their work groups as will typical men leaders who often present themselves as self-motivated. Thus, a simple, self-presentational technique has the potential to mitigate the problems of women leaders in the difficult relationships they encounter at work.

A follow-up study by Shackelford, Wood, and Worchel (1996) confirmed and extended Ridgeway's results. Along with presentation as group motivated, they also investigated the effects of demonstrating competence and assertive behavior on the influence of women in work groups. They found that all three strategies—demonstrated competence, assertive behavior, and presentation as group motivated—increased the influence of women in work groups. Also as expected, they found that assertive behavior necessary for effective leadership produced resistance and created problems for women who tried it. In contrast, women who presented themselves as group motivated attained higher status without encountering the resistance usually encountered by women leaders.

The research on power and status we have described both explains and offers a partial solution to the difficult relationships encountered by women and minorities who become leaders. A leadership position requires the use of power that creates resistance and resentment among those on whom it is used. Because of their low status, women and minorities who become leaders will likely need to use their power more than will White men. Thus, women and minority leaders face greater difficulty in relationships with their subordinates. The research on group motivation, however, suggests that by presenting themselves as group-motivated, women and minority leaders can use power without creating significantly more resentment than do White male leaders. Further research, especially in applied settings, could be beneficial.

Emotion at Work

Leaders face the dilemma of having to motivate followers while limiting power use. The discovery by status researchers that the effects of status characteristics and other factors combine to determine a person's influence on others in a work group may help resolve that dilemma. When group members follow the advice of a high-status individual, they do so willingly because they perceive it to be in the best interest of the group and, to the extent they are invested in group goals, of themselves (Berger et al., 1977).

Lovaglia and Houser (1996) investigated the relationship between status and emotion. They found that a person could increase her influence by creating positive emotion in a member of a work group and decrease her influence by creating negative emotion in others. Interestingly, they found that the emotion need not be directed at the leader to have the effect. People who feel happy and more satisfied in general will be more likely to follow a leader's direction than will people who feel angry and resentful. Baron (1987) demonstrated that job interviewers in a bad mood rated a job candidate lower than did job interviewers in a good mood.

Leaders can use the influence produced by their high status and the positive emotions they generate to motivate followers without the negative side effects of power use. Women and minority leaders may initially have to use more power because of their low status, but that can be mitigated. A leadership position is itself a status characteristic, and a record of previous accomplishments has more impact on influence than diffuse status characteristics such as race or sex. Thus, a leadership position and competent performance countervail the initially lower status of women and minority leaders. In sum, recent research in social psychology suggests that women and minorities can increase their influence, effectiveness, and acceptance as a leader by (a) clearly demonstrating their competence, (b) showing assertive, confident behavior, and (c) presenting themselves as group motivated to defuse resistance and negative emotion in their group.

HOW POWER AND STATUS ARE RELATED

Effective leaders can use their knowledge of status processes to manage their relationships with coworkers. Recall that work relationships are characterized by unequal power needed to coordinate the work of large numbers of people. However, power use produces resentment that strains relationships. Recent research has progressed by first separating the concepts of power and status and then showing how they are related. Recall that power as we use the term refers narrowly to the ability to reward or punish another person that emanates from a social position. Status, also narrowly defined, refers to the hierarchy formed when group members are ranked in terms of the prestige and honor in which they are held. For example, when a boss orders an employee to work late on a Friday evening, she uses power. In contrast, when an employee decides on her own to stay late to finish an important job because she knows that her boss would approve, she does so out of respect for her boss, that is, for her boss's high status.

Attaining a Position of Power

In modern organizations, no leader can be effective without attaining a formal leadership position. Climbing the corporate ladder is an important goal for workers who aspire to lead. That climb is often characterized negatively by people who see organizations primarily in terms of power differences and power use. If people rise in an organization by winning power struggles, then those who succeed to leadership have done so by damaging the careers of others. Research on status and power suggests that a focus on power processes in organizations is myopic for both leaders and researchers. There is a better way to succeed.

Effective leaders have both power and high status. That is, they have attained a position that gives them control over the working lives of other people, and they also have earned respect, honor, and prestige from coworkers. Because power and high status are positively correlated in society, an interesting research question asks whether power can be used to gain high status. That is, can a person who uses power gain honor and prestige from that power use? A person could then use power knowing that high status would follow and provide the tools needed to smooth relationship problems created by power use.

In theory, it would seem likely that power produces high status although it might be wise to temper power use during one's rise to the top. Lenski (1966) noted, "Honor is denied to those who rule by force alone" (p. 52). The phrase "force alone," however, leaves much room for power use before a leader risks being denied honor. Lovaglia (1994) proposed three theoretical mechanisms by which power use could increase an individual's status. First, an individual can use power to increases resources. Others who observe those resources may well assume that they were acquired at least in part because of the competence of the power user. Stewart and Moore (1992) found that those who were paid more for a job had increased influence over a coworker who was aware of their pay rate. These expectations for the competence of the power user should then translate into increased status. Second, the resources acquired by the power user can be used to accomplish group goals (Ridgeway 1991). Thus, resources are direct evidence of potential contributions by the power user to the group and increase expectations accordingly. Third, people have good reasons for deferring to those in power who can reward or punish them. When people develop a pattern of deference (Fisek, Berger, & Moore, 2002), they may then come to assume that it is the result of the higher status rather than the power of the person to whom they are in the habit of deferring.

In practice, however, demonstrating an increase in status for those who use power has proven extremely difficult. Lovaglia (1995) found that power use can increase expectations for the competence of the power user, but no increase occurred in the power user's influence, perhaps because of the negative emotional reactions engendered by power use (Willer et al., 1997). It may be possible for power users to gain status by using their power on people outside their own group and refraining from its use within the group (Lovaglia, Willer, & Troyer, 2004), but even that strategy may not be effective for leaders who must manage unequal power relationships within their group. Power use, then, may not represent an effective strategy for leaders aspiring to a position that combines high power with the influence, prestige, and honor that accompany high status.

Using Status Processes to Attain Power

It is also possible that power and status are causally related but in the opposite direction. Recent research shows that it is relatively easy to use status to attain power. Thye (2000) reasoned that because high-status individuals are expected to make valuable contributions to the group, those expectations would generalize such that resources associated with high-status people would also be expected to have greater value. In his study, high-status and low-status individuals were assigned different colors of poker chips that could be acquired in identical ways. That is, it was equally easy for high-status and low-status individuals to acquire their chips, and there was no advantage for a person to acquire or hold one color of chip over the other. Nonetheless, Thye found that people were willing to pay more for the chips of the color associated with high status. Here we see the advantage of seeing work situations from a perspective of status rather than power. People *resent* giving up resources demanded by a more powerful person. In contrast, people *willingly* pay more for resources associated with a high-status person. The implication for leaders is that workers resent being told what to do. In contrast, they willingly follow the lead of a person whom they honor and respect.

USING STATUS TO LEAD

Leaders can maintain positive relationships with their people using the same techniques that are effective for attaining high status without creating resentment: demonstrated competence, assertive, confident behavior, and willingness to contribute to group goals rather than selfish goals.

Effective leaders regularly demonstrate their competence, resisting the temptation to rest on the laurels that resulted in their promotion. The expectations that coworkers hold for the leader's competence fade with time and require renewal. The challenge to regularly demonstrate their competence is made easier for leaders by the phenomenon of status generalization. For example, it is not necessary to continually make new breakthroughs in the technical areas that result in many leaders' success. Rather, demonstrated competence in any salient arena generalizes to higher expectations by coworkers and continued high status for the leader.

Assertive behavior is also important. While effective leaders refrain from the direct use of power over coworkers, assertive, confident behavior ensures that their ideas are heard and respected.

Effective leaders continually demonstrate their willingness to sacrifice merely personal goals to contribute to group success. For example, new executives are taught to be the first one in the office in the morning and the last one to leave at night, not because workers require their supervision, but because the leaders' sacrifice increases their status and influence.[3] Workers who see the boss giving up her leisure time to contribute to their success will be more likely to follow her lead.

Status as a Solution to the Problem of Unequal Contributions

Resentment over who has contributed more or less than their fair share is a major impediment to maintaining positive relationships. Effective leaders can use their understanding of status processes to dramatically reduce the negative effects of the equity problem, both in their relationships with coworkers and in the resentments of coworkers for each other.

We noted that status hierarchies form naturally in work groups and may be necessary for the efficient completion of many group tasks. That is, coworkers form expectations for each other's contributions to group success that vary from large to small. Because of differences in workers' competence, motivation, and the self-fulfilling nature of status processes, workers also range widely in their actual contributions from those who contribute little or nothing to those who seem to always put in the extra work needed for the group to succeed.[4] It is easy for those who contribute more to resent those who share in the rewards of group success while apparently contributing little to it. Equity theory and research has shown that when individuals feel underrewarded or overrewarded, they are motivated to redress the inequity (Hatfield & Sprecher, 1984). Perceived inequity has been shown to produce physiological arousal (Markovsky, 1988). Negative emotions and attempts to redress inequity are more likely when individuals perceive themselves to be underrewarded, while cognitive reassessments are more likely when individuals feel overrewarded (Hatfield & Sprecher, 1984). Moreover, those who contribute little often justify their work with resentment of the way they are treated. Leaders too are prone to resentment due to the isolation of their position. It is easy for leaders to begin thinking that they are doing most of the work while their coworkers are idling along behind them.

To resolve the difficulty in relationships produced by the unequal contributions of workers, a manager could attempt to use power to equalize contributions. Underperforming workers could be punished with a resulting increase in their resentment. Underperforming workers that increase performance could also be rewarded but that would likely increase the resentment of overperforming workers who might reasonably expect additional rewards. In sum, negative reactions to power use are difficult to avoid.

Research on the benefits of high status suggests that workers who contribute more than their share *are* being rewarded for it. The rewards of high status are so great that the responsibility to contribute more than others is trivial in comparison. Further, those rewards would be impossible without the smaller contributions of low-status workers who set the standard that allows high-status workers to excel. The rewards of high status that result from contributing more than one's fair share to group success go beyond increases in pay and the likelihood of promotion. High-status workers are happier at work (Bokemeier & Lacy, 1987, Grunig, 1990; Lucas, 1999). They feel less stress and are healthier in general (Matthews & Power, 2002; Turner & Avison, 2003).[5] Making clear the value of the indirect benefits of contributing to a work group could help alleviate much of the difficulty in worker relationships caused by their unequal contributions. More research, especially in applied settings, could be fruitful here.

Thinking in Terms of Status Rather Than Power

The temptation is great for leaders to think of their position in terms of power use. What good is the ability to reward and punish if never used? Yet as Emerson (1962, 1972) noted, to use power risks setting in motion forces of resentment and discontent capable of reducing a leader's power. Leaders who think in terms of power ask: How can I reward or punish my people to get them to do a job they otherwise would not do? It usually will be more effective, however, to think in terms of status: How can I show people that doing a job that contributes to the group's success increases their prestige as well? Then their desire to attain status will provide the motivation without resentment.

A classic example of invoking status to motivate comes from a field experiment that sought to determine how best to motivate fifth-grade students in an antilittering campaign (Miller, Brickman, & Bolen, 1975). Two different techniques were used on different classes. Teachers used proven persuasive techniques in some classes such as repetition, explaining the benefits, and active role playing. In other classes, teachers made no attempt to persuade students but instead informed students that they had been recognized as among the most responsible and neatest classes in school. Labeling the students as responsible and neat gave them a status to maintain; they were ranked above students in other classes in terms of prestige and honor. The effect was dramatic. Students whom teachers attempted to persuade not to litter improved little and soon reverted to their earlier behavior. In contrast, students who had a status position to protect littered much less and the effect persisted.

While the negative effects of power use can be lessened by relying primarily on rewards rather than punishments, even rewards have limited motivational effect. After all, the withdrawal of an expected reward feels similar to punishment. Moreover, workers would like to maximize their rewards. The tendency is to try to gain the greatest reward for the least effort. While workers want rewards and will work for them, they nonetheless resent the feeling of dependency that develops toward the leader who dispenses those rewards. (See Emerson 1962, 1972 for the reciprocal relationship between power and dependency.)

Understanding the importance of status as a motivator and the benefits of limiting power use also underscores the value of patience in a leader. Leadership is the management of relationships of unequal power to create a group that can effectively address a wide variety of problems. Using power to solve an immediate problem efficiently can damage relationships in ways that reduce the effectiveness of the group. Understanding status allows one to motivate workers to achieve without telling them what to do while at the same time earning their appreciation rather than their resentment. The next problem a team encounters may well be solved before their leader hears about it. When motivated by status, members of task groups will compete with each other to be first to identify and solve problems. Effective leaders realize that the relationship is more important than any individual task outcome.

NOTES

1. Recent research on power has developed away from previous thinking that conceived virtually all social interaction as some kind of power, primarily because confusion over what constitutes power slowed progress. Particularly difficult was deciphering whether each use of the term referred to "power to" accomplish something or "power over" another person. For example, French and Raven (1968) proposed a number of bases of power only some of which refer to power as we use it here in this chapter, the ability to reward or punish others. Of particular relevance for our later discussion is their concept of *expert power* as an individual's ability to influence others due to technical expertise relevant to a group's goals. It is possible that technical expertise could produce power in the sense that we use the term, but only to the extent that the expert could use her knowledge to reward or punish others by sharing or withholding it. Emerson's (1962) power–dependence theory suggests that power would then be limited by the availability of the knowledge from other sources. Thus expertise may or may not be a source of power but always confers some degree of prestige and influence on the expert.

2. The reverse process can also be seen, that is, competence implies expectations for leadership. The common problem of those with technical expertise rising to management positions in which they are less competent is the basis for the Peter Principle.

3. One might ask who would know that the boss is the first to arrive and last to leave, which would seem to limit the effectiveness of the strategy. It is common, however, for workers to make a game of trying to come in earlier or stay later than the boss, especially if the boss is well respected. Not only does this produce the desired effect but word spreads as workers recount their successes or failures.

4. As explained in the section Status in Work Groups and Society, high status individuals receive more opportunities to perform, perform more and receive higher evaluations for performances than do those with lower status. Thus, not only is it likely that those with high status will contribute more to group success, but even if they contribute less, group members are likely to give them more credit than they deserve. Because expected contributions to group success form the basis for status, high status is self-fulfilling.

5. While it can be argued that high-status positions in society also usually come with a high degree of power and these examples do not adequately separate the two, it is unlikely that power in the sense of rewarding and punishing others produces the social, emotional, and health benefits found. Rather, high-status positions confer prestige, honor, and their attendant social benefits largely to the extent that individuals in them refrain from using the power that comes with those positions. High-status workers with relatively little power, ministers and professors for example, seem to derive these benefits in greater measure than do high-status workers with more power such as lawyers and judges. Politicians may be the best example of professionals who wield great power but whose status, job satisfaction, and sometimes health suffer.

REFERENCES

. Baron, R. A. (1987). Mood interviewer and the evaluation of job candidates. *Journal of Applied Social Psychology, 17*, 911–926.

Berger, J., Fisek, M. H., Norman, R. Z., & Zelditch, M., Jr. (1977). *Status characteristics and social interaction: An expectations states approach.* New York: Elsevier.

Berger, J., Norman, R. Z., Balkwell, J., & Smith, R. F. (1992). Status inconsistency in task situations: A test of four status processing principles. *American Sociological Review, 57*, 843–855.

Bokemeier, J. L., & Lacy, W. B. (1987). Job values, rewards, and work conditions as factors in job satisfaction among men and women. *The Sociological Quarterly, 28*(2), 189–204.

Brass, D. J., & Burkhardt, M. E. (1993). Potential power and power use: An investigation of structure and behavior. *Academy of Management Journal, 36*(3), 441–470.

Bruins, J., Ellemers, N., & De Gilder, D. (1999). Power use and differential competence as determinants of subordinates evaluative and behavioural responses in simulated organizations. *European Journal of Social Psychology, 29*, 843–870.

Cohen, W. (2000). *The new art of the leader.* New Jersey: Prentice-Hall Press.

Elliott, J. R., & Smith, R. A. (2004). Race, gender, and workplace power. *American Sociological Review, 69*, 365–386.

Emerson, R. M. (1962). Power-dependence relations. *American Sociological Review, 27*, 31–40.

Emerson, R. M. (1972). Exchange theory, Part I: A psychological basis for social exchange. In J. Berger, M. Zelditch, Jr., & B. Anderson (Eds.), *Sociological theories in progress* (Vol. 2, pp. 38–57). Boston: Houghton-Mifflin.

Fisek, M. H., Berger, J. & Moore, J. C., Jr. (2002). Evaluations, enactment, and expectations. *Social Psychology Quarterly, 65*, 329–345.

Frank, R. H. (1985). *Choosing the right pond.* New York: Oxford University Press.

French, J. R. P., Jr., & Raven, B. (1968). The bases of social power. In D. Cartwright & A. Zander (Eds.), *Group dynamics* (pp. 259–269). New York: Harper & Row.

Greenberg, J. (1988). Equity and workplace status: A field experiment. *Journal of Applied Psychology, 73*, 606–613.

Grunig, L. A. (1990). An exploration of the causes of job satisfaction in public relations. *Management Communication Quarterly, 3*, 355–375.

Hatfield, E., & Sprecher, S. (1984). Equity theory and behavior in organizations. *Research in the Sociology of Organizations, 3*, 95–124.

Hermann, C. P., Lovaglia, M. J., Mannix, E. A., Samuelson, C. D., Sell, J., & Wilson, R. K. (2005). Conflict, power and status in groups. In M. S. Poole & A. B. Hollingshead (Eds), *Theories of small groups: An interdisciplinary perspective* (pp. 139–184). Thousand Oaks, CA: Sage.

Hobbes, T. (1881). *Leviathan.* Oxford, UK: James Thornton.

Lawler, E. J., & Yoon, J. (1993). Power and the emergence of commitment behavior in negotiated exchange. *American Sociological Review, 58*, 465–481.

Lawler, E. J., & Yoon, J. (1996). Commitment in exchange relations: Test of a theory of relational cohesion. *American Sociological Review, 61*, 89–108.

Lawler, E. J., & Yoon, J. (1998). Network structure and emotion in exchange relations. *American Sociological Review, 63*, 871–894.

Lenski, G. (1966). *Power and privilege: A theory of stratification.* McGraw Hill: New York.

Lovaglia, M. J. (1994). Relating power to status. *Advances in Group Process, 11*, 87–111.

Lovaglia, M. J. (1995). Power and status: Exchange, attribution and expectation states. *Small Group Research, 26*, 400–26.

Lovaglia, M. J., & Houser, J. A. (1996). Emotional reactions and status in groups. *American Sociological Review, 61*, 867–883.

Lovaglia, M. J., Willer, R., & Troyer, L. (2004). Power, status and collective action: Developing fundamental theories to address a substantive problem. In S. R. Thye, J. Skvoretz, & E. J. Lawler (Eds.), *Advances in Group Processes* (Vol. 20, pp. 105–131). San Diego, CA: Elsevier.

Lucas, J. W. (1999). Behavioral and emotional outcomes of leadership in task groups. *Social Forces, 78*, 747–776.

Lucas, J. W. (2003). Status processes and the institutionalization of women as leaders. *American Sociological Review, 68*, 464–480.

Lucas, J. W., & Lovaglia, M. J. (1998). Leadership status, gender, group size, and emotion in face-to-face groups. *Sociological Perspectives, 41*, 617–637.

Markovsky, B. (1988). Injustice and arousal. *Social Justice Research, 2*, 223–233.

Matthews, S., & Power, C. (2002). Socio-economic gradients in psychological distress: A focus on women, social roles and work-home characteristics. *Social Science and Medicine, 54*, 799–810.

Miller, R. L., Brickman, P., & Bolen, D. (1975). Attribution versus persuasion as a means for modifying behavior. *Journal of Personality and Social Psychology*, *31*, 430–441.

Ridgeway, C. L. (1982). Status in groups: The importance of motivation. *American Sociological Review*, *47*, 76–88.

Ridgeway, C. L. (1991). The social construction of status value: Gender and other nominal characteristics. *Social Forces*, *70*, 367–386.

Ridgeway, C. L. (2001). Gender, status and leadership. *Journal of Social Issues*, *57*, 637–655.

Ridgeway, C. L., & Berger, J. (1986). Expectation, legitimation, and dominance behavior in task groups. *American Sociological Review*, *51*, 603–617.

Ridgeway, C. L., & Berger, J. (1988). The legitimation of power and prestige orders in task groups. In M. Webster, Jr. & M. Foschi (Eds.), *Status generalization: New theory and research* (pp. 207–231). Stanford, CA: Stanford University Press.

Rodriguez-Bailon, R., Moya, M., & Yzerbyt, V. (2000). Why do superiors attend to negative stereotypic information about their subordinates? Effects of power legitimacy on social perception. *European Journal of Social Psychology*, *30*, 651–671.

Shackelford, S., Wood, W., & Worchel, S. (1996). Behavioral styles and the influence of women in mixed-sex groups. *Social Psychology Quarterly*, *59*, 284–293.

Shelly, R. K., & Webster, M., Jr. (1997). How formal status, liking and ability status structure interaction: Three theoretical principles and a test. *Sociological Perspectives*, *40*, 81–107.

Stewart, P. A., & Moore, J. C. (1992). Wage disparities and performance expectations. *Social Psychology Quarterly*, *55*, 78–85.

Thye, S. R. (2000). A status value theory of power in exchange relations. *American Sociological Review*, *65*, 407–432.

Turner, R. J., & Avison, W. R. (2003). Status variations in stress exposure: Implications for the interpretation of research on race, socioeconomic status and gender. *Journal of Health and Social Behavior*, *44*, 488–505.

Tyler, T. R., & Blader, S. L. (2002). Autonomous vs. comparative status: Must we be better than others to feel good about ourselves? *Organizational Behavior and Human Decision Processes*, *89*, 813–838.

Waller, W. W., & Hill, R. (1951). *The family: A dynamic interpretation*. New York: Dryden Press.

Willer, D., Lovaglia, M. J., & Markovsky, B. (1997). Power and influence: A theoretical bridge. *Social Forces*, *76*, 571–603.

Weber, M. (1968). *Economy and society* (G. Ross & C. Wittich, Eds.). Berkeley: University of California Press. (Original work published 1920)

Webster, M., Jr., & Foschi, M. (1988). Overview of status generalization. In M. Webster, Jr. and M. Foschi (Eds.), *Status generalization* (pp. 1–22). Stanford, CA: Stanford University Press.

Webster, M., Jr., & Driskell, J. E. (1983). Beauty as status. *American Journal of Sociology*, *89*, 140–165.

Wrong, D. H. (1979). *Power: Its forms, bases, and uses*. Chicago: University of Chicago Press.

Yukl, G., Kim, H., & Falbe, C. M. (1996). Antecedents of Influence Outcomes. *Journal of Applied Psychology*, *81*, 309–317.

Chapter 5

Money and Relationship Difficulties

Graham Allan
Christian Gerstner
Keele University, England

Material resources are clearly of major consequence in people's lives. Much of our daily activity is spent in work with the goal of generating the resources necessary for us to achieve an acceptable—or at least tolerable—standard of living. For most people, especially within industrialized or postindustrialized societies, the predominant means of doing this is through waged or salaried labor. Such labor generates an income which is then transformed through consumption and unpaid work into living standards. However, employment is not the only means by which we acquire resources. At different phases of the life course, individuals may rely on other forms of income—pensions, welfare payments, investments, or the earnings of other family or household members. Whatever the source, it is obvious that obtaining money is central for sustaining well-being and lifestyle at an individual and a household level.

Given this centrality, it is not surprising that money is of consequence in many personal relationships, both inside and outside the family, though it is the former we will be focusing on in this chapter. It is particularly important in those household/family relationships in which there is some form of shared domestic economy—typically relationships involving spouses or other such partners, and parent(s) and dependent children. As much feminist literature has argued over the last 30 years, the distribution of resources—and especially money—within households is far more complex (and often a good deal less equitable) than cultural ideals and, indeed, many welfare policies would imply (Blumberg, 1991; Delphy & Leonard, 1992; Oakley, 1974; Pahl, 1989). Negotiations between partners about the distribution of finances within households are certainly a common source of argument, as are discussions between children and parents over pocket money or contributions to domestic up-keep. While love of money may not really be "the source of all evil," issues around its control, management and use are, at the very least, potentially conflictual elements within the complex of household/familial relationships.

The distribution and use of money are likely to become more contentious when the available amount is limited. Poverty generates tensions that are hard to accommodate, frequently resulting in attribution of personal blame and inadequacy even though the underlying causes are evidently structural. For example, studies of unemployment or of economically marginalized localities illustrate how the difficulties of coping with the pressure of poverty impact negatively on the personal relationships maintained within a household, especially between spouses or partners (Gallie, Marsh, & Vogler, 1994; Morris, 1990). Even if poverty itself is not an issue, "ownership" of household finances often is. Under wage labor systems, income tends to be seen as belonging to those who actually go to the workplace to earn it rather than being defined communally as belonging to the wider family or household grouping. Thus, the commonly perceived rights over household income are less secure for those who do not earn, or who do not earn much, than for those to whom the money is paid, irrespective of the contribution the former may make to the transformation of that money into household living standards.

In this chapter, we concentrate on a number of illustrative examples of situations in which money matters become a focus of difficulties and concern within relationships. We have chosen these examples to highlight the theme that within relationships money needs to be understood in its social context rather than being seen in a solely "economic" or "financial" light. In particular, while poverty and economic hardship can certainly generate or exacerbate tensions within relationships, these are by no means the only circumstances in which money plays some part in relationship difficulties. Indeed, a part of our argument is that money issues can act as a symbol of relationship tensions rather than necessarily being the cause of these, as a focus on, say, debt, unemployment, or other aspects of poverty might suggest.

In the rest of this chapter, we will discuss our theoretical perspective on money, emphasizing the need to set it within a social as well as financial framework. We will then discuss more substantive issues, focusing on four themes that arise in "money transactions" within different family relationships and which can, at times, prove problematic. These themes are fairness, compromise, negotiation and dependence. To illustrate these themes we will draw on four case examples of common experiences within the complex of household/family relationships in which money matters can become problematic. These examples focus on inheritance; separation and divorce; money management between couples; and dependence in later adolescence. In our conclusion, we will draw together some of the key themes we have been discussing to enable these to be located within a broader understanding of difficulties in relationships.

UNDERSTANDING MONEY

The majority of research on money in relationships has applied the market model of money. Historically there are three strands of theory on money. While all three strands differ in their assessment of money's effects on society, it is apparent that they share a common technical definition of and assumptions about money (Parry & Bloch, 1989; Economist Books, 2000; Simmel, 1990; Tawney, 1972). This is the backdrop of the market model of money, which defines money as a qualitatively neutral object, and defines its functions in economic terms. All Western monies are treated as functionally the same and differ only in quantity, not in quality. "Money thus served as the fitting neutral intermediary of a rational, impersonal market, expressing the economic relations between objects ... in abstract quantitative terms, without itself entering into those relationships" (Zelizer, 1997, p. 7).

We reject the premise of this model because it is not strong enough to explain much that happens during complex social interactions. This may be illustrated by the example of a parent paying a child to wash the car. If the parent pays the child the same amount as would be paid at the car wash, the market model of money is sufficient to explain the negotiation and transaction of money. However, if the parent pays more than the typical market price, the market model of money can explain the exchange only as irrational behavior. Furthermore, if the financial transfer causes conflict in the relationship or if it worsens an already difficult relationship, the market model cannot explain the role of money as a causal factor or as an expression of these relational difficulties. We argue that when we apply the sociological understanding of exchange and objectification we arrive at a much more valid and meaningful conceptualization of money that is capable of explaining the role and use of money in relationships in general and the possible difficulties in these relationships in particular.

Objectification refers to a process of externalization fundamental to the development of an object. Simmel argues that it is "the precondition for culture and thus society, but it is mediated by exchange, which as the expression of the relationship between things and desires, is the source of all value" (as cited in Miller, 1991, p. 71).

During exchange two things happen: (a) a transaction of material or nonmaterial goods from A to B, and (b) symbolic interaction. Carrier (1995) points out that these objects acquire social meanings that are based "on their position in a public code that relates objects and differences between objects to social positions and differences between social positions" (Carrier, p. 5). Money when exchanged acquires social meanings from the cultural context and from the setting of the social situation between the exchange partners. There are two notions of meanings; one is that of the public uses and meanings of money that allow the social actors to use money in the first place, and the other is those uses and meanings that the social actors ascribe to money in their particular relationship and situation. Thus during the transaction/exchange of objects and in this case money, people's "understanding of the object interacts with their understanding of the relationship, strengthening or weakening it, modifying or reproducing people's understanding of each other in their relationship and of the object involved" (Carrier, 1995, p. 8).

The transaction of material or non-material goods is a symbolic interaction where the "thing" exchanged

> may be said to release symbolic meaning in the context of the relationship. The general meaning of the symbol is then the social implications and consequences of the perpetuation of this particular culturally recognised relationship of exchange as distinct from other such relationships. (Parkin, 1976, p. 171)

One example is the case of gifted money. Two actors construct money within a particular exchange of their relationship as a gift and thus assign the particular £5 note, say, a specific social and cultural meaning. This is expressive of their relationship in the wider social context but only important and recognized within their particular exchange and relationship. Because money can be a symbol of the relationship, gifting money is a challenging social interaction. Gifting the "wrong" amount can easily lead to conflict and create difficulties in relationships, or it can be an expression of already difficult relationships.

The symbol itself may be considered as Saussure's sign and can be broken down into two components, one being the *signifier* constituted by the locus or object exchanged itself, and the other being the *signified* constituted by the social relationship. As an outcome of this, it may even be the case that transacted objects take on meanings that are over and above, and may even contradict, their meanings as a commodity-sign or even its utility (Carrier, 1995). An illustration of this is inherited money. People construct inherited money in the context of their relationship with the deceased. This can lead to instances where the amount received is felt to be more important than its economic value would merit and may be expressed by the refusal to spend it or to at least keep it to be spent on something special that would do their relationship justice (Finch, Hayes, Masson, Mason, & Wallis, 1996). Understanding this symbolic function of money helps explain difficulties in relationships between the bereaved and deceased and/or between different bereaved relations, such as siblings. As the money inherited is a symbol of the strength and nature of the relationship between the bereaved and the deceased and among the bereaved themselves, the amount given and received is judged on the background of concepts of fairness and equality. Thus, where people feel an imbalance, this can lead to or further express difficulties in relationships.

Against this background the artefact "money" has to be defined in very different ways than the market model of money, resulting in an alternative sociological or social model of money. Key authors of this approach are Zelizer (1989, 1997), Falicov (2001), and Helleiner (1998, 2003). From this perspective, the artefact money is not meaningless and uninfluenced by extra-economic factors, but instead, is deeply shaped by the social and cultural structure in which it is used. It is embedded in particular times, places, and social relationships. It is accepted that money can "corrupt" values and social ties, transforming them into numbers; however, followers of this perspective argue that money itself is being endowed with meanings and social patterns. The model argues "for a plurality of qualitatively distinct kinds of money shaped by different networks of social relations and varying systems of meaning" (Zelizer, 1989, p. 370). This means that market money is not the only but just one type of money.

Therefore, the term *money* used in this chapter describes an artefact that is not just a medium of exchange but also a medium of communication that simplifies and expresses complex social relationships. All monies are based within particular, overlapping social networks, which actively decide on the form of money and what its meanings and uses are in particular social settings and situations. Therefore, money can only exist within the practices of these networks, as outside of them it is rendered meaningless. It can take physical (banknotes, coins, gift vouchers, credit or debit cards, checks, gold, diamonds, tobacco, cigarettes) and nonphysical forms (e-money/virtual money).

The point of this approach is that value and meaning cannot be taken for granted as inherent in the object; rather, it is pointing to a fundamentally sociocultural model of value. Moreover, it is also suggesting the complex interaction between individual judgments about value, fairness, compromise, negotiation, and independence, and how those are resolved in daily life. The resolution of different value schemes is central to successful relationships. In our analysis, we explore what happens when dissonances occur in these relationships, focused on the exchange of the artefact of money. We draw on Britain for our legal and policy frameworks around money. These frameworks are of course somewhat different in other societies, as are norms and expectations about how different relational matters are best handled. However, the underlying arguments we are making about relationships and money apply more broadly, even if the details differ.

INHERITANCE

We start by considering inheritance. Given the importance of the topic, it is surprising how little research there has been on the personal and social, rather than financial, dimensions of this form of property transfer, especially given the significant changes there have been in patterns of inheritance over the last two generations in most Western countries. In the past, the great majority of people had relatively little to leave at the time of their death. Their property was largely limited to artefacts like furniture or jewelry which typically had limited monetary worth. However, the rise in home ownership, together with other elements of greater affluence, has altered this and resulted in increasing numbers of people leaving estates that have significant monetary value. Of course, this change has not occurred uniformly; it is very much shaped by aspects of social inequality including especially class, sex/gender, and ethnicity. Nonetheless, in Britain and other Western countries, transfers of property at death are now of far more social and personal, as well as financial, significance than ever before (Finch & Hayes, 1994). This trend is likely to continue, as current cohorts of home owners reach the end of their life, although future shortfalls in pension provision could affect this.

Central to any inheritance is the question of "Who gets what?". How are decisions reached? What principles, if any, do people follow? What moral and legal legitimations are drawn on? In turn, what *rights*, if any, do people have to benefit from an inheritance? Of course, some people die intestate, and so, explicitly at least, do not make any decisions. In such cases, the state provides a framework for determining who has the right to inherit, normally based on established kinship principles. While decisions reached through legal process can be contested, the legislative framework is by its nature usually clear-cut. Increasingly though, people are writing wills and making active decisions about who is to benefit from their estate. While these frequently involve leaving specific artefacts to different individuals, they also now commonly involve the leaving of money. This is particularly so where there is no surviving spouse, so that equity from the person's home is included in the inheritance. Such capital sums can easily be divided in a variety of ways, unlike artefacts whose value is often sentimental rather than financial (Finch et al., 1996).

In many ways, the easy division of money, together with the decreasing incidence of intestacy, renders conflict between family members following bereavement less likely. Rows over who is to have the piano, the brooch or the dressing table were likely to be more common in the past. Yet at the same time, the higher value of modern estates leaves individuals with a greater material interest in their division. Half of nothing much is nothing much. Half of an apartment or house is a different matter. Equally, the writing of a will makes the implicit explicit. It symbolizes the value placed on different relationships by the deceased. Yet, inheritance and wills also carry other moral overtones, especially where there is no surviving spouse. Essentially the property of an individual is their own to use and dispose of as they wish. Nonetheless, despite the discretion people can rightly—that is, morally—exercise, the way in which property is bequeathed is still normatively framed, with the breaking of these normative conventions or "guidelines" being a matter of potential conflict and dispute for those involved.

In many regards, the key issue in determining who should inherit what revolves around the concept of "fairness" (Finch et al., 1996; Finch & Mason, 2000). What it appears testators usually wish to do is to be fair to those to whom they leave their wealth. In the majority of cases, this seems to be a relatively straightforward matter. For example, leaving the whole or substantial majority of an estate to a surviving spouse is uncontentious and recognized as wholly appropriate. It is, in normal circumstances, the "right" thing to do. Where there is no surviving spouse, then the normal and acceptable principle, in the absence of any expectations of *primogeniture*, is to divide the bulk of the estate equally among any children. Some particularly prized possessions may be left to specific individuals to celebrate the relationship there was; other beneficiaries, for example, grandchildren, siblings, friends, or charities, may be left sums of money. Overall though, there is a general expectation that children will inherit equally (Finch & Mason, 2000). Mirroring the normative convention of loving all children equally and not having explicit favorites, "fairness" decrees that children benefit in broadly equal ways. Indeed if a child has pre-deceased a parent, then there is also an expectation that any children that child had will inherit his or her share.

The potential for relationship difficulties to emerge here is clear. While there are general normative principles about inheritance, these are not legally or morally binding. When they are not followed, there is some potential for relationship difficulties to arise between actual or putative beneficiaries. Whether difficulties arise or not is likely to be influenced by the degree to which the testamentary decision is understood by those involved to meet the criteria of fairness. Here what counts as fair is not as straightforward as it first appears. When, for example, is it fair for one child to be advantaged over others? Under what circumstances is it reasonable for a child to be left less than siblings? Would it be understood as fair to favor one child over others because the parent had a closer emotional bond with that child? Would it be fair if they had provided a disproportionate amount of care for the parent when it was needed? Is such favoring acceptable if one child is seen as in greater material need than the others, because of, say, disability, familial circumstance, or career disadvantage? Alternatively, if a parent disapproves of a lifestyle choice made by the child, is some degree of disinheritance then acceptable?

At issue here are the competing notions of what counts as fair that those involved may hold in the given circumstances (Finch & Mason, 2000). There is no necessary agreement between them. When one party feels that they or their (descendent) family have been treated unfairly, tensions may emerge or, more likely be exacerbated, in their relationships with other family members. In particular, this difficulty is likely to arise if the advantaged beneficiaries are seen by those who are disadvantaged as somehow exercising undue influence over the testamentary decisions, though of course what counts as "undue influence" is as contestable as the notion of fairness. Importantly, while conflict over inheritance currently appears to be relatively uncommon, it is likely that it will become more frequent in the future as a consequence of the increasingly complex demographic and family patterns people are now creating. In particular, remarriage, second families, reconstituted families, and births outside marriage can render decisions about inheritance far more problematic than previously, in the process making issues of fairness more contestable. As with other aspects of reconstituted family life, normative guidelines over the management of these matters are comparatively ill-defined. Classically, issues arise with remarriage, particularly in later life, and the competing claims the new spouse and children from a previous union have over the estate. The concern from the children's perspective is that their "rightful" inheritance will either be spent by the new spouse or else be passed to his or her children who are seen as having no legitimate claim on the inherited money (Burgoyne & Morison, 1997).

DIVORCE AND SEPARATION

We started by discussing inheritance as a source of difficulties in relationships because it is the simplest of the issues we are focusing on. Where conflict arises over inheritance, it is commonly concerned with constructions of fairness and, as implied earlier, often mirrors tensions that existed previously within relationships. Our second topic—divorce and separation—is far more complex, with money matters frequently being central to the relational difficulties experienced. Indeed, much of the legal framework of divorce is centrally concerned with the distribution of property consequent on the ending of the marital contract. This and the arrangements made for the care and custody of any dependent children are the matters that most exercise the courts, though the judgments made about contested issues obviously depend on the particular laws governing these issues in different legal jurisdictions. Of course, in some cases the courts may do little more than rubber stamp agreements previously reached by the couple before any court hearing, though these too will normally be framed by the partners' understandings of current legal judgments. Yet, whatever principles and means of settlement are applied, the division of money and other property following separation and divorce is frequently experienced as both practically complex and emotionally distressing.

In part, this is a consequence of the competing material interests of the couple. Assuming new partnerships are not immediately formed, separation and divorce necessarily represent a decline in each person's standard of living. The break up of what previously was a single domestic unit into two separate ones inevitably involves greater costs, and consequently a reduction in the resources available for nonessential items. Two homes cannot be run as cheaply as one. Moreover, the couple is involved in a zero-sum game: what one side gains, the other loses (Kurz, 1995). Yet, as important in many cases, the very act of negotiating separate financial arrangements represents an extremely powerful symbol of what has been lost with the ending of the marriage. Continuing conflict around the division of resources can often become the more intense because the arguments are not solely about resources, important though these are. These arguments over financial settlements come to embody each spouse's views and feelings about the relationship and about the behavior of the other in the periods before and after the separation. In effect, conflict over money can serve as the arena through which the couple express their emotional antagonisms and sensitivities (Simpson, 1998).

In general, the intention of laws governing divorce is to protect the interests of those involved and ensure an equitable and fair distribution of resources. Even more than with inheritance though, the concept of fairness is contestable. What the two parties understand as fair may be at considerable variance, depending on the weight being attached to the different elements that contributed to the welfare of their shared domestic union. Where there are no young children involved and where the marriage was relatively short-lived, negotiations around the distribution of money, pensions, and other possessions following separation are likely to be less protracted than in other cases. Both sides are more likely to want to make a "clean break" and to end their involvement speedily. Little collective capital will have been built up and fewer financial sacrifices made for the collective good. In consequence, agreeing on an equitable division of shared resources is likely to be a more straightforward matter, often only requiring court approval rather than intervention.

With marriages that are longer-lasting and/or where there are children involved, financial settlements are more likely to be marked by sustained antagonism and disagreement over what counts as equitable and fair. In part, this is fueled by the difficulty of calculating the contribution husband and wife have each made to the marriage and the costs that each has borne. In particular, issues arise around the implicit agreements the spouses reached about the division of work and employment inside and outside the home. The impact this has on future earning potentials, especially for women who have spent periods outside the workforce focusing on home and family, is problematic (Davies, Joshi, & Peronaci, 2000). Equally though, financial settlements are complicated by the need to provide for dependent children. Because they share a household with the residential parent, whatever financial contribution is made for them by the nonresidential parent also contributes to the living standards of the residential parent. This can generate conflict, with one side believing they are contributing too much and the other that they are receiving too little.

Under these circumstances, negotiation of financial settlements that are deemed satisfactory by both sides can be extremely difficult. However, in Britain at least, the normal outcome is clear-cut. Divorced mothers with dependent children are typically in greater poverty than married mothers, with a comparatively high proportion dependent on state benefits (Rowlingson & McKay, 1998). In recent years, policy initiatives have attempted to reduce state expenditure consequent on increased levels of divorce, as well as generating mechanisms to reduce conflict over financial, and other post-divorce, settlements. One element of this has been to emphasize the role of divorce mediation in reaching settlements rather than immediate recourse to the more disputational approach of lawyers. A second element has been to emphasize clean-break principles in settlements between spouses, so that there is no need for continuing financial dependency, or other involvement, once the divorce has been granted. However, this is somewhat contradicted by a third element of policy development, which has emphasized the continuation of parenting responsibilities inside or outside of marriage, thereby fostering a continuing degree of involvement by the now separated parents (Simpson, 1998; Smart & Neale, 1999). In Britain, a major plank of this policy has been an attempt to standardize and regulate the financial contribution nonresidential parents pay toward their child(ren)'s upkeep. Over the last decade, this has led to much political debate, in part because of the complexity of the rules governing the calculations made, though these have recently been simplified (see http://www.csa.gov.uk/).

It is clear that money issues are far more liable to generate relationship difficulties in the context of divorce than they do with inheritance. Issues arise in both contexts over constructions of fairness, although with inheritance there is a wide recognition that the testator has the right to dispose of money as desired. Moreover, the possibilities of negotiation are, for obvious reasons more limited. The case of divorce is quite different. Here it is normal for extensive and, frequently, antagonistic negotiations to take place over the division of money and other material resources. In other words, what counts as fair is highly contestable. While there is a legal framework for adjudicating these issues, within this there is still room for dispute and argument about how the framework should be interpreted in any particular case. As noted earlier, the judicial process itself often encourages such argumentation. To put this a little differently, what tends to be lacking is a moral or social agreement over the rules to be applied. Arguably this is beginning to develop as the number of couples experiencing divorce increases. In particular, financial and other mediation is likely to be more successful if common ground rules for determining disputes become more widely accepted socially and thus more normative. Similarly, if as with the Child Support Agency in Britain, there are established and relatively straightforward principles governing maintenance decisions, then the likelihood of conflict emerging is reduced. However, divorce involves emotional sores as well as material conflicts. Conflict over money issues may well be prolonged through serving as an outlet for feelings of jealousy, rejection and other such emotional hurt.

DOMESTIC MONEY MANAGEMENT

With the two areas discussed so far, inheritance and divorce, disputes over money can ultimately be determined through legal process. Courts can make rulings that are binding on the parties. Of course, while this offers a route for formal settlement, it does not mean that the disputes are satisfactorily resolved from the perspectives of those involved. While they may accept the judgments reached, they can continue to harbor feelings of resentment. Indeed, this is more likely, as often the disputes over money are in part consequent on deeper resentments and dissatisfactions within the relationships in question. That is, disputes over money serve to express other antagonisms in the relationships rather than being the sole or primary source of the tensions. In the last two areas we focus on, there is no legal framework that can be applied to settle matters. In each of these areas, power and dependency, as well as implicit negotiation, play a much larger part.

The first of these concerns the distribution of material resources, and especially money, within marriage. While present-day ideologies of partnership and marriage in the West emphasize love and emotional compatibility as the bases of the union, marriage also involves the material construction of a home and family life. In other words, as well as love and commitment, marriage is about a shared domestic economy, which involves the coordination of household and nonhousehold labor and the transformation of this labor into individual and collective living standards (Allan & Crow, 2001). It also normally involves a gendered division of labor and an accompanying division of rewards; this becomes more marked when there are children in the household. There can be debate about the extent to which the gendered character of this division of labor has altered over the last two generations in line with wives' changed involvement in employment, but nonetheless in most marriages domestic coordination, management, and servicing typically remain more a female than a male responsibility. In turn, husbands' primary, though not sole, responsibility lies in the realm of income provision.

In Britain, as elsewhere, various studies have examined the ways in which money is allocated between spouses. While there is a good deal of diversity in the arrangements couples negotiate over the course of their relationship, a number of distinct patterns of money management have been identified (Pahl, 1989; Vogler & Pahl, 1994). While there is no need to discuss these different allocation systems in detail here, it is important to recognize the dimensions entailed in them. In particular, Vogler and Pahl (1994, p. 273) make the important distinction between the strategic control of household money and the day-to-day management of that money. The latter may appear to indicate power and control over resources, although this can be quite misleading. Even if, say, a wife is responsible for paying bills, this may represent the burden of trying to make ends meet from inadequate household budgets rather than the exercise of any real determination of overall financial resourcing. Strategic control, on the other hand, may entail infrequent routine decision making but still represent a dominant control of the overall distribution of financial resources within the family and household.

What matters most is the overall outcome of household allocation systems in terms of the distribution of resources between individuals. In their British research, Vogler and Pahl (1994) addressed this in two ways. They asked each spouse in their sample of couples about the extent to which they had had to do without specific items (food, clothing, leisure activities, etc.) when the household was short of money. They also asked each spouse about the personal spending money they normally had access to. In couples where there was joint strategic control and joint management—about 20% of the 1,211 couples in their sample—there were few differences between husbands and wives. In the remaining couples though, husbands tended to experience less financial deprivation than their wives at times of shortage and/or to have greater personal spending power. Most interestingly, even in the 40% of couples where the wife had responsibility for managing money, there was "a disjuncture between control over finances and access to money as a resource," with wives having less personal spending money and higher levels of personal deprivation (Vogler & Pahl, 1994, p. 283). In other words, husbands' needs tended to be prioritized over those of the wives. As Vogler and Pahl suggest, this raises issues about the nature of the control those wives who exercise day-to-day financial management actually have. In many cases, especially where the household is not affluent, such control may offer few freedoms and be better understood as constraining. Indeed, the recent ideological emphasis on equality within marriage may often serve to mask "the real extent of inequality in access to money as a resource" (Vogler & Pahl, 1994, p. 283; see also Nyman, 1999; Vogler, 1998; Wilson, 1987).

Studies of household allocation systems within marriage have not focused explicitly on difficulties in relationships stemming from the methods in which money is managed by the couple. Instead, the focus has been more on exploring the systematic inequalities in the benefits and costs to husbands and wives entailed in the different allocation systems. In particular, these studies explore how marital ideologies emphasizing equality and sharing often disguise the continuing operation of male hegemonic power, rooted in men's higher earning capacity and their primary attachment to employment. Yet within these analyses, it is clear that there is potential for challenge, conflict, and disagreement over the uses to which money is put. Such conflict is less likely where both individuals are responsible for their own budgeting and have negotiated how household expenses are to be divided, which is most likely when both sides have significant income of their own and/or when they are in "nonstandard" unions, that is, cohabitation or remarriage (Burgoyne & Morison, 1997; Elizabeth, 2001). Conversely, disputes would seem more likely to arise in situations where there is a relative shortage of resources.

In the absence of more research on the topic, it is difficult to decide which money allocation systems are most likely to generate relationship difficulties. It could be that the more "joint" the decision making is, the more likely disagreements and arguments are to arise (Schwartz, 1994). The "rules" of the couple's relationship allow for each side to express different views so that even robust disagreement is acceptable. In other words, whether such conflict is seen as positive or negative is moot. It may be seen as a sign of relational strength rather than as a sign of relational difficulty. Equally, while other systems of money management may be shown to have unequal consequences, this of itself does not mean the relationships are in difficulty. This depends on the legitimacy given to the differentials that emerge. For example, a wife who is given a fixed budget to manage—what Vogler and Pahl (1994) call a "housekeeping allowance" system (pp. 268–269)—may not regard this as problematic within the relationship even if she struggles financially. What is likely to matter is whether she and others within her primary network consider such an allocation system to be fair and reasonable. Equally, the extent to which she defines herself as financially dependent is of consequence in her judging what is reasonable "under the circumstances." Moreover, in the context of wider inequality and male hegemonic power, acquiescence and an absence of disagreement cannot be read as relationship satisfaction. It may represent contentment with the marital status quo or it may be more an indicator of differentials in power and dependence, as it clearly is in cases of domestic violence.

It would undoubtedly be useful to have more research focusing on the significance of monetary management issues in marital disharmony. Better knowledge of the processes of negotiation between husbands and wives over time, including how power is exercised and legitimacy achieved or challenged, would be of particular value.

PARENTS AND YOUNG ADULTS

The final case illustration of money and relationships we consider in this chapter also raises issues of power, legitimacy, fairness, and negotiation within a family context. It concerns the ways in which money can become a problematic element within relationships between parents and their young adult children, defined loosely here as children aged between 18 and 23. As we will see, this topic also raises questions about the definitional boundaries of relational "difficulties." A key point here is that while difficulties around money in these relationships are not by any means inevitable, they are quite commonly experienced and involve structural issues concerning the transitions of the younger generation to economic and social independence from their parents.

As is widely recognized, childhood is socially constructed with significant cultural differences in what is expected of children of different ages at different times and in different societies. Within Western societies, there has tended to be an elongation of childhood dependency. With changing employment structures and longer periods of schooling, the transition to independent adulthood has become more complex with new phases of childhood emerging. The social recognition of adolescence in the mid-20th century was a part of this, as has been the continuing development of youth movements and markets more recently (Miles, 2000). In other words, there has been a shift in the patterning of parental involvement in their children's lives during late adolescence/early adulthood. For most of the 20th century, in Britain at least, children were expected by their early 20s to be living away from the parental home and no longer reliant on parental support. At times, parents may have chosen to provide piecemeal or more substantial material support, often in kind, depending on the circumstances of the two generations. This often needed managing with some care so as not to threaten the younger generation's independence—prized as the symbol of adulthood. (For a classic study of this, see Bell, 1968.)

In countries like Britain, the social and economic experiences of many young adults have changed significantly over the last generation. There have been major demographic shifts in terms of partner formation, cohabitation, marriage, and childbirth (see Allan & Crow, 2001). There have also been shifts in the patterning of education, with higher proportions of young people staying in education until their late teens and early 20s. The job market has also changed, with significant numbers of young people being employed in relatively low-paid and insecure jobs, especially in the service sector (Macdonald, 1997). Moreover, pathways out of the parental home have become more varied and less certain, in part because of inflation in the housing market (Goldscheider & Goldscheider, 1999; Jones, 1995). Indeed increasingly there is a tendency for young people to return to the parental home after one or more periods of greater housing independence (Heath, 1999; Jones, 2003; Peters, 1987). The impact of these changes has been to reduce the significance of what previously were the three main markers of adulthood: leaving home, marriage, and secure employment. Instead, young people are now in more of an interstitial social and economic location, at times reliant on their parents' patronage for some matters but more independent of them in others.

A range of problematic issues arises when young adults are materially dependent on their parents. Whereas this is "normal" and expected for younger children, in young adulthood there remains an assumption of at least "proto-independence." In other words, even if it is common for parents to provide degrees of financial and other material support for their young adult children, there are no clear socially institutionalized norms governing what the extent of this should be. Young adult children are not expected to be cast adrift by their parents, but at the same time there is a normative assumption of a broad independence. Thus, young adults do not have the right to demand material support from their parents. What their parents give them, how they help them out, and in what circumstances are, in principle, for their parents to decide.

In practice, it is likely a process of negotiation occurs. Sometimes this negotiation may involve parents and an adult child purposefully discussing issues around the distribution of resources, though more frequently it is negotiation in the sense developed by Finch and Mason (1993) in their work on kinship obligations and solidarities. What is particularly important in these negotiations is the imbalance in resources and power between the two parties. It is the parents who have the power, as it is their resources which are in question. In determining what resources to give to their adult child, numerous issues come into play (Allatt & Yeandle, 1992). There are likely to be judgments about, inter alia how deserving the child is, the legitimacy of the current need for resources, the past history of support, the needs of other children (adult or dependent) and the desire to be fair to them, the resources available, and what is thought to be in the best interests of the young adult (including the possibility of "forcing" a greater independence).

None of these issues is straightforward, and none is determined in isolation. At the heart of the decisions lies the history of the relationship in question and, in particular, the dynamics of previous support that has been given. Often no significant difficulties arise with these transactions. They are managed in ways acceptable to all. At other times though, frustrations and tension can develop, whether the support is direct or in kind, for example, through subsidizing domestic living costs. Typically at the heart of the disputes are matters of control and dependency. In other words, when parents provide financial support for their adult child, they normally expect that adult child to respond appropriately. In practice, what this usually entails is an element of gratitude, a recognition of the parents' right to influence the child's lifestyle, relative thrift rather than financial profligacy, appropriate efforts to become more independent, and so forth. Where this does not happen—where the adult child wastes money on items the parents consider to be superfluous, where overspending continues, where insufficient effort is made to sustain domestic order, where they keep irregular hours, where gratitude and recognition of the subsidization are lacking—then it is likely that parents will demonstrate their power through tempering their support. A degree of parental control, subtly or otherwise exercised, is the tacit price of financial dependency.

MONEY AND RELATIONSHIP DIFFICULTIES

In this chapter, we have been arguing that money can be a source of difficulties and tensions in family relationships and that there are wide differences in the extent to which this happens and in the consequences that follow such difficulties. In particular, we have focused on four key elements: fairness, negotiation, power, and dependency. We have also argued that money carries more than just economic or financial meaning. The use of money is embedded within the different relationships we have discussed, and its management reflects other aspects of these relationships. In other words, money in relationships needs to be understood as socially constructed; its significance and meaning should be seen as an integral element of the relationship as it is constituted. In this, the use of money comes to be morally framed, with issues of right and wrong, appropriate and inappropriate feeding into relational disagreements and tensions.

Thus, from the viewpoint of a social model of money, relationship difficulties that involve monetary transactions are not simply about money as a commodity but as a symbol. Of course, money causes conflict in many circumstances. In large part, contract law is concerned with the rights and obligations involved in financial and other material agreements. However, these typically involve relationships that are defined in essentially financial terms. Put simply, most relationships involving financial transactions—for example, with a salesperson, tax official, or a bank manager—are purely instrumental ones. Disagreements and conflicts may arise, but they are generally about a specific transaction, though it is possible for them to build up over a series of similar transactions. The kinds of relationship that this chapter examines are not of this order. They are longer-term, multiplex, personal relationships involving complex patterns of exchange and transaction. As such, the monetary transactions involved cannot be considered separately or as necessarily predominant, even when they explicitly serve as the focus of the disagreement.

We have emphasized fairness as a key notion in understanding monetary difficulties that arise in the types of personal relationships we have been discussing. It is when people feel they, or someone they care for, have been treated unfairly that tensions and conflicts emerge. However, the notion of fairness is clearly complex, perhaps especially in the realm of sustained personal relationships. While there may be a degree of consensus over what counts as fair or reasonable in any type of relationship, such normative agreement at best provides a framework within which those involved constitute and enact the details of their various relational transactions. In other words, what is taken as constituting fairness in any relationship is effectively negotiated rather than given. Such negotiation is, of course, contextual and emergent. It does not normally involve a formal process of discussion; rather, it is implicit in the development of the relationship. It is influenced by previous experience and knowledge of the ways others manage their relationship. Equally, it involves the particular circumstances of both sides and the changes there are in these over time. Such negotiations also involve the moral standing of the parties, not just in their own or each other's eyes, but also in terms of the moral reputation they have established within their networks (Finch & Mason, 1993).

A consequence of this is that there can be substantial disagreement over what constitutes fairness in any particular instance. Moreover, the factors that are seen as pertinent to any calculation of fairness can also be disputed and given different weighting. Inheritance is a good example. In principle, normative convention has it that children should be treated equally. However, this might be compromised if there has been a history of antagonism with one child, if one child has provided considerably more care, if one child has a disability and requires costly support, if one child is thought to be particularly reckless with money, and so forth. In other words, all sorts of contextual considerations can, in principle, alter the equation of fairness that claims children must be treated equally. So too with divorce settlements. There are all sorts of factors, leaving aside self-interest, which can influence views of what comprises a fair division of resources. Not least among these are the levels of blame that each side attaches to the other for their marital separation. In summary here, tensions in personal relationships are likely to emerge when one party perceives he or she is being treated unfairly, but fairness itself is essentially contestable. Moreover, more than other aspects of relationships, because money is easily measurable, imbalances in its division are readily apparent. It is in part because of the precise calculation possible with money that it comes to symbolize and express relational tensions around contestable issues of fairness.

It is important to recognize that negotiations around ideas of fairness in relationships are frequently structured by issues of power and dependency, which have a legitimacy sanctioned within their broader social and economic context. Thus, despite ideological shifts seeing contemporary marital relationships as egalitarian, in many marriages the realities of the gendered employment structure ensure men's position is privileged. As we argued earlier in this chapter, when wives work full-time in the home, or even when they are employed part-time, most are financially dependent on their husband's earnings. In other words, their husbands are structurally more powerful. While at times such power may be challenged, it nonetheless has a legitimacy that is built into everyday assumptions governing domestic organization. Thus, even where wives appear to make decisions about expenditures, it is common for those decisions to favor husbands' interests—a clear manifestation of power (Lukes, 2004). When these arrangements become issues of dispute within a marriage, when their fairness is challenged, the negotiations that arise are inevitably framed by these relative inequalities in power and dependency. In other words, they help shape the understandings developed of what constitutes fairness in these matters.

So too differentials in power and dependency are of consequence when it comes to financial arguments in relationships between parents and their late adolescent/young adult children. Here disputes can often arise over what financial subsidies it is reasonable and fair for the younger generation to receive and what is required in return, especially when the young adult is still living in the parental home. Quite evidently, the negotiations occurring are not premised on equality of position. It is the parents who hold the resources; it is they who can set the conditions of any subsidy. The young adult may chafe at these conditions and find ways to undermine them, but ultimately the more claims that are made on parents for support, the more dependency is apparent, and the stronger the liability for the young adult to acquiesce to parental control. Constructions of fairness are central within the negotiations that arise, but so too are these issues of power and dependency. It is the parental view of fairness that carries the most weight.

In summary, our argument in this chapter has been that money issues may be the focus of dispute in the forms of personal relationship we have considered, but the nature of the difficulties that arise cannot be properly understood or analyzed as being simply about money. Rather, money issues are embedded within broader aspects of relationships. They are an element within their construction which may come to the fore at times, but which when they do still need to be understood within the wider framing of those relationships. We have consequently argued that issues of fairness, negotiation, power, and dependency need considering in analyzing how difficulties over money in personal relationships arise and are managed. Although in this chapter we have focused on a small number of illustrations of relationship difficulties involving money, the general themes we have addressed could usefully be applied to a wider range of money-related relationship problems.

ACKNOWLEDGMENT

We are grateful to Rebecca Leach for the significant contribution she made to the development of this chapter.

REFERENCES

Allan, G., & Crow, G. (2001). *Families, households and society.* Basingstoke, UK: Palgrave.

Allatt, P., & Yeandle, S. (1992). *Youth and unemployment: Voices of disordered times.* London: Routledge.

Bell, C. (1968). *Middle class families.* London: Routledge & Kegan Paul.

Blumberg, R. L. (Ed.). (1991). *Gender, family and economy.* Newbury Park, CA: Sage.

Blumstein, P., & Schwartz, P. (1991). Money and ideology: Their impact on power and the division of household labor. In R. L. Blumberg (Ed.), *Gender, family and economy* (pp. 261–288). Newbury Park, CA: Sage.

Burgoyne, C. B., & Morison, V. (1997). Money in remarriage: Keeping things simple—and separate. *Sociological Review, 45,* 363–395.

Carrier, J. G. (1995). *Gifts and commodities.* London: Routledge.

Davies, H., Joshi, H., & Peronaci, R. (2000). Forgone income and motherhood: What do recent British data tell us? *Population Studies, 54,* 293–305.

Delphy, C., & Leonard, D. (1992). *Familiar exploitation: A new analysis of marriage in contemporary Western societies.* Cambridge, UK: Polity.
Economist Books. (2000). *Pocket money.* London: Profile Books.
Elizabeth, V. (2001). Managing money, managing coupledom: A critical examination of cohabitants' money management practices. *Sociological Review, 49,* 389–411.
Falicov, C. J. (2001). The cultural meanings of money: The case of Latinos and Anglo-Americans. *American Behavioural Scientist, 45,* 313–328.
Finch, J., & Hayes, L. (1994). Inheritance, death and the concept of the home. *Sociology, 28,* 417–433.
Finch, J., Hayes, L., Masson, J., Mason, J., & Wallis, L. (1996). *Wills, inheritance, and families.* Oxford, UK: Oxford University Press.
Finch, J., & Mason, J. (1993). *Negotiating family responsibilities.* London: Routledge.
Finch, J., & Mason, J. (2000). *Passing on: Kinship and inheritance in England.* London: UCL Press.
Gallie, D., Marsh, C., & Vogler, C. (1994). *Social change and the experience of unemployment.* Oxford, UK: Oxford University Press.
Goldscheider, F., & Goldscheider, C. (1999). Changes in returning home in the United States, 1925–1985. *Social Forces, 78,* 695–720.
Heath, S. (1999). Young adults and household formation in the 1990s. *British Journal of Sociology of Education, 20,* 545–561.
Helleiner, E. (1998). National currencies and national identities. *American Behavioural Scientist, 41,* 1409–1436.
Helleiner, E. (2003). *The making of national money: Territorial currencies in historical perspectives.* Ithaca, NY: Cornell University Press.
Jones, G. (1995). *Leaving home.* Buckingham, UK: Open University Press.
Jones, G. (2003). Youth, dependence and the problem of support. In S. Cunningham-Burley & L. Jamieson (Eds.), *Families and the state: Conflicts and contradictions* (pp. 187–204). London: Palgrave.
Kurz, D. (1995). *For richer, for poorer: Mothers confront divorce.* New York: Routledge.
Lukes, S. (2004). *Power: A radical view.* London: Macmillan.
Macdonald, R. (1997). *Youth, the "underclass" and social exclusion.* London: Routledge.
Miles, S. (2000). *Youth lifestyles in a changing world.* Buckingham, UK: Open University Press
Miller, D. (1991). *Material culture and mass consumption.* Oxford, UK: Basil Blackwell.
Morris, L. (1990). *The workings of the household: A U.S.-UK comparison.* Oxford, UK: Polity Press.
Nyman, C. (1999). Gender equality in "the most equal country in the world"? Money and marriage in Sweden. *Sociological Review, 47,* 766–793.
Oakley, A. (1974). *The sociology of housework.* London: Robertson.
Pahl, J. (1989). *Money and marriage.* Basingstoke, UK: Macmillan.
Parkin, D. (1976). Exchanging words. In B. Kapferer (Ed.), *Transaction and meaning* (pp. 163–187). Philadelphia: ISHI.
Parry, J., & Bloch, M. (1989). Introduction: Money and the morality of exchange. In J. Parry & M. Bloch (Eds.), *Money and the morality of exchange* (pp. 1–33). Cambridge, UK: Cambridge University Press.
Peters, J. F. (1987). Youth, family and employment. *Adolescence, 22,* 13–27.
Rowlingson, K., & McKay, S. (1998). *The growth of lone parenthood: Diversity and dynamics.* London: Policy Studies Institute.

Schwartz, P. (1994). *Peer marriage*. New York: Free Press.

Simmel, G. (1990). *The philosophy of money* (2nd enlarged ed.). London: Routledge.

Simpson, B. (1998). *Changing families*. Oxford, UK: Berg.

Smart, C., & Neale, B. (1999). *Family fragments*. Cambridge, UK: Polity.

Tawney, R. H. (1972). *Religion and the rise of capitalism*. Harmondsworth, UK: Penguin.

Vogler, C. (1998). Money in the household: Some underlying issues of power. *Sociological Review, 46*, 687–713.

Vogler, C., & Pahl, J. (1994). Money, power and inequality within marriage. *Sociological Review, 42*, 263–288.

Wilson, G. (1987). *Money in the family*. Aldershot, UK: Avebury.

Zelizer, V. A. (1989). The social meaning of money: Special monies. *American Journal of Sociology. 95*, 342–377.

Zelizer, V. A. (1997). *The social meaning of money*. Princeton, NJ: Princeton University Press.

Chapter 6

The Difficulties
of In-law Relationships

Mary Claire Morr Serewicz
University of Denver

Although popular culture presents stereotypes of negative in-law rela-tionships, complete with demanding or intrusive mothers-in-law, domineering or indifferent fathers-in-law, ungrateful or irresponsible children-in-law, and boorish or gossipy siblings-in-law, empirical re-search demonstrates that in-law relationships, like other close relation-ships, can range from satisfying and beneficial to disappointing and detrimental. This chapter, however, will focus on difficulties and will present evidence that characteristics of the structure and formation of in-law relationships result in difficulties. Although relationships with siblings-in-law (Floyd & Morr, 2003) and more extended in-law rela-tionships (Duvall, 1954) can be difficult and have received research attention, this chapter focuses on the relationship between parents-and children-in-law from the point of view of the child-in-law. Not only have relationships with parents-in-law received the most research attention, but relationships with parents-in-law (and especially moth-ers-in-law) are most frequently perceived as the most difficult of in-law relationships (Duvall, 1954).

Although this chapter primarily considers parents- and children-in-law in Western culture, it is important to note that in-law relationships in non-Western cultures also appear to be difficult. The similarities and differences in Western and non-Western in-law relationships shed light on the sources of difficulty for Western parents- and children-in-law. In Western cultures, in-law relationships are often characterized as distant and negative (Duvall, 1954), but cross-cultural research has found sim-ilarities between Western and non-Western cultures in perceptions of distance and negativity toward in-laws. For instance, people from the United States, Egypt, Kuwait, and Sudan express similar preferences for a distant relationship with the mother-in-law (Adler, Denmark, & Ahmed, 1989). Likewise, research with caregiving daughters (-in-law) in India and Belgium found that both Indian and Belgian women felt greater love and affection for their mothers than for their mothers-in-law, even though Indian women are traditionally expected to transfer their love and responsibilities from their mother to their mother-in-law on marriage (Datta, Poortinga, & Marcoen, 2003). Indian women, but not Belgian women, also reported feeling more of a burden to care for their mothers-in-law than for their mothers and reported greater conflict with their mothers-in-law than with their mothers (Datta et al., 2003). Apparently, then, negativity and distance are not restricted to Western in-law relationships.

Along with these similarities between Western and non-Western relationships, some contrasts can be observed between cultural expectations for in-law relationships. For instance, traditional Indian (Datta et al., 2003) and Taiwanese (Altman, Brown, Staples, & Werner, 1992) cultures set clear expectations and roles for the mother-in-law/daughter-in-law relationship. In these cultures, it is traditional for daughters-in-law to reside with their husband's family, and the mother-in-law holds greater power in the relationship. For example, in Indian culture, the daughter-in-law is expected to care for the mother-in-law as she grows old, and one participant in Datta et al.'s (2003) research described the ultimate power that the mother-in-law has to decide whether her daughter-in-law's life will be happy. Another example illustrating the power difference and tension between mother- and daughter-in-law exists in a Taiwanese wedding tradition in which the mother-in-law places the wedding ring on the bride's finger during the wedding ceremony, but the bride bends her finger so that the mother-in-law cannot slide the ring all the way onto her finger (Altman et al., 1992). Although the new wife in a traditional Taiwanese family has low status, her status increases in time as she bears sons and makes connections within the community (Altman et al., 1992), but the overall character of the relationship with in-laws is a difficult and distant one based on initial differences in status.

In contrast to some non-Western cultures, Western married couples are relatively autonomous from the in-laws (Altman et al., 1992). The relative independence of Western couples is observed in the expectations that they will have a residence separate from the in-laws (Altman et al., 1992) and that Western adults hold more responsibility for their own aging parents than for their parents-in-law (e.g., Datta et al., 2003). Less frequent contact and less obligation toward parents-in-law reduces the power of parents-in-law because they have less opportunity to influence the rewards and costs obtained by the child-in-law. Moreover, cultural differences including the lower degree of filial reverence in Western than in non-Western cultures and the primacy of the Western marital relationship over the parent–adult child relationship reduce the status difference between parents- and children-in-law.

Overall, although Western and non-Western cultures may experience negativity and prefer distance in their in-law relationships, Western parents-in-law have less relative power and status than do non-Western parents-in-law.

These comparisons of Western and non-Western in-law relationships offer clues to the special sources of difficulty with in-law relationships in Western culture. The difficulty that children-in-law have interacting with their parents-in-law includes handling negativity, managing appropriate distance, and negotiating power and status. These challenging situations stem from the nature of the in-law relationship as involuntary and triadic. The triadic structure makes maintaining a satisfactory relationship complex, and the nonvoluntary nature of the relationship further complicates its maintenance. The remainder of the chapter will examine the triadic, nonvoluntary structure of relationships with Western parents-in-law as the source of difficulty. Difficulties in negotiating roles will then be considered as a problem arising from the nature of the parent-in-law/child-in-law relationship.

THE NONVOLUNTARY, TRIADIC NATURE OF IN-LAW RELATIONSHIPS AS THE SOURCE OF DIFFICULTY

The structure of in-law relationships poses particular challenges. Specifically, the properties of in-law relationships as triadic and nonvoluntary serve as the source of difficulty in dealing with parents-in-law. Although many relationships can be analyzed at the triadic level, and many relationships are involuntary, the combination of these two factors results in special circumstances for the parent- and child-in-law. Because they are brought together by a third party, the child/spouse, in-laws have no choice in the initiation of their relationship. However, their relationship with the child/spouse necessitates the maintenance of the relationship. Research conducted on relationships following marriage indicates that, at least early in the in-law relationship, in-laws are aware of this intersection of the triadic and involuntary qualities of the relationship. For instance, most mothers- and daughters-in-law in Pfeifer's (1989) study defined their relationship with each other as associates by marriage, rather than as a parent–child, friend, or extended family relationship. They also reported using the son/husband as a mediator as their most frequent method of conflict management. Thus, in their perception and behavior, these mothers- and daughters-in-law recognize the involuntary definition of their relationship through the intersection of the parent–child and marital relationship and use their triadic connection to maintain the relationship. Although it is the interaction between these two qualities that define the complexity of in-law relationships, the following discussion highlights one factor at a time to clarify the analysis.

Implications of the Triadic Relationship

The relationship between the parent-in-law and the child-in-law is involuntary and exists by virtue of their relationship with a third party: the child/spouse. Moreover, for both the parent-in-law and child-in-law, the relationship with that third party is likely to be more salient and more rewarding than their relationship with one another. Thus, the relatively weak connection between parent-in-law and child-in-law is made by virtue of their strong connections with the child/spouse. The involuntary quality of the in-law relationship structure contributes to the salience of the triad for parents- and children-in-law: in their relationship, the triadic bonds are stronger than the dyadic bonds.

Examining the triadic relationship from a social exchange perspective leads to the consideration of rewards and costs in the relationship among the three members. In a triadic relationship, each member incurs rewards and costs due to the actions of all members (Thibaut & Kelley, 1959). Many means exist for a triad to succeed in providing beneficial outcomes to its members. Beneficial outcomes are obtained in the case of joint cost-cutting (Thibaut & Kelley, 1959), as when two spouses dread interacting with the parent (-in-law) individually but can make the interaction less upsetting if they provide each other moral support and interact with the parent (-in-law) together. Mutual facilitation of enjoyment (Thibaut & Kelley, 1959) occurs when, for example, the triad has a common interest that causes them to enjoy an activity together more than they would separately. Sequential patterns of interdependence (Thibaut & Kelley, 1959) benefit the triad when each member gives rewards to another member but receives rewards from the third member. For instance, a son-in-law may help his mother-in-law with household repairs, freeing the mother (-in-law) to help her daughter with child care, for which the daughter/wife praises her husband. This last example shows that interaction between dyads within the triad has the potential to influence the third member of the triad.

The influence of the third triad member, the child/spouse, prevents the parent- and child-in-law from forming a truly dyadic relationship. The actions of this third party in the triad can function to benefit or harm the parent- and child-in-law. For instance, the child/spouse might act in such a way as to facilitate positive interaction between the parent- and child-in-law. As an example, a son might selectively repeat only the positive comments that his father has made about his wife, improving his wife's rewards and increasing her motivation to interact with his father in anticipation of further rewards, or a wife might feel such happiness when her husband and her father are pleasant to each other that her positive regard provides rewards to both men. Conversely, the child/spouse might interfere with the interaction between the parent- and child-in-law in a negative way. For instance, a wife may show boredom and change the subject when her husband and her father begin to discuss their common interests because she does not share the same interest, or a husband might disclose to his wife a resentment that he holds against his mother. In the context of the husband's relationship with his mother, the resentment might appear to be slight, but to the wife, who does not know the whole context of their relationship, the resentment might appear to be very significant. She may find it very difficult to interact positively with her mother-in-law with this knowledge.

Even when the child/spouse does not actively interfere with or facilitate the parent-in-law/child-in-law relationship, the connection with that third party places constraints on the interaction between the parent-in-law and child-in-law. The in-laws might feel less free to interact with each other in the way that they would prefer because of potential effects on the third party. For instance, a husband might be reluctant to express his anger to his mother-in-law for fear that his action would upset his wife. A more complex influence of the presence of the third party is related to Thibaut and Kelley's (1959) description of a common tension in triadic relationships in which member A of the triad prefers a dyadic relationship with triad member B over the triadic relationship among A, B, and C; however, B does not reciprocate A's preference. In the case of the in-law triad, it is likely that the child-in-law would prefer the marital dyad over the triad and that the parent-in-law might prefer the parent-child dyad over the triad, though, of course, these dyads likely differ in the absolute value placed on them by each triad member. Empirical evidence for this pattern of preferences is provided by Floyd and Morr's (2003) finding that greater affection is expressed between spouses than between siblings and between siblings than between siblings-in-law. The child/spouse is unlikely to reciprocate the preference for either dyad over the triad, but it is likely that, if forced to choose one dyad over the other, the child/spouse would choose the marital dyad. The costs incurred in such a choice, though, would likely be great for all three individuals. At the same time, resentment at having to maintain a dispreferred relational status might motivate in-laws to punish one another, and perceptions of the child/spouse's preference for one dyad over another might affect an in-law's perception of power or status over the other in-law.

Constraints of the Involuntary Relationship

The preferences that the triad members hold for their relationships are further constrained by the involuntary dyadic relationship. Nonvoluntary relationships are those which a person effectively cannot leave because the costs of leaving would be so great (Thibaut & Kelley, 1959).[1] In this case, the relationship between in-laws is initiated in such a way that the parent- and child-in-law have little choice about the relationship, and they would incur great costs in dissolving their relationship. Parents in Western culture typically have little influence over their children's choice for a spouse. Spouses have no choice at all in selecting the parents of their spouse (unless, of course, they choose a spouse specifically because they like his or her parents or, somewhat more likely, disqualify a potential spouse because of dislike for his or her parents). Though lack of choice is relevant, it appears that negativity and preferences for distance exist even in non-Western cultures in which the families have more influence over the choice of their child's mate (e.g., Datta et al., 2003). More salient than choice are the barriers to ending the in-law relationship.

Once the relationship has been formed, dissolution is very difficult because of the high costs to all parties involved. In this case, dissolving the in-law dyad necessitates splitting up the triad. At least one link, between parent and child, between parent-in-law and child-in-law, or between spouses, would have to be dissolved to end the maintenance of a relationship between in-laws. Hence, in-laws are in the position of maintaining a nonvoluntary relationship. As Thibaut and Kelley (1959) explain in their discussion of nonvoluntary relationships, "the greater the penalties for escape (or attempted escape), the poorer the outcomes that a prisoner can be forced to endure" (p. 170). The metaphor of prison is a bit excessive for the discussion of in-law relationships, but the effect of constraints does apply: The stronger the forces (e.g., love for the child/spouse, fear of financial repercussions and social disapproval) are for preventing a member from leaving, the greater the costs he or she may be made to suffer in the relationship.

However, similarities and differences in power (defined as the ability to affect another's outcomes; Thibaut & Kelley, 1959) between in-laws may attenuate this effect. That is, the parent-in-law will have greater power to affect the child-in-law's outcomes negatively as a function of the child-in-law's love for the child/spouse, desire to raise his or her children within the extended family, financial dependence on the child/spouse, and so on. The child-in-law will have greater power to affect the parent-in-law's outcomes negatively as a function of the parent-in-law's love for the child/spouse, dependence on the child/spouse for care, desire to spend time with his or her grandchildren, and so on. If both parent- and child-in-law experience strong constraints to remain within the triadic relationship, both will have high power to influence each other's outcomes. Given the interdependence created by constraints on members to remain in the triad and the mutual influence of triad members, power similarity would make in-laws more reluctant to increase each other's costs for two reasons: Imposing costs on a person who also has power over one's own outcomes increases the probability that the other person will retaliate and increase one's own costs, and the best way to improve one's own outcomes in this situation may be to improve the outcomes of the other triad members.

No doubt the personal characteristics and interpersonal interaction of the in-laws also influence their behavior. Specifically, liking for the in-law would be apt to increase rewards in the relationship, in that in-laws would derive enjoyment from spending time together, and liking also reflects rewards gained in the relationship in the past. Evidence exists that liking moderates the effect of the voluntary or nonvoluntary nature of a relationship on relational partners' behavior. Hess (2000) examined differences in relational maintenance of voluntary relationships with liked partners (VR/Ls), nonvoluntary relationships with liked partners (NR/Ls), and nonvoluntary relationships with disliked partners (NR/Ds). Voluntary relationships with disliked partners were not investigated because of the assumption that these relationships would be unusual and would not be long-lasting. He argued that "NR/Ds pose a special challenge for their participants because social conventions, especially civility norms, dictate that people behave in all relationships in a manner consistent with the way we treat people we like" (Hess, 2000, p. 460). Thus, people in NR/Ds are placed in the uncomfortable position of feeling an obligation to behave pleasantly with people they dislike. Interestingly, reported importance of the relationship did not differ for those participants who reported on VR/Ls and NR/Ls, but importance was rated considerably lower by those participants who reported on NR/Ds. In social exchange terms, perceiving the NR/D as unimportant would reduce the effects of the negative outcome of that relationship.

Liking was also related to the behavior participants reported using in their relationships. Specifically, Hess (2000) considered enactment of hostile and distancing behaviors. Hostility is a common response to being constrained in an unsatisfactory relationship, and distancing can be used as a way to minimize the influence that a disliked partner can exert on one's outcomes (Thibaut & Kelley, 1959). Participants in relationships with people they liked were far less likely to report enacting distancing or hostile behaviors toward their partner than were participants in relationships with people they disliked (Hess, 2000). Also, participants with relational partners they liked reported using specific distancing behaviors much less frequently than did those with disliked partners (Hess, 2000). Hence, some of the constraints on interaction in a nonvoluntary relationship might be moderated by the degree to which in-laws feel affection and liking for each other. The likelihood that in-laws will perceive their relationship as difficult due to its involuntary nature probably depends largely on whether the in-laws actually like each other. Affinity between in-laws probably causes them to perceive the relationship as similar to voluntary relationships and to behave accordingly.

If a person likes his or her partner in a nonvoluntary relationship, that relationship probably also compares more favorably with the person's alternatives and with his or her standards for a satisfactory relationship. In this case, liking the in-law may make the in-law triad appear more rewarding than other possibilities, including the possibility of excluding the in-law from the relationship. This favorable comparison with alternatives would reduce the person's desire to leave the relationship. Without the feeling of constraint, he or she would be less likely to enact hostile or aggressive behaviors toward the other triad members, because feeling constrained is often a cause of hostility (Thibaut & Kelley, 1959). Rather, the desire to continue the relationship would motivate the person to maximize the outcomes of all triad members. Evidence for this argument may be found in the research of Timmer and Veroff (2000), who discovered that a wife's closeness to her husband's family predicts marital happiness. Moreover, when either the wife's or the husband's parents are divorced, wife's closeness to the husband's family decreases the risk of divorce (Timmer & Veroff, 2000). Thus, the positive enactment of the in-law relationship reduces the desire to dissolve the triad through divorce and is related to improved outcomes to the triad members.

Rewards and Costs in a Nonvoluntary, Triadic Relationship

The foregoing discussion defines in-law relationships as triadic and nonvoluntary. In summary, then, parent-in-law/child-in-law relationships come into being through the actions of a third party, the child/spouse. Thereafter, the actions of the three parties affect the triad as a whole, and the relationship between the parent- and child-in-law involves and is affected by the third party. Their communication with each other is constrained by the influence of the child/spouse. Moreover, the parent- and child-in-law have powerful disincentives to leave the relationship. Regardless of their satisfaction or dissatisfaction with the in-law triad, they effectively must remain in the triad. However, satisfaction level and degree to which they are constrained to remain in the relationship affect their behavior in the relationship. This behavior affects the outcomes of the triad member to whom the behavior is directed. The mutual influence that exists in the triad, though, means that their own actions will also have an impact on the triad as a whole and on their own outcome.

Crucial to this argument is the interdependence of rewards and costs in the parent-in-law/child-in-law relationship. Existing research has documented a variety of rewards and costs exchanged in the in-law relationship, and not surprisingly, the triadic nature of the relationship is often evident in this research. In Golish's (2000) study of turning points in relationships of parents and their adult children, the parent's acceptance or rejection of the child's spouse emerged as a turning point. Rejection of the spouse tended to decrease closeness between parent and child, whereas acceptance of the spouse increased parent–child closeness. Researchers have also found connections between in-law relationship processes and marital quality. Bryant, Conger, and Meehan (2001) found that conflict with in-laws was negatively related to both spouses' reports of marital quality later. Morr's (2003b) research on newlyweds' relationships with their in-laws found that private disclosure from in-laws was positively related to newlyweds' feelings of acceptance by the family and to satisfaction with the in-laws. Together, acceptance by and satisfaction with the in-laws explained 43% of the variance in the newlyweds' marital satisfaction (Morr, 2003b). Based on these findings, it can be concluded that communicative actions of acceptance, rejection, disclosure, and conflict result in rewards and costs for all members of the triad, not just the two members involved in the communicative episode. The potential impact of the in-law relationship on the child/ spouse and on the parent-child and marital dyads demonstrates the interdependence of outcomes for members of the triad.

The clearest example of the interdependent reward/cost pattern in the in-law relationship is demonstrated in the mutual exchange of support between married couples and their parents. The involuntary nature of the in-law relationship is evident in this pattern, too, in that the expectation to provide aid to one's parents and children ends up with parents providing support to their children-in-law along with their children and with children providing support to their parents-in-law as well as their parents. Support exchanged in the in-law triad can ease the strains of everyday life and of important life transitions, and these expectations can also place a heavy burden on these relationships. Parents (-in-law) typically provide a great deal of instrumental support through financial assistance early in marriage and service support during their grandchildren's preschool years (Goetting, 1990). Married couples are in turn expected to provide instrumental support (i.e., financial, task related, and personal/medical care) as their parents (-in-law) grow older (Goetting, 1990). The functioning of the relationship may or may not be related to the provision of support: the nonvoluntary nature of the relationship might cause the obligation to provide aid to hold even when the triadic relationship is unsatisfying, or members in strained relationships may miss out on potential sources of instrumental help because the already high costs of the relationship might discourage the aid provider from incurring even higher costs by providing support. On the other hand, members in positively functioning relationships may receive much help from in-laws because the high rewards provided by the relationship and the promise of reciprocity offset the costs of providing support, but they may also incur great costs in fulfilling their duties to provide aid to in-laws. By the same token, poor relationships with in-laws, in which few rewards are gained, may free the parties from the costs related to obligations to provide care and support to in-laws.

INTERPERSONAL NEGOTIATION OF IN-LAWS' ROLES

The difficulty with in-law relationships rests on the structural factors discussed previously: The in-law relationship is triadic and nonvoluntary. That combination of structural features gives rise to a further complication in that in-laws must negotiate ambiguity about their roles in the relationship. Thibaut and Kelley (1959) explain that roles are constellations of norms about a person's behavior in a given relationship. Norms are rules for behavior to which members of a relationship subscribe (Thibaut & Kelley, 1959). Established norms for behavior (e.g., that spouses will take turns washing the dishes) improve outcomes in relationships (Thibaut & Kelley, 1959) because the members are saved the costs of negotiating every situation individually (e.g., nightly discussions about which spouse will do the dishes) and of possible conflict (e.g., fights about inequity in dishwashing responsibilities). Roles, as sets of norms, also function to improve outcomes in relationships, and in order to minimize their costs, people may rely on culturally or socially based roles that specify the norms a person will follow in a given relationship, rather than explicitly negotiating every expected norm for the role they play in every relationship.

However, in-laws in Western cultures are placed in a situation for which cultural roles are quite ambiguous. In fact, scholars argue that the in-law's position in the family is a roleless one (see, e.g., Pfeifer, 1989). Factors including the relatively high autonomy of Western married couples from their extended family (Altman et al., 1992), the high level of choice involved in developing and maintaining contemporary family relationships (Stein, 1993), and the increasing provision of care (once expected to be provided by family) by public and governmental institutions (Riley & Riley, 1993) introduce ambiguity into in-laws' expectations for the enactment of their role in the relationship. In the triad under consideration, the marital and parent-child relationships do have culturally defined roles that they may choose to apply or to adapt.

In attempting to establish a framework in which they can improve the outcomes of the triad members and enable themselves to predict the outcomes that will result from their behaviors, members of the in-law relationship will attempt to establish roles. Their choices are likely to proceed by drawing an analogy between the in-law relationship and another, more familiar relationship with established roles. In-laws might use their experience in parent-child relationships to understand how to be an in-law, or they might draw on experiences from other relationships, such as friendships. The particular choice of an analogous relationship affects the in-laws' relationship outcomes because drawing an analogy to a parent-child relationship will set up different standards for satisfaction within the relationship than would drawing an analogy to a friendship. Moreover, in-laws might disagree about their preferred roles in the relationship, with the parent-in-law choosing to behave as a parent and the child-in-law choosing to behave as a friend, for example. Such mismatches between role choices are likely to cause difficulty for the in-laws.

Ambiguity in Family Membership and Roles

Although in-law relationships have an ambiguous structure in contemporary society, it is important to note that present-day family relationships are less clearly defined than they once were. Social scientists argue that kin relationships in the present-day United States are largely a matter of choice rather than strict roles and obligations (Riley & Riley, 1993). In fact, some researchers argue that this state of affairs has existed for more than a century (Stein, 1993). Examples of research findings supporting this notion include research on boundary ambiguity, in which family members are uncertain about who belongs as a member of the family. For instance, families launching an adolescent sometimes experience boundary ambiguity as the child leaves home (Pasley & Ihinger-Tallman, 1989), some recently divorced couples may have ambiguous feelings about the ex-spouse's membership in the family (Madden-Derdich, Leonard, & Christopher, 1999), and some families of men who were declared missing in action in Vietnam may experience ambiguity about whether the man who is MIA is a family member (Boss, 1977). Similarly, Jorgenson (1989) asked her participants to explain whom they considered to be their family members. There was much variation in the particular individuals named, but relational factors were a common theme: Participants decided who "counts" as a family member according to their time spent with one another and their participation in important family activities.

These studies demonstrate the notion that the roles of family members and the boundaries of the family are not clearly defined in modern American culture. Families sometimes experience ambiguity in designating family members, and they tend to use interpersonal, rather than structural, features of the relationships as criteria for determining membership status. Likewise, membership status is granted in interpersonal, rather than structural, ways. For instance, Petronio (2002) argues that group members confer membership status by disclosing the group's private information to a new member. Similarly, Pfeifer (1989) described acceptance of an in-law as demonstrated by conferring "family privileges of behavior, knowledge, and permission" (p. 220). Indicators of acceptance within the family include "being privy to insider information, included in decision making policies, and asked for advice and/or assistance" (Pfeifer, 1989, p. 223). Thus, defining an individual as a member of a family and assigning this member an appropriate role is not always a clear-cut process. Family members use cues such as physical presence and behavior to make decisions about a person's role in the family, and they act on those decisions in the ways they communicate with members and nonmembers.

Roles Established by In-laws

Evidently, the role of "in-law" in a family is an ambiguous one. This ambiguity opens possibilities for in-laws to improvise roles, with various results. Furthermore, the dynamic nature of relationships in general is heightened by the flexibility allowed by role ambiguity. Hence, in-law relationships have potential to change over time, with the parties to the relationship trying out different roles and adapting their interaction to their personal preferences and to changes that occur with time. However, although precisely defined roles for in-laws do not exist, there are a few norms for behavior expected from and toward one's in-laws. In-law relationships obligate individuals to form some sort of familial bond with people to whom they are not related by blood and who may be strangers when the relationship begins (Bryant et al., 2001). The exact nature and extent of that bond are not clearly agreed on, but researchers argue that some sense of reciprocal obligations and fulfillment of those expectations is beneficial for family relationships in general.

The construct of "felt obligation" deals with issues including frequency of contact, personal assistance, avoidance of conflict, communication, and disclosure (Stein, 1993). Stein's research shows that married individuals feel fewer obligations toward in-laws than toward their own parents. However, some level of felt obligation toward in-laws seems to serve a positive function. In research conducted by Jackson and Berg-Cross (1988), women's adjustment to their mothers-in-law was positively correlated to variables related to felt obligation, specifically, dependency on mother-in-law, compliant problem-solving strategy, and frequency of phone contact. Stein (1993) points out the benefits that can be gained by fulfilling such reciprocal obligations. By meeting their responsibilities to each other, family members are likely to increase their "solidarity and connectedness" (Stein, 1993, p. 83). Furthermore, in an explanation of intergenerational family obligations, Bengtson (1993) argues that family members typically recognize and do not resent their obligations. Thus, a norm associated with the roles that in-laws define for themselves is some obligation for contact and communication with one another, assistance, and avoidance of conflict.

The contrast that Stein (1993) discovered in the comparison of obligations toward parents and parents-in-law is consistent with cultural expectations. American culture clearly demarcates the status of family by nature and family by law (Stein, 1993). Family members by nature are those with whom one shares genetic material. Family members by law include any relations acquired as the result of law or custom. Stein argues that there are clear differences in these relationships: People typically feel fewer obligations to family members by law than to family members by nature. For instance, Coleman, Ganong, and Cable (1997) found that women's obligations to their mothers and daughters were perceived to be greater than to their mothers-in-law, and Coleman and Ganong (1998) found that men's obligations to their fathers and sons were perceived to be greater than to their stepfathers and former fathers-in-law.

Status as member of the family is a significant aspect of the role of an in-law. As discussed earlier, ambiguity about the membership of a family can exist. Family membership is one basis on which an in-law's role can be based. If an in-law is a family member, then family member norms can serve as the basis for the constellation of norms that will make up the in-law's role. If the in-law is not a family member, then decisions can be made about which, if any, family norms will be incorporated into the in-law's role. Changes in family member status appear to be associated with major turning points in the lives of the in-laws. Emerging research indicates that newlyweds identify private disclosures from their in-laws as signals of the degree to which the newlywed is considered to be a member of the family (Morr, 2003a). Furthermore, the overall amount of information disclosed by in-laws is positively related to the newlywed's perception that he or she is accepted as a family member (Morr, 2003b). In this research, newlyweds typically identified significant disclosures occurring at the points of engagement and marriage (Morr, 2003a). Thus, the disclosure of the family's private information signaled the change in family membership status that occurred with engagement and marriage. A second critical event, the birth of a couple's first child, has been investigated in relation to women's relationships with their mothers and mothers-in-law. Fischer's (1983) investigation found that, with the birth of a woman's first child, her relationship with her mother improved, but her relationship with her mother-in-law declined. A specific issue of contention with the mother-in-law was her criticism about the daughter-in-law's childrearing methods. Such critical statements at the time of this major event may be perceived as rejection and could influence the daughter-in-law's perception of her acceptance as a member of the in-laws' family.

Beyond the basic designation of the in-law as a member or nonmember in the family, analogies drawn between the in-law relationship and some other relationship contribute more specific sets of norms to the in-law's role. Participants in Pfeifer's (1989) study chose from four options to define their mother-in-law/daughter-in-law relationship. In-law relationships were rated most highly in quality when a relationship was defined as a parent-child or as a friend relationship by the parties involved (Pfeifer, 1989). The other two options for definition were associate by marriage (the most frequently chosen option) and extended family relationship, both of which are closer to the literal definition of an in-law relationship than are the parent-child and friend definitions. Choosing to define their relationship in parent–child or friendship terms likely causes the in-law relationship to actually involve more obligations than would the choice to define the relationship as an associate or extended family connection. Although the norms associated with these roles demand greater contributions from the in-laws, they also must include greater rewards, since the quality of these relationships was high.

Implications of In-laws' Roles

Defining the in-law relationship by drawing comparisons with parent-child, extended family or friendship relationships allows in-laws to establish roles for one another. This choice, however, has its own implications for the relationship. Choosing to define an in-law relationship as analogous to a parent–child relationship implies different standards for satisfaction than does choosing to define that in-law relationship as analogous to an extended family relationship. A parent–child relationship likely has a comparison level (the minimum outcome level, in terms of rewards and costs, at which a relationship will be satisfying; Thibaut & Kelley, 1959) that is greater than the comparison level of an extended family relationship. A parent–child-type in-law relationship likely requires more costs and promises more rewards to the in-laws than does the extended-family-type in-law relationship. Choosing a particular set of roles for the parent-in-law and child-in-law not only designates the norms for behavior of the in-laws, but also sets the threshold for a satisfactory relational outcome.

Further difficulties arise when the parent-in-law and child-in-law choose different relational definitions and, with them, different roles for the in-laws. For instance, as mentioned earlier, a parent-in-law might act under the assumption they have a parent-child-type relationship, while the child-in-law acts under the assumption they have a friendship-type relationship. Of course, those assumptions assign roles, with assumed norms for behavior, for both in-laws. If the child-in-law acts in a way consistent with a friend role, he or she might violate the expectations of the parent-in-law, who expects the child-in-law to act consistently with a child role. Role incompatibility is likely to lead to frustration and disappointment in the in-law relationship. Evidence for this phenomenon is found in the circumstances of mothers- and daughters-in-law in Pfeifer's (1989) study who reported poor quality in-law relationships. Participants who described their relationships as unsatisfactory included mothers-in-law who expected a very close relationship with their daughter-in-law and daughters-in-law who expected their mother-in-law to grant them rights equal to those of the mother-in-law's children immediately. These unhappy in-laws appear to have chosen roles for the in-law relationship that are inconsistent with those that the other member had chosen. Jackson and Berg-Cross (1988) found a similar result in their study focusing on Black women's relationships with their mothers and mothers-in-law. Results indicated a negative relationship between participants' need for inclusion (the desire for the relational partner to actively invite and include the participant in activities) and mother-in-law adjustment (which included measures of affection, intimacy, tension, and involvement). In both the Pfeifer (1989) and the Jackson and Berg-Cross (1988) studies, the disappointed party had placed high expectations on the in-law. This is not surprising, in that the person who chooses roles for the in-laws that reflect a higher standard for satisfaction would be more likely to be disappointed than the person who chooses roles with a lower standard for satisfaction. Whether or not the mother-in-law or daughter-in-law of the disappointed woman was aware of these high demands, she failed to meet them, and the discrepancy was related to poor relational quality.

Discrepancies in role definition might be due to a large number of factors. However, the evidence that critical life events affect the designation of family members suggests that differences in perception of these events might be related to differences in the perception of in-laws' roles. For example, in Pfeifer's (1989) study, daughters-in-law stated that they had begun preparing themselves to be family members from the first meeting with their spouse's family. On the other hand, mothers-in-law did not begin to view the daughter-in-law as a potential family member until their son told them he was considering marriage. In this case, the mother-in-law and daughter-in-law defined different critical events for beginning the transition to family membership. Such discrepancies could result in contradictory role definitions, especially early in the in-law relationship.

The definition of in-laws' roles also influences relationships beyond the triad of the parent (-in-law), child-in-law/spouse, and child/spouse. Individuals in a family deal with relationships and boundaries on many levels simultaneously (Petronio, 2002). Role definitions and communication in the triadic relationship affect and are affected by other relationships within the family system and relationships with others outside of the family. Defining the roles of the parent-in-law and child-in-law relates to the roles these individuals play in other relationships. For instance, Jorgenson's (1994) study of address terms used for parents-in-law revealed that some married couples consider relationships with other family members in deciding what to call their parents-in-law. In considering whether to call the parents-in-law "Mom and Dad," these individuals consider their own loyalties to their parents as well as the claim of the spouse's siblings to have exclusive rights to call their own parents "Mom and Dad." In considering these factors, these individuals wrestle with the questions of whether a parent-in-law is the same as a parent and whether a child-in-law is the same as a child. In-laws also evaluate other family members' management of roles. The daughters-in-law who participated in Pfeifer's (1989) study assessed the quality of their relationship with their mother-in-law by comparing their own contact with their mother-in-law with the frequency of her contact with her other children and in-laws. Thus, in working out relational issues, in-laws consider their own and others' roles in the larger family system, and they consider each others' role performance outside of the triad when they evaluate the quality of the triadic relationship.

CONCLUSION

Difficulties in in-law relationships are rooted in the nature of the relationships themselves. Parents- and children-in-law find themselves in a nonvoluntary, triadic relationship. They are unable to leave this relationship because of the high potential costs to all three members, but their behavior is constrained by the influence of the child/spouse. Because of the ambiguous nature of the in-law relationship, they also must define their own roles. Drawing an analogy to another type of relationship, such as a friendship relationship, can help to establish clear roles and expectations, but further difficulties will arise if the two in-laws choose incompatible roles.

Much remains unknown about the relationships of parents- and children-in-law. More research is required to explore and test the claims made in this chapter. First of all, very little research includes all three members of the triad. Furthermore, what little research exists on relationships of parents-in-law and children-in-law focuses almost exclusively on mothers- and daughters-in-law. As a result, it is difficult to say how many of the research findings discussed in this chapter are unique to women or to same-sex in-law relationships. Research most often addresses in-law relationships from the point of view of the child-in-law, and the possibilities of connections between the in-law triad and the larger family system, though deserving of research attention, pose challenges to researchers because of the necessarily complex research design that would be required.

Incorporating in-law relationships into theories and research about relationships in general poses challenges for many reasons. The relationship's complexity and ambiguity make it difficult to draw points of similarity and difference between in-law relationships and other types of relationships, but these attributes also make in-law relationships that much more interesting as a basis for theory. Furthermore, our knowledge of in-law relationships is limited by the small amount of existing research on involuntary relationships in general and on in-law relationships in particular. In the future, research should investigate the in-law relationship from the points of view of all of the members of the triad. The existing research on mothers- and daughters-in-law should be matched by research including fathers-in-law and sons-in-law in all possible combinations to clarify sex differences and similarities in in-law relationships. Moreover, our knowledge of in-law relationships tends to cluster around points of marriage of the child and child-in-law, birth of the first child/grandchild, and health crises of the older parent-in-law. Research that extends our understanding of the in-law relationship across the life of the relationship is needed. In reference to the claims in this chapter, a better understanding of the nature of interdependence in triadic relationships, circumstances that lead to satisfaction and dissatisfaction in the in-law triad, and causes of beneficial and harmful behavior within the triad all deserve attention. The process of establishing roles for parents- and children-in-law and the causes of changes in those roles over time are also topics about which little is known.

In 1954, Duvall's research revealed that mothers-in-law were the most difficult of in-laws, but that in-law relationships can be both wonderful and miserable. Fifty years later, the same cultural stereotypes of in-law relationships exist, but we still have much to learn about why in-law relationships are difficult. This chapter takes a step toward explaining the difficulty of parents- and children-in-law, and it remains for further research to fill in the gaps in our knowledge of this complicated, ambiguous relationship.

NOTE

1. Thibaut and Kelley (1959) also stipulate as part of their definition that a person in a nonvoluntary relationship must be dissatisfied with that relationship. They argue that a person in a satisfactory relationship might be unable to leave, but the point is moot because the person would choose that relationship even if leaving were a possibility. However, current understanding of nonvoluntary relationships defines them solely by the criterion of the inability to leave the relationship, whether or not the person likes the partner (e.g., Hess, 2000) or is satisfied in the relationship. In this chapter, "nonvoluntary relationships" refers to relationships in which the extremely high costs of dissolving the relationship force the members to continue, regardless of whether the relationship is satisfactory or unsatisfactory.

REFERENCES

Adler, L. L., Denmark, F. L., & Ahmed, R. A. (1989). Attitudes toward mother-in-law and stepmother: A cross-cultural study. *Psychological Reports, 65,* 1194.

Altman, I., Brown, B. B., Staples, B., & Werner, C. M. (1992). A transactional approach to close relationships: Courtship, weddings, and placemaking. In W. B. Walsh, K. H. Craik, & R. H. Price (Eds.), *Person-environment psychology: Models and perspectives* (pp. 193–242). Hillsdale, NJ: Lawrence Erlbaum Associates.

Bengtson, V. L. (1993). Is the "contract across generations" changing? Effects of population aging on obligations and expectations across age groups. In V. L. Bengtson & W. A. Achenbaum (Eds.), *The changing contract across generations* (pp. 3–23). New York: Aldine de Gruyter.

Boss, P. (1977). A clarification of the concept of psychological father presence in families experiencing ambiguity of boundary. *Journal of Marriage and the Family, 39,* 141–151.

Bryant, C. M., Conger, R. D., & Meehan, J. M. (2001). The influence of in-laws on change in marital success. *Journal of Marriage and the Family, 63,* 614–626.

Coleman, M., Ganong, L., & Cable, S. M. (1997). Beliefs about women's intergenerational family obligations to provide support before and after divorce and remarriage. *Journal of Marriage and the Family, 59,* 165–176.

Coleman, M., & Ganong, L. H. (1998). Attitudes toward men's intergenerational financial obligations to older and younger male family members following divorce. *Personal Relationships, 5,* 293–309.

Datta, P., Poortinga, Y. H., & Marcoen, A. (2003). Parent care by Indian and Belgian caregivers in their roles of daughter/daughter-in-law. *Journal of Cross-Cultural Psychology, 34,* 736–749.

Duvall, E. M. (1954). *In-laws: Pro and con*. New York: Association Press.

Fischer, L. R. (1983). Mothers and mothers-in-law. *Journal of Marriage and the Family, 45*, 187–192.

Floyd, K., & Morr, M. C. (2003). Human affection exchange: VII. Affectionate communication in the spouse/sibling/sibling-in-law triad. *Communication Quarterly, 51*, 247–261.

Goetting, A. (1990). Patterns of support among in-laws in the United States. *Journal of Family Issues, 11*, 67–90.

Golish, T. D. (2000). Changes in closeness between adult children and their parents: A turning point analysis. *Communication Reports, 13*, 79–97.

Hess, J. A. (2000). Maintaining nonvoluntary relationships with disliked partners: An investigation into the use of distancing behaviors. *Human Communication Research, 26*, 458–488.

Jackson, J., & Berg-Cross, L. (1988). Extending the extended family: The mother-in-law and daughter-in-law relationship of Black women. *Family Relations, 37*, 293–297.

Jorgenson, J. (1989). Where is the "family" in family communication?: Exploring families' self-definitions. *Journal of Applied Communication Research, 17*, 27–41.

Jorgenson, J. (1994). Situated address and the social construction of "in-law" relationships. *Southern Communication Journal, 55*, 196–204.

Madden-Derdich, D. A., Leonard, S. A., & Christopher, F. S. (1999). Boundary ambiguity and coparental conflict after divorce: An empirical test of a family systems model of the divorce process. *Journal of Marriage and the Family, 61*, 588–598.

Morr, M. C. (2003a, February). *Focus group investigation of private disclosure in a family membership transition: In-laws' disclosures to newlyweds*. Paper presented at the annual meeting of the Western States Communication Association, Salt Lake City, UT.

Morr, M. C. (2003b, November). *Newlyweds' relationships with in-laws: Relationships among disclosure, family privacy orientation, and relational quality*. Paper presented at the annual meeting of the National Communication Association, Miami Beach, FL.

Pasley, B. K., & Ihinger-Tallman, M. (1989). Boundary ambiguity in remarriage: Does ambiguity differentiate degree of marital adjustment and integration? *Family Relations, 38*, 46–52.

Petronio, S. (2002). *Boundaries of privacy: Dialectics of disclosure*. Albany, NY: State University of New York Press.

Pfeifer, S. K. (1989). *Mothers'-in-law and daughters'-in-law perceptions of interpersonal interaction*. Unpublished doctoral dissertation, University of Delaware.

Riley, M. W., & Riley, J. W., Jr. (1993). Connections: Kin and cohort. In V. L. Bengtson & W. A. Achenbaum (Eds.), *The changing contract across generations* (pp. 169–189). New York: Aldine de Gruyter.

Stein, C. H. (1993). Felt obligation in adult family relationships. In S. Duck (Ed.), *Social context and relationships* (pp. 78–99). Newbury Park, CA: Sage.

Thibaut, J. W., & Kelley, H. H. (1959). *The social psychology of groups*. New York: Wiley.

Timmer, S. G., & Veroff, J. (2000). Family ties and the discontinuity of divorce in Black and White newlywed couples. *Journal of Marriage and the Family, 62*, 349–361.

Chapter 7

The Trouble With Distance

Erin M. Sahlstein
University of Richmond, Virginia

Various problems can plague personal relationships and threaten their existence (e.g., serial conflict, wavering commitment, angry exes, and unsupportive friends and family). One of the most difficult problems to manage in any relationship is distance. Because we tend to associate relationships with closeness, whether metaphorical or real, and with face-to-face interaction or physical co-presence, distance is primarily considered to be a barrier to relating that needs to be overcome, whether it is physical, psychological, emotional, or all three interdependently.

If one or both relational partners perceive dissimilarities, then they may view the relationship as doomed since they cannot "see eye to eye." Partners also can intentionally increase psychological distance between them in order to slow or cease relational development (Hess, 2002). Within personal relationships, emotional closeness and intimacy, not distance, are hallmarks of success and satisfaction (Baxter & Montgomery, 1996). Distance of any kind is certainly not perceived as indicative of a good relationship and is more likely to be viewed as problematic. Long-distance relationships are typically viewed as negative, abnormal, or doomed (Sahlstein, 2004a). People do not typically display excitement when they find out they will be separated for unexpected or extended periods of time, and they often have trouble initially seeing positive possibilities for being apart (Sahlstein, 2004b).

Despite the negative connotations surrounding distance, long-distance relationships (LDRs) are becoming a frequent part of modern experience. With the increased affordability and availability of communication technologies, as well as increased mobility in our population, many individuals participate in long-distance relationships with romantic partners (sometimes several), hometown friends, college buddies, and family members. Research on LDRs has often shown that they are satisfying and sustainable relationships with many redeeming qualities (Sahlstein, 2004a, 2004b); however, many problems facing LDRs have been reported in the literature. In this chapter, I briefly discuss some of the challenges of long-distance relating and then focus on one particular problem for LDRs—their simultaneous management with proximal relationships (PRs). Taking a relational dialectics perspective, I will describe some of the contradictions experienced within this matrix of relating and conclude by offering directions for future research.

THE DIFFICULTIES OF LONG-DISTANCE RELATING

Long-distance relating has been primarily studied in the context of romantic connections (i.e., dating relationships or marriages), although research has also been conducted on long-distance parenting and friendships. Each LDR type has its unique challenges, yet they all present the difficult task of partners maintaining a sense of a relationship despite their physically separate existence. The challenges that partners face can be located at the level of the individual (e.g., feelings of abandonment or jealousy), the relationship (e.g., conflicts regarding how to manage the household), or the social network (e.g., family members' disapproval of the distal configuration of a commuter marriage). In the subsequent sections, I present the difficulties reported within five LDR types (romantic, military, commuter, parental, and friendship). Although these are not actually mutually exclusive, researchers have tended to pick one or the other for their research, a problem to which I shall return.

Problems With Long-Distance Romance (i.e., Dating)

Actually, the term *long-distance romance* is always used by researchers to refer to dating relationships specifically, and the following discussion is about dating, not about the romance in long-distance marriages, for example, which I treat separately. Researchers have discussed various problems of long-distance dating relationships (LDDRs), although they have invariably labeled the relationships Long Distance *Romantic* Relationships and only a few have solicited the specific details of the relational difficulties. Westefeld and Liddell (1982) reported five challenges for LDDRs: (a) financial strains due to high costs of travel and telephone bills, (b) emotional strains on the partners due to extreme feeling changes, (c) time management issues, (d) relational assessment difficulties, and (e) negotiating other relationships. Although travel and communication have become more affordable than when this study was published, the seamless movement and interactions of proximal romantic relationships (PRRs) remain in contrast to the "marked" patterns of relating within LDDRs. LDDR couples continue to experience emotional strain because they are hyper-conscious of the transitions between moments of being together and being apart. For example, Sahlstein (2004b) reported that couples recognized themselves strategically planning for their time together. According to Guldner (1996), LDDR partners report more symptoms of depression than PRR partners, and they feel uneasy in large group situations where their partner is absent, possibly due to being in relational "liminal" spaces (i.e., being in a relationship but primarily living an "individual" life). Dainton and Aylor (2001) address how levels of relational uncertainty may affect LDDR functioning. LDDR partners with some face-to-face contact and LDDR partners without face-to-face contact were significantly different with respect to their relational uncertainty levels; participants who saw their partners from time to time throughout the separation were less uncertain and more trusting of their relationship than participants who could not ever see their partners during the separation. Similarly, Holt and Stone (1988) reported that couples who are in LDDRs for more than 6 months and who live at least 250 miles apart have less satisfaction and intimacy than couples in LDDRs for less than 6 months. Clearly, reduction of contact can lead to problems in LDDRs, and physical distance has been reported to contribute to relationship demise (Knox, Zusman, Daniels, & Brantley, 2002).

A specific problematic outcome of restricted communication that has been posited is idealization (Stafford & Reske, 1990), which could cause future problems within these relationships. Stafford and Reske argue that LDDR partners who idealize their relationships likely do not have realistic assessments of their relationships and have overly positive views of the partners given their limited amount and frequency of interaction. Idealization may cause difficulties for LDDR partners when spending time together, as they may have to (re)negotiate their ideal views of the relationship with its reality. Furthermore, they may not like the relationship once they are in either temporary or permanent proximity to one another. However, no research directly examines the influence of idealization levels for LDDR couples once they become PRRs.

Sahlstein (2004b) has identified several areas of concern for people in LDDRs. Couples in her study reported that periods of separation create intense pressure on them to have quality/positive time when together, thus raising the bar for such meetings. They also noted that friends, family, and work suffer as a result of being in a LDDR and that their conversations are too often meta-communicative. Partners also often feel as if they are living separate lives, and this can construct uncertainty around their relationship and the time they spend together. After their periodic face-to-face visits, LDDR partners feel let down and they have to go through periods of adjustment that can be emotionally and physically draining. They also have difficulties managing conflict; couples reported avoiding conflicts or saving them for face-to-face visits. Conflicts often feel unresolved because of their inconsistent and intermittent management.

Problems With Long-Distance Marriage

Similar issues arise within long–distance marriages, yet distinct concerns emerge as well. Long–distance marriage occurs in several forms: two of the most widely researched are military marriages (MMs) and commuter marriages (CMs). "The most frequently identified sources of stress for [military] families have been separation, deployments, and reunions" (Knox & Price, 1999, p. 131), specifically "separation of family members; fear of capture, injury or death; shifts in family roles; disruption of normal routine; [and] increased financial pressures" (Norwood & Ursano, 1996, p. 6). The research in this area primarily focuses on the female's experience and reveals the many emotional challenges that face military wives (McCubbin, Dahl, & Hunter, 1976). The spouse left behind during deployments (most often the female) has almost the entire responsibility for household management and child care. Military families do not have high incomes and many live at or below the poverty line (Knox & Price, 1999). Given these conditions, military spouses encounter a variety of problems during the deployment of the partner.

Norwood, Fullerton, and Hagen (1996) describe the emotional and practical issues faced by military families across the three primary stages of deployment: anticipation, separation, and reunion. During the anticipation stage, spouses experience a range of emotions. They move through fear, denial, anger, resentment, and hurt immediately after the deployment announcement up to a week before the spouse leaves for his or her tour of duty. These emotions turn into confusion, ambivalence, anger, and withdrawal in the final days before deployment. The anticipation stage is extremely challenging for the marital partners; they are experiencing such strong emotions but need to address the reality of the impending changes ahead. Plans need to be made about management of the household (e.g., bills, child care, home and auto repair) as well as the relationship (e.g., when and how to communicate). During the separation, the spouses who remain are left with a significant amount of responsibility. They must maintain the family both practically and emotionally, all the while feeling abandoned, alone, and fragmented (Norwood et al., 1996). Once they have adjusted to the separation, the partners feel more confident and calm as they settle into their new routines and roles. As the reunion draws near, their feelings of uncertainty and expectation increase as they start to plan for their spouse's homecoming. The reunion occurs in two substages: honeymoon and readjustment. The honeymoon spans from the first day home up until the first conflict. Spouses experience a state of euphoria during this period; they are so excited to be together and to re-form their bonds. The first fight initiates the readjustment phase where spouses feel uncomfortable and confused, yet happy, as they renegotiate their roles and routines.

Commuting couples experience similar financial and emotional strain as LDDRs and MMs, because satisfaction can decrease as the time apart increases (Rhodes, 2002). Because they have regularly moved through the phases of separation and do so more frequently than MMs, they are highly aware of the quantity, frequency, and quality of their time together, which can be viewed as both positive and negative for the relationship (Jackson, Brown, & Patterson-Stewart, 2000). Unique to military and commuter marriages, in comparison to LDDRs, is the couple's perception of a "home base" (i.e., one residence is typically viewed as temporary and primarily for the absent partner, and the other is joint living space where the couple resides). Problems, such as deciding how to divide household labor, arise out of this context that do not occur in LDDRs where the partners have separate households or MMs where deployments construct rigid role definitions (i.e., the deployed partner is completely absent for an extended period of time vs. frequent, intermittent absences). Some commuter couples do set up two entirely different households where neither space is a home; thus, partners feel dislocated and without a sense of place (Gerstel & Gross, 1984). The physical separation affects the relational dynamics similar to LDDRs: less face-to-face contact, physical intimacy, and knowledge of each other's daily experiences. According to Gerstel and Gross (1984), up to one third of CMs experience infidelity, which can cause a host of problems within marriage (e.g., physical or verbal abuse, distrust, and divorce).

Commuter couples also have trouble maintaining and developing their friendships in the larger network beyond the romantic pairing. Network members may start to view the partner "at home" as a single person (Gerstel & Gross, 1984) and therefore different from the network when the spouse is away. When the CM partners are together, on weekends and vacations, they likely spend the time together, which isolates the couple from family and friends. Partners who move away struggle to cultivate social networks due to their married-singleton lifestyles; they typically work during the week, and on the weekends, for example, they visit (or are visited by) their spouses/families. CM partners are legally bound together and yet are socially separate in ways that cause confusion for everyone involved.

Problems With Long-Distance Parenting

Commuter marriages among couples with children can create difficulties over parenting; however, children of commuter marriages have received little attention from CM researchers (Rhodes, 2002). Specific studies concerning long-distance parenting and kinship are dispersed across several areas of research, such as military families (Norwood & Ursano, 1996), noncustodial parenting as a result of divorce (Stewart,

2003), commuter marriages (Jackson et al., 2000), and transnational families (Parrenas, 2001). Sahlstein (2004a) identified some of the potential negative qualities of long-distance kinship (LDK):

1. LDKs are difficult to maintain (inconvenient, expensive).
2. They can cause tension and stress on the individual.
3. Family members have difficulty maintaining current information about each other.
4. The distance makes it difficult to reassure, comfort and support one another.
5. Family members have low frequency and quantity of interaction.
6. LDKs are difficult to manage during challenging times (i.e., for either the family or individual members).

Children in military families often experience a variety of problems when one or both parents are deployed (McCubbin et al., 1976). During the deployment, children can have feelings of abandonment, confusion, and anxiety; parents can feel guilty, disconnected, and depressed. Parent–child interaction can be awkward during the reunion stage of deployment; children do not know how to relate to their newly present parent.

Divorce spawns LDKs of varied degrees, which can significantly affect parent–child relationships. For example, divorced fathers have less contact, more physical distance, and are less likely to reside with their children (Rollie, chap. 10, this volume; Shapiro, 2003). When divorces happen later in life, fathers often become estranged from their adult children in part due to the geographic distance between them (Shapiro, 2003). Generally, both nonresidential mothers and fathers primarily spend leisure time with their children and are less involved in their academics and daily activities. Parents' involvement in their children's schooling decreases as their physical distance increases (Stewart, 1999). Divorce can create some complex parenting arrangements given that many individuals remarry, have "new families," and move to new homes. My brother, for example, has been married three times and has three children as a result. He lives with his youngest daughter, his son lives in the same metropolitan area, and his eldest daughter lives several thousand miles away. Fathers with more than one set of parenting responsibilities, such as my brother, are less likely than fathers with only one set to see their nonresidential children (Manning, Stewart, & Smock, 2003), a situation which certainly affects the children and their relationships with their father. Although the research in the areas of divorce, noncustodial parenting, and blended families does not distinguish distal and proximal relationships, many do include variables such as frequency of contact and number of miles between family members (Rollie, chap. 10, this volume).

The perspectives of the children in commuting households have received practically no attention from researchers. Jackson et al. (2000) report that children in commuter families experience negative emotions similar to those of children in military families. They also report that commuter children feel a lack of concern on the part of the absent parent. There remains, however, a significant gap in the LDR research concerning the children within these commuter families.

Transnational families—and specifically those involving mothering at a distance—have gained attention from some scholars (Parrenas, 2001). An extreme form of CM, transnational families occur when one or both parents move to another country (even continent) in order to provide for the family. Transnational motherhood, in particular, is fraught with "numerous costs and [is] attained in a context of extremely scarce options" (Hondagneu-Sotelo & Avila, 1997, p. 567). These relationships emerge out of the financial difficulties of the family and are simultaneously both a blessing and a burden for the familial system; one parent's income supports the needs of the family, but his or her absence creates individual and relational problems. The absent parent is displaced in a foreign land with little to no social support either in the immediate proximity or back home (i.e., she is not being a "good mother"). Absent parents are likely performing physically laborious jobs with little cultural capital. The children are left with only one parent to care for them, yet child care is often left to other family members (e.g., aunts or grandparents) or hired help (Parrenas, 2001). Children may not see their displaced parent for years, and this engenders resentment and anger for both the child and the spouse. Parrenas reports that children "are racked with loneliness, insecurity, and vulnerability" and "they crave greater intimacy with their migrant parents" (p. 131). While the parent can rationalize the distance through the financial rewards obtained for the family, the children feel abandoned and would rather have the parent present instead of having increased economic resources (Parrenas, 2001). Their differing perceptions lead to repetitive conflicts within the parent-child relationship.

Problems With Long-Distance Friendships

LDFs have received little attention from relationship researchers but have been indirectly examined through the study of computer-mediated communication (e.g., Parks & Floyd, 1996). Friendships often deteriorate due to distance, and the financial strains placed on the maintenance of the relationship are similar to those for LDDRs (Rohlfing, 1995). However, many friendships are initiated and maintained at a distance (Johnson, 2001), especially now that e-mail and other forms of computer-mediated communication are widely available. According to Rohlfing (1995), LDF partners "experience a slight decrease in satisfaction and intimacy during the early stages of geographic separation" although these effects diminish over time (p. 192). Some of the frustrations with LDFs are that conversations primarily bring partners up to speed on one another's lives and do not include much intimate talk (Rohlfing, 1995). LDF partners do not visit one another frequently, and this can decrease relational satisfaction. However, due to the increased use of electronic mail, cell phones, and instant messaging, LDFs are more easily maintained than even a few years ago. LDFs can also be considered difficult because partners change during absence, which can cause strain on the relationship (Rohlfing, 1995). Given that LDFs are the "most voluntary" form of LDRs, their attrition likely impacts research results. Proximal friendships that are challenging likely do not transition well, if at all, into LDRs. Those that do make the transition, yet experience trouble, will fade away or exist in an extended holding pattern of pleasant interactions that involve very few problems. It remains for researchers in this area to examine deteriorated LDFs in order to identify the range of problems specific to these relationships.

Putting Problems in Perspective

LDRs are more often than not perceived as difficult when compared to proximal relationships (PRs), but more research needs to be done to identify their difficulties and how they are managed. Researchers usually lump LDRs into one homogeneous group and compare them only to proximal romantic relationships (PRRs) with respect to certain variables: frequency and amount of contact (Holt & Stone, 1988), relational uncertainty (Dainton & Aylor, 2001), maintenance strategies (Carpenter & Knox, 1986; Johnson, 2001), mediated communication (O'Sullivan, 2000), social networks (Sahlstein, 2004b), and coping methods (Holt & Stone, 1988). Only a few scholars have differentiated between types of romantic LDRs (Dainton & Aylor, 2002; Holt & Stone, 1988; Sahlstein, 1999) and all do so using different factors (e.g., miles apart and frequency of contact, pre-separation origins, or discontinuities) in their typologies. Many of the researchers operationally define and differentiate romantic LDRs from PRRs in terms of miles apart or frequency of contact and usually in reference to PRR standards (Carpenter & Knox, 1986; Helgeson, 1994a, 1994b; Holt & Stone, 1988; Schwebel, Dun, Moss, & Renner, 1992; Stafford & Reske, 1990). It would be interesting to examine closely whether it is misleading to judge long-distance relationships by the standards of proximal relationships or whether people in LDRs do the same things as those in PRRs so far as they can.

The most puzzling, albeit implicit, assumption of this literature is that individuals are involved in isolated relationships (e.g., if someone is in a long-distance romantic relationship, the focus never falls on simultaneous involvement in any proximal romantic relationships). What I have experienced as difficult is the *simultaneous* management of my LDDR and my long-distance friendships (LDFs), long-distance kin relationships (LDKs), and numerous PRs. In the next section, I will discuss matrices of relating and argue that LDR/PR systems should be a primary focus of future long-distance relationship research.

RELATIONAL DIALECTICS AND RELATING AT A DISTANCE

"Any particular personal relationship is part of a matrix of other relationships."
—Baxter & Montgomery (1996, p. 168)

"The belief that personal relationships are purely private entities is a myth."
—Parks (1997, p. 368)

Baxter and Montgomery (1996), working from the perspective of relational dialectics, have made links between contradictions of connectedness and separateness with problems partners face in commuter marriages (pp. 97–98). Relatedly, Bridge and Baxter (1992) examined how individuals maintain relationships that have multiple definitions (e.g., Jay is both my romantic partner and my coworker). There exists only one published study on the relational dialectics of long-distance relating (Sahlstein, 2004b).

Relational dialectics (Baxter & Montgomery, 1996) is a theoretical framework that can provide valuable insight to relating at a distance because it can be used to specifically locate and explore the negotiation of contradictions in personal relationships. A relational dialectics perspective assumes that "social life is a dynamic knot of contradictions, a ceaseless interplay between contrary or opposing tendencies" (Baxter & Montgomery, 1996, p. 3). For example, in many relationships partners experience the management of tendencies to both autonomy and connection or to both certainty and uncertainty. Baxter and Montgomery (1996) assert that multiple contradictions are being negotiated in relationships. LDRs can usefully be framed and examined to determine the ways in which they are intertwined with proximal relationships (i.e., PRs) and how contradictions emerge from their intersections of the requirements of these two sorts of relationships.

There are four main assumptions of any dialectical approach: contradiction, change, praxis, and totality (see Baxter & Montgomery, 1996, for a detailed discussion of the four assumptions). For this discussion, I choose to focus on contradiction and totality. Contradiction is the "dynamic interplay between unified opposites" (p. 8). Various contradictions have been identified in the literature; one of the most widely examined dialectical contradictions in personal relationships is that between autonomy and connection (Baxter & Montgomery). For example, a personal relationship can be defined as a connection shared between two individuals. Thus, personal relationships are at their very heart about individuals being connected and interdependent. However, at the same time, the relationship depends on the individuals having some level of autonomy. People want to be a part of relationships, but they also desire to be their own person: Being your own person is accomplished by being defined in relation to others. Autonomy and connection are in opposition, and we cannot understand one except in conjunction with the other. Thus, autonomy and connection are not only in opposition, but they are *unified* opposites; "they negate one another at the same time as they are interdependent ... with one another" (Baxter & Montgomery, pp. 9–10). Moreover, relational contradictions do not always occur in isolation; rather, several contradictions may be at play simultaneously or overlap with one another at various points in time (i.e., a form of totality).

People wake up to their family members, roommates, spouses, and/ or children every day. Many trek off to work or school and interact with coworkers, peers, teachers, and members of their communities. These relationships not only exist within immediate, daily experience; many relationships with family members, romantic relationships, friendships, and coworker relationships are negotiated at a distance. The management of distant and proximal relationships can be both productive and stressful for the individual and his or her total set of relations. For example, the organization of one's time between different sets of relational partners can prove to be an important dynamic. On one hand, time spent with family and friends who live close by is valuable, but if someone who lives in a different state is visiting, the proximal partners can be put aside in deference to the visitor. Proximal partners can be seen at any time and will always be available in ways the visitor will not. On the other hand, spending time with long–distance friends requires effort and planning, while one can spontaneously invite proximal partners to dinner at short notice. Having long-distance relationships often puts stress on one's time (e.g., "Who should I visit this summer?"), while having proximal relationships can be taken for granted (e.g., "I can see him anytime"). The choices made about distributing time between two sets of relations can be difficult (Milardo, 1982). Trying to reach every relationship and maintain it with an appropriate level and type of communication can be a daily concern.

In this section, I explore how individuals negotiate multiple relationships in their lives, both proximal relationships and long-distance relationships. I examine how these two sets of relations are interrelated and have mutual influence on one another with both positive and negative results. Framing the issues from a relational dialectics framework (Baxter & Montgomery, 1996), I discuss LDR experiences as situated within the simultaneous management of both PRs and LDRs.

Individuals and Networks

Individuals (and partners) are a part of a multiplex of relationships. For example, I am involved in a PRR along with many friendships, peer relationships, neighbors, and coworker relationships, but I also have numerous LDRs (with family members, friends, ex–romantic partners, and coauthors). These different relationships in my life are managed on a daily basis. Research has shown that relationships are influenced by other relationships within a person's social network (Baxter, Dun, & Sahlstein, 2001; Parks & Adelman, 1983; Parks & Eggert, 1991; Surra, 1988). One clear example of the interdependence of an individual's many relationships is displayed in Altman and Ginat's (1996) description of the lives of polygamous Mormon families. The wives all have one relationship in common, a marriage to the same husband, but the wives also have relationships with one another. Their children all have relationships with each other and they each have relationships with the community. The marriages do not exist in isolation; rather, each member of the network navigates matrices of relating. LDR partners' relationships inform one another, which has not been explored as a primary element of this type of relating.

Parks and colleagues have done extensive work on communication networks (see Parks, 1997 for an extended description of these works). Based in a systems perspective, these researchers typically discuss network qualities (e.g., network strength and overlap) and also address the emergent qualities that result from the negotiation of communication/personal relationship networks. I believe that a relational dialectics approach provides a sense-making device for examining the ongoing management of long-distance and proximal relationships.

Totality and LDRs

Scholars have not gathered substantial empirical data exemplifying the relational dialectics concept of totality. Totality illustrates how phenomena are interdependent with other phenomena· how phenomena are connected and how they influence one another (e.g., contradictions, partners, and different relationships). Although an unfortunate choice of terms that implies completion, totality is used by scholars of relational dialectics to emphasize that there exist dynamic relationships between various parts of the system at different levels. A relational dialectics approach does not assume that a complete picture is ever possible because the relational matrix is always changing, albeit insignificantly at times. Baxter and Montgomery (1996) conceptualize totality as the interconnectedness between contradictions within a relational context. Relational partners do not experience one contradiction at a time; rather, contradictions are at play and intertwine with each other. For example, the contradiction between autonomy and connection may be at play with the contradiction between openness and closedness. For example, a LDR couple may be working out how to spend their time when they are together, and in that process they have to disclose what else is happening in their lives. For some couples, this could be problematic if they want to try to keep their lives separate in some ways. Yet in order to have a better connection, they need to reveal aspects of their individual arrangements. Moreover, the experience of contradictions occurs within a particular relational and historical context. In addition, close relationships exist within a multiplex of other, perhaps distant, relations and should not be isolated for analysis.

I use relational dialectics as a springboard for exploring totality in the simultaneous maintenance of proximal and long-distance relationships. My previous LDR research has indicated that LDRs are influenced by PRs and that the negotiation of one's LDRs is interdependent with the negotiation of one's PRs (Sahlstein, 2004b). In the remainder of this chapter, I explore how this framework is useful for making sense of the difficulties inherent in totality of individuals' relationships, both proximal and long-distance simultaneously.

Proximal Relationships, Long-Distance Relationships, and Relational Dialectics

Partners in LDRs have noted that their network members influence their relational experiences (Sahlstein, 2004b). Persons in LDDRs report that their relationships are strained or limited because of the negotiation that needs to take place between their LDDR partner and (potential and current) PR partners. For example, some couples report that they are unable to devote the necessary time to making "couple friends" with others because they want to spend the time they have together alone. Being apart constrains couples' abilities to socialize with other people because they feel pressure to spend all of their time together with one another. LDDR partners reported having difficulties with network negotiation when they are apart because of the time they spend when they are together (Sahlstein, 2004b). LDDR partners remarked that being in a relationship and spending time with their partners on the weekends negatively affects their "apart" friendships by being a constant presence during that time. This work provides the initial empirical evidence that LDDRs and PRs have to be negotiated and do not exist in existential isolation, and the work provides the impetus to explore further the simultaneous management of these two types of relationships.

In a recent study, Sahlstein and Truong (2002a, 2002b) interviewed 47 students who were involved in LDRs and PRs simultaneously. We asked them to discuss how their LDRs and PRs[1] enabled and constrained one another. For the purpose of discussing LDR difficulties, I will review the ways in which the relationships constrained one another only.

PRs Constrain LDRs. Several themes demonstrate that PRs constrain LDRs: (a) forced choices, (b) out of sight, out of mind, (c) organizational hassles, (d) presence/comparison, and (e) jealousy. The first theme in this category is "forced choices." The presence of PRs presents choices for the individual that do not often favor LDRs. PRs are perceived as "easier" and thus are often chosen for attention over LDRs, leading to the decreased quality of LDRs. The second theme is "out of sight, out of mind." When PR partners are present and LDR partners are absent (most of the time physically), people will often be unmindful of LDR partners because PR partners are present and the PR partners are more available for interaction. When LDR partners are "out of mind," there is the potential for the relationship to weaken or even lapse. The third theme is "organizational hassles." The existence of LDRs makes it difficult to manage PRs. PRs are perceived as hindrances to LDRs because time is finite, LDRs take time, and PRs are perceived as taking very little time and effort to maintain. When managing time, individuals will often choose to spend time with PR partners over LDR partners because of the aforementioned perceptions. "Presence/comparison" is the fourth theme in this category. The physical presence of PR partners makes LDR partners seem even more distant. Seeing PR partners on a regular basis makes the individual recognize the absence of his or her LDR partners, which can cause the individual to not want to continue the relationship, to miss the partner, and/or to pressure the LDR partner to see the individual. The final theme in this category is "jealousy." The immediacy of PR partners and the perceived ease of their management and time spent with the partner create negative feelings within LDRs. LDR partners become jealous, and this leads to negative interactions between the individual and his or her LDR partners.

LDRs Constrain PRs. However, the direction of constraints can work in converse. LDRs can work to constrain an individual's PRs through: (a) high expectations, (b) presence, (c) organizational hassles, (d) mental connections, and (e) negative spillover. LDRs serve as a deterrent for "new" or "different" kinds of relational partners, and thus LDR partners set up high expectations for what is a "good" relationship, not allowing individuals to explore freely other relationships for fear of making mistakes, wasting time, or taking time away from other things. A second way in which LDRs can constrain PRs is simply through their cognitive and emotional "presence." Already having LDR partners (e.g., good friends back home) can decrease the individual's desire to explore other relationships. This is an "if it isn't broke, don't fix it" mentality. LDRs also can constrain PRs by making life feel like an "organizational hassle." Having LDRs makes the maintenance of PRs difficult. If LDRs were not part of life, PRs would be much easier to negotiate on a daily basis (especially on the weekends, during vacation breaks and holidays). The fourth issue identified by participants is that their LDRs can constrain the management and maintenance of their PRs by producing mental connections that cannot be (perceived) as possible in one's PRs. The mental connections with LDRs make it difficult to develop PRs (although they are the partners who are more often physically present) because the LDR connections can be quite strong and have endured over time and space. The final way in which LDRs constrain PRs is through "negative spillover." When problems arise in LDRs, the problems can "leak" into the individual's PRs. Individuals experience difficulties separating their LDRs and PRs, which constructs problems for both types of relationships because they are experienced as interdependent with one another.

The management of LDRs and PRs is experienced as a complex process of negotiating competing desires, wants, and needs. Three primary contradictions emerge as salient across participant experiences: similarity-difference, uncertainty-certainty, and autonomy-connection.

Similarity-Difference.   The contradiction of similarity and difference emerged out of participants' reports of how their LDRs and PRs simultaneously enabled and constrained one another. The contradiction is produced by the simultaneous need for LDRs and PRs to hold similar and different qualities or functions for the participant. On one hand, participants reported wanting their LDR partners and PR partners to interact and have a good time together, for example, when a LDR romantic partner would come to visit. However, many of our participants reported that once put in the same room, LDR partners and PR partners did not "mesh." One woman named "Alice" said:

> My friends, they're so different and it's the same ... when I was back home. My girlfriends and I were all planning to go into the city [for New Year's]. We got a hotel room and everything .... I really wanted some of my other friends from here to come so I had three girls that go to school with me here ... I called them up and I [said]: "Yeah, you guys have to meet us in the city" and all that stuff so they came and it was just, it was weird because they're, you know my groups of friends are so different and like, to have them interact it was just, I don't know, it was kinda complicated. {Tape 15, lines 2108–2223}

Clearly, "Alice" experiences tensions across her friendship network when her "back home" friends come into contact with her "here" friends. They are "different" and yet she appreciates having both sets of friends in her life. "Alice" is one example from a series of participants who noted that difference is problematic, yet differences are what make their individual lives richer and more exciting.

Participants expressed excitement about having different sets of friends (and thus different areas of their lives), but they also noted the importance of having similar values across their different relationships. PRs were often initiated due to their perceived similarity with LDRs from back home. "Lucy," an international student, disclosed that she appreciates the similar values of her PR partners (who are primarily other international students) and LDR partners. At the same time, "Lucy" recognized that her PR friends have different daily practices and mindsets.

> But on the other side they [her PR partners] have different habits. So that's something I really like. And they really see the world in a different way. So that's something which goes in everything we do. Back home, my

school and my friends, obviously I love them. But we, they are very close[d minded] …. I mean we dress all the same and we go [to] exactly the same places. And we do pretty much the same thing. So coming here, I feel more relax[ed]. Back home sometimes you cannot really be what … the way you feel. {Tape 19, lines 264–303}

"Lucy" recognizes that she is exposed to different types of people, and she feels liberated through her PR partners to see and do things in a different way. She continues to love and miss her friends at home, but she recognizes the "closed-minded" manner in which they relate. She is struggling with what to think about each set of friends and what they mean for her personal growth.

A final issue related to similarity and difference was that if the participants did have similar PR partners and LDR partners, they had to decide with whom to spend their time. Participants, while interested in seeing continuity across their relationships, also wanted to have differences emerge from them. If a LDR and a PR are perceived as too similar, then choices need to be made about the maintenance of each. Participants often ask themselves questions such as "If I can have the same amount of fun with less effort by staying at school and hanging out with my PR friends, then why should I drive three hours to visit a LD friend?" or "If my LD friends, whom I have known for longer than my PRs, are so similar to my PRs, then I would rather not invest in 'new' friends? But they are nice to have around because I feel comfortable with them." Notions of similarity and difference worked with and against one another in the relationships of our participants but at times are intertwined with notions of uncertainty and certainty.

Uncertainty-Certainty.   A second contradiction that emerged from Sahlstein and Truong's (2002) data was between the simultaneous needs for uncertainty and certainty in their LDRs and PRs. For example, having more certainty about LDR partners' lives was productive for managing PRs in positive ways. When there was certainty in one's LD romantic relationship, participants could tolerate more uncertainty in their PRs and/or explore those relationships more rigorously because they did not question issues in their LDRs.

LDR partners, because they share a history with the participant, were often viewed as the stable entities in the participants' lives. Their LDR partners "know" them and can give them informed support. They can seek their support for the friends in their PRs. Participants seemed to treat LDR partners as the pillars of strength when their immediate lives were chaotic, stressful, or unsatisfying. "Jody" recognized how her sister helped her with difficulties in her PRs.

Sometimes my sister can just bring out the best in me. She can just help me. Since she knows me and I tell her what's going on, she can help me relate with professors and/or my roommate. Since she's been through those kinds of things. I mean [it's the] same with my brother sometimes. Since they've been through it, they can help me with my relationships. {Tape 7, lines 1587–1593}

Certainty, or stability, in one's LDRs also led some of our participants to be laissez-faire about their PRs. One woman did not care much about knowing more about her PR partners or having a secure future with them because she felt she had it all with her LDR partners. "Sandra" stated:

Because I have so many friends back home, I didn't feel this great urge to make you know a big, big friendship here. That is the main reason because I feel so, so safe [with my friends from home]. {Tape 20, lines 1339–1343}

The satisfying certainty that relational partners construct in their longer lasting long-distance relationships serves to decrease participants' urgency to initiate new relationships. Nevertheless, participants reported that maintaining strong connections with LDR partners was not always ideal for their connections with PR partners, and they needed "space" from their LDR partners even when separated by great physical distances.

Autonomy-Connection.   Negotiating various connections can be a strain on any one relationship. Spending more time with, and potentially increasing the level of intimacy in, one relationship may negatively affect time spent with another relational partner, resulting in a stagnant (or decreased) level of intimacy. However, spending time with other people can help promote or reinforce a relationship with someone and vice versa (i.e., spending time with one person may help relations with several others). Participants in Sahlstein and Truong's (2002a, 2002b) research reported the mutually enabling and constraining forces of autonomy and connection for their LDRs and PRs. One participant, "Penny," reported how being away from her LDR partners allowed her to become closer to her PR partners. The autonomy from her LDRs opened up potential spaces of connection with the people around her.

Well, because I can't always be with all of these people who have always been so close ... I've become closer with my proximal ones and they have become the ones that I can actually sit down and talk to about things. And they're also ones that if I'm having problems with anything here I can just let steam out here real quickly. I can have my friend come down and ... we talk for an hour about everything. Or if something's going wrong [with] my boyfriend, I usually will talk to my best guy friend, but then I can ... hit ideas off of everybody and [my LDRs] have a lot of different views than [my PRs]. So it's good to have a whole overall perspective on things. {Tape 3, lines 1308–1322}

"Penny" cannot physically be with her LDR partners when she needs to discuss sensitive topics, and her PR connections are fostered through her increased autonomy from her LDR partners. "Penny" also reported that the connections could be too great between her LDRs and PRs. When conflicts occur in one or the other relational type, "spillover" can occur.

> I mean, I'm sure it's shown when I'm having a rough day and when I'm with my friends. I'm just frustrated and stressed out because [my LDR partners] are nagging me to do something and mad that I can't get there and [they are] disappointed. It's not all my fault. It's other things in [my LDRs] that are affecting my relationships here at school. {Tape 3, lines 1337–1383}

Participants noted these kinds of connections in various configurations (e.g., LDRs "spilled" over positively into PRs and vice versa) constructing a clear pattern of interdependence between the LDRs and PRs in their lives.

Some of the participants perceived no overlap between their LDRs and PRs (e.g., international students). These participants appear to have cleanly segmented their PR and LDR lives, promoting the perception of independent relational systems. Participants indicated several accounts for the differentiation and separation, but overall these participants either avoided or denied the possible contradictions between autonomy and connection or had found a way to manage the contradiction practically, through rigid separation.

STUDYING LDRs AS DIFFICULT RELATIONSHIPS

As noted earlier, scholars have treated LDR participants as if they were only in one type of relationship (i.e., in only LDRs). In light of this discussion and Sahlstein and Truong's (2002a, 2002b) empirical data, isolated views of relating are problematic. Partners have many different relationships occurring simultaneously (i.e., both LDRs and PRs, romantic relationships, friendships, and familial relations). LDR scholars should recognize and examine the complex reality of long-distance relating (and its interrelationship with proximal relating). Specifically, LDR scholars should begin to focus on how the individual's (and the dyad's) network contributes to the "primary" relationship being examined. Many challenges, difficulties, and problems stem from the maintenance of different relationships, and continuing to view relationships as isolated experiences is myopic.

A second area of research is to address not only how PRs influence LDRs but also that they are in dynamic interplay with one another in practice. Individuals are likely to manage both LDRs and PRs simultaneously due to society's increased mobility and advances in communicative technologies. Scholars need to attend to the multiple relations at

play in people's lives because a person's LDRs are connected to and influenced by his or her PRs (and vice versa). Researchers in this area should
not assume that what takes place in one relationship is isolated from the
other relationships in partners' lives. LDR scholars should no longer
continue to primarily isolate the LDR from the PRs. Clearly, there is
much to be gained from close analysis of the interconnections between
these two relational types both for the individuals and for their relationships. If scholars want to promote stronger, healthier LDRs and address
their difficulties, they must attend to the dynamics of the whole system
of relating.

A third line of research is to closely examine difficulties of LDRs at the
level of conversation (e.g., conflicts, the unsupportive communication
of network members, the discussion of "how things are changing," and
how "distance" is constructed within interactions; e.g., Hess, 2002).
LDR scholars have not studied how conflicts are managed in these relationships, despite the likelihood that conflict management at a distance
has significant influence on relational stability and satisfaction.
Sahlstein (2004b) and Gerstel and Gross (1984) both report that LDDR
partners experience difficulty managing conflicts because they spend
such concentrated amounts of time together, and ideally partners want
the face-to-face moments to be fun, exciting, and memorable for *good*
reasons. Partners do not want to spoil their time together addressing
conflicts. Scholars need to study how conflicts are managed and the
long-term effects of refraining from "negative" conversations and
experiences.

One type of difficult conversation occurs when partners reveal, decide, or are informed that they will henceforth be in a LDR. A son telling
his parents that he has decided to enroll in a university 2,000 miles
away creates an emotional moment. A couple with equal career ambitions must decide if their relationship can survive living in different
states. The moment an army soldier tells her husband and children that
she is being deployed to Iraq must be extremely challenging for her marriage and her relationships with her children. Understanding how partners manage these difficult conversations would help identify
productive management techniques as well as the decision-making processes used within LDRs. Both lines of research are currently unrepre-
sented in this area. Related is the issue of how many relationships never
turn into LDRs. Conceivably many partners discuss moving apart but
decide against it. What are these conversations like, and who is less
likely to take on a LDR?

A final line of future research is to identify, and subsequently give attention to, the most difficult LDRs (e.g., soldiers with families who are
involuntarily called back up for duty, Sudanese families fleeing their
homeland, families becoming "transnationals" as a result of globalization) and the partners who experience the most problems within LDRs
(e.g., mothers of young children who are left behind during war, the
child whose father lives in another state since his parents' divorce). Re-

sources are limited, and continuing to utilize our energy for the study of convenient samples of voluntary, educated, relatively affluent, and satisfied populations should be reconsidered. The college couple who has even reasonable access to instant messaging, cell phones, Blackberry® text message devices, web cams, dependable transportation, and the funds to underwrite the entire relationship likely needs our research and advice less than the mother who is working in this country in order to feed her children back in the Philippines. White, middle- to upper-class American citizens likely have qualitatively and quantitatively different experiences with distance in their relationships. If class and race were seriously considered, then researchers could no longer treat LDRs as one homogeneous group.

Difficulties in Studying LDRs

LDRs still remains an understudied area of research more than a decade after Rohlfing (1995) first noted the fact. In part, this is due to the difficulties of studying relationships that are primarily managed in a state of absence. A significant challenge for researchers is gaining access to all of the partners in a LDR. By definition, LDR partners live in separate locations and when they are together, they may not want to spend time completing surveys or participating in interviews. LDR couples experiencing the most difficulty are unlikely to participate, for example, if they need their time to work out conflicts and rejuvenate the relationship or if they are on the verge of dissolution. Potential participants may also have confidentiality or economic concerns due to their position in the community (e.g., see Parrenas, 2001). Partners that do participate are typically quite satisfied with their relationship (Sahlstein, 2004b). The moderate to high satisfaction levels reported for LDRs (both friendship and romantic relationships) may be due to self-selecting samples of nondistressed, well-adjusted relationship partners willing to reveal the details of their successful LDRs.

Difficulties with Distance

Distance, as displayed in this discussion, can produce a variety of problems within personal relationships, but the most significant difficulty of distance for LDR scholars is recognizing that LDRs are not inherently a negative form of relating (Sahlstein, 2004b). For example, physical distance can provide relational partners with opportunities otherwise unavailable when they are together, and psychological distance can provide perspectives unthinkable when partners are like-minded. A more significant problem for the study of personal relationships is the stabilization of the individual within one particular relationship (e.g., long-distance or proximal relationship). Scholars should work to dislocate their hard positioning of these concepts (i.e., the individual, the relationship, other relationships) and look at the (dis)placement of the individual across multiple locations of self and in relation to others. The dislocation of a "relational self" is arguably the key element of difficulty in LDRs.

NOTE

1. The participants were students at a small, private liberal arts institution. They reported having 14 LDRs and 16 PRs on average. The relationship types participants reported for both their PRs and LDRs were friends, parents, siblings, extended family members, roommates, peers, coworkers, faculty/staff, teammates, coaches, and romantic partners.

REFERENCES

Altman, I., & Ginat, J. (1996). *Polygamous families in contemporary society.* New York: Cambridge University Press.

Baxter, L. A., Dun, T., & Sahlstein, E. (2001). Rules for relating: Communication among social network members. *Journal of Social and Personal Relationships, 18,* 173–199.

Baxter, L. A., & Montgomery, B. (1996). *Relating: Dialogues and dialectics.* New York: Guilford Press.

Bridge, K., & Baxter, L. A. (1992). Blended friendships: Friends as work associates. *Western Journal of Communication, 56,* 200–225.

Carpenter, D., & Knox, D. (1986). Relationship maintenance of college students separated during courtship. *College Student Journal, 28,* 86–88.

Dainton, M., & Aylor, B. (2001). A relational uncertainty analysis of jealousy, trust, and maintenance in long-distance versus geographically close relationships. *Communication Quarterly, 49,* 172–188.

Dainton, M., & Aylor, B. (2002). Patterns of communication channel use in the maintenance of long-distance relationships. *Communication Research Reports, 19,* 118–129.

Gerstel, N., & Gross, H. E. (1984). *Commuter marriage: A study of work and family.* New York: Guilford Press.

Guldner, G. T. (1996). Long-distance romantic relationships: Prevalence and separation-related symptoms in college students. *Journal of College Student Development, 37,* 289–295.

Helgeson, V. S. (1994a). The effects of self-beliefs and relationship beliefs on adjustment to a relationship stressor. *Personal Relationships, 1,* 241–258.

Helgeson, V. S. (1994b). Long distance romantic relationships: Sex differences in adjustment and breakup. *Personality and Social Psychology Bulletin, 20,* 254–265.

Hess, J. A. (2002). Distance regulation in personal relationships: The development of a conceptual model and a test of representational validity. *Journal of Social and Personal Relationships, 19,* 663–683.

Holt, P. A., & Stone, G. L. (1988). Needs, coping strategies, and coping outcomes associated with long distance relationships. *Journal of College Student Development, 29,* 136–141.

Hondagneu-Sotelo, P., & Avila, E. (1997). "I'm here, but I'm there": The meanings of Latina transnational motherhood. *Gender & Society, 11*, 548–571.

Jackson, A. P., Brown, R. P., & Patterson-Stewart, K. E. (2000). African-Americans in dual-career commuter marriages: An investigation of their experiences. *The Family Journal, 8*, 22–37.

Johnson, A. J. (2001). Examining the maintenance of friendships: Are there differences between geographically close and long-distance friends? *Communication Quarterly, 49*, 424–435.

Knox, D., Zusman, M. E., Daniels, V., & Brantley, A. (2002). Absence makes the heart grow fonder? Long distance dating relationships among college students. *College Student Journal, 36*, 364–367.

Knox, J., & Price, D. H. (1999). Total force and the new American military force: Implications for social work practice. *Families in Society, 1*, 128–136.

Manning, W. D., Stewart, S. D., & Smock, P. J. (2003). The complexity of fathers' parenting responsibilities and involvement with nonresident children. *Journal of Family Issues, 24*, 645–667.

McCubbin, H. I., Dahl, B. B., & Hunter, E. J. (1976). Research on the military family: A review. In H. I. McCubbin, B. B. Dahl, & E. J. Hunter (Eds.), *Families in the military system* (pp. 291–319). London: Sage.

Milardo, R. M. (1982). Friendship networks in developing relationships: Converging and diverging social environments. *Social Psychology Quarterly, 45*, 162–172.

Montgomery, B., & Baxter, L. A. (Eds.). (1998). *Dialectical approaches to studying personal relationships.* Mahwah, NJ: Lawrence Erlbaum Associates.

Norwood, A. E., Fullerton, C. S., & Hagen, K. P. (1996). Those left behind: Military families. In R. J. Ursano & A. E. Norwood (Eds.), *Emotional aftermath of the Persian Gulf War: Veterans, families, communities, and nations* (pp. 163–196). Washington, DC: American Psychiatric Press.

Norwood, A. E., & Ursano, R. J. (1996). The Gulf War. In R. J. Ursano & A. E. Norwood (Eds.), *Emotional aftermath of the Persian Gulf War: Veterans, families, communities, and nations* (pp. 3–24). Washington, DC: American Psychiatric Press.

O'Sullivan, P. (2000). What you don't know won't hurt me: Impression management functions of communication channels in relationships. *Human Communication Research, 26*, 403–431.

Parks, M. R. (1997). Communication networks and relationship life cycles. In S. Duck (Ed.), *Handbook of personal relationships* (2nd ed., pp. 351–372). London: Wiley.

Parks, M. R., & Adelman, M. (1983). Communication networks and the development of romantic relationships: An expansion of uncertainty reduction theory. *Human Communication Research, 10*, 55–79.

Parks, M. R., & Eggert, L. L. (1991). The role of social context in the dynamics of personal relationships. In W. H. Jones & D. Perlman (Eds.), *Advances in personal relationships* (Vol. 2, pp. 1–34). London: Jessica Kingsley.

Parks, M. R., & Floyd, K. F. (1996). Making friends in cyberspace. *Journal of Communication, 46*, 80–94.

Parrenas, R. S. (2001). *Servants of globalization: Women, migration, and domestic work.* Stanford, CA: Stanford University Press.

Rhodes, A. R. (2002). Long-distance relationships in dual-career commuter couples: A review of counseling issues. *The Family Journal: Counseling and Therapy for Couples and Families, 10*, 398–404.

Rohlfing, M. A. (1995). Doesn't anyone stay in one place anymore? An exploration of the under-studied phenomenon of long–distance relationships. In S. Duck & J. Wood (Eds.), *Under-studied relationships: Off the beaten track* (pp. 173–196). London: Sage.

Sahlstein, E. (1999). *Presences, quasi-presences, and absences: An investigation of long-distance relational types.* Paper presented at the annual convention of the National Communication Association, Chicago.

Sahlstein, E. (2004a). *Perceptions of long-distance relationships: Kinship, friendship, and romance.* Unpublished manuscript.

Sahlstein, E. (2004b). Relating at a distance: Negotiating long-distance and proximal relationships. *Journal of Social and Personal Relationships, 21,* 689–702.

Sahlstein, E., & Truong, T. (2002a). *Long-distance and proximal relations: Totality in practice.* Paper presented at the annual meeting of the International Communication Association, Seoul, Korea.

Sahlstein, E., & Truong, T. (2002b). *Long-distance and proximal relations: A web of contradictions.* Paper presented at the National Communication Association convention, New Orleans.

Schwebel, A. I., Dunn, R. L., Moss, B. F., & Renner, M. A. (1992). Factors associated with relationship stability in geographically separated couples. *Journal of College Student Development, 33,* 22–30.

Shapiro, A. (2003). Later-life divorce and parent–adult child contact and proximity: A longitudinal analysis. *Journal of Family Issues, 24,* 264–285.

Stafford, L., & Reske, J. R. (1990). Idealization in communication in long distance premarital relationships. *Family Relations, 39,* 274–279.

Stephen, T. D. (1986). Communication and interdependence in geographically separated relationships. *Human Communication Research, 13,* 191–210.

Stewart, S. D. (1999). Disneyland dads, Disneyland moms? How nonresident parents spend time with absent children. *Journal of Family Issues, 20,* 539–556.

Stewart, S. D. (2003). Nonresidential parenting and adolescent adjustment: The quality of nonresidential father-child interaction. *Journal of Family Issues, 24,* 217–244.

Surra, C. A. (1988). The influence of the interactive network on developing relationships. In R. Milardo (Ed.), *Families and social networks* (pp. 48–81). Newbury Park, CA: Sage.

Westefeld, J. S., & Liddell, D. (1982). Coping with long distance relationships. *Journal of College Student Personnel, 23,* 550–551.

Chapter 8

Beer Goggles, Catching Feelings, and the Walk of Shame: The Myths and Realities of the Hookup Experience

Elizabeth L. Paul
The College of New Jersey

While casual sexual interaction occurs in many different social and developmental contexts, the casual sexual practice of the "hookup" is especially characteristic of late adolescent Western college students (Lambert, Kahn, & Apple, 2003; Paul & Hayes, 2002; Paul, McManus, & Hayes, 2000). A hookup is a brief sexual encounter between two youths who either do not know each other at all or who are just acquainted. The sexual encounter may range from kissing and petting to various forms of penetrative sexual interaction. Typically, hookup partners expect that this will be a temporary one-time sexual encounter—perhaps even anonymous—with "no strings attached" (i.e., minimal or no expectation of follow-up interaction) and most hookups are intended "generally" but not necessarily with the specific partner. For example, most youths describe going to a party with the intention of hooking up, but they don't have a specific "target hookup partner" in mind (Paul et al., 2000).

Hookups are commonplace on college campuses. Two thirds of college students report having hookup experience; about half of those students have experienced penetrative sex during a hookup (Paul & Hayes, 2002; Paul et al., 2000). The frequency of hookup experiences varies: Some students hook up weekly with different partners, other students hook up occasionally, and some students hook up only once. Intoxication from alcohol use is a common precipitant of hookups, particularly those that involve penetrative sexual acts. A proclivity toward risk taking as well as views of romantic relating as game-playing or a conquest also predict hookup experience (Paul et al., 2000).

141

Students perceive hooking up to be a prominent characteristic of college social culture. On average, college students believe that about 85% of college students have hooked up (Paul & Hayes, 2002) while studies have suggested that about 70% of college students have hookup experience (Paul & Hayes, 2002; Paul et al., 2000). This inflated perception—and indeed, the significant actual occurrence of hookups—creates pressure for some students to hook up because they don't feel like they "fit in" to the college culture and lack a sense of social acceptability (Lambert et al., 2003), and they don't want to miss out on the fun that is assumed to be characteristic of hooking up.

Despite the popular myth that hookups are "emotion-free sexual abandon," oftentimes they are *difficult* experiences—intra- and interpersonally (Paul & Hayes, 2002). Research on the casual sexual practice of the hookup has revealed a complex subjective and emotional texture often with contradicting emotions. There is a striking disconnect between the persistent belief that hookups are positive and "easy" and the felt emotional complexity of hookups. College students' emotionally complex descriptions of their own hookup experiences contrast with their standardized relatively one-dimensional views of a *typical* hookup. More research is needed into how and why so many students create this singular perception of a *typical* hookup that is far removed from their real experiences.

FOCUS GROUP METHODOLOGY

Exploring sources of difficulty besetting many hookup experiences is necessary for gaining a more realistic picture of the college norm and for providing students with supportive scaffolding as they make behavioral decisions and process difficult experiences. Students' own perceptions and experiences of difficulty are essential for understanding what the hookup means to them. To gain insight into students' experiences and views of hookups, a series of eight focus groups with diverse college students at a mid-sized northeastern 4-year state college was conducted in spring 2004; an additional focus group was conducted in September, 2004. Focus groups, each involving 8 to 12 students, included males and females (four focus groups were co-ed, two included males only, three included females only), students of different ethnic groups (Hispanic, Asian, African American, Caucasian) and sexual orientations (homosexual, heterosexual), students at different stages of progress toward their college degree, athletes, Greek social organization members, and students living on and off campus. A total of 86 students participated actively in the focus groups.

Focus groups were formed with the assistance of select student leaders representing different segments of the student population (e.g., an athlete, a leader of a fraternity, residence hall staff members, a commuter student). They were asked to gather 8 to 12 students who would feel comfortable talking about the college hookup culture. Students were asked to share their perspectives only to the degree they were comfortable and were assured of confidentiality; sharing personal experience was not required and was entirely their choice. All student participants in the focus groups participated actively in discussion and most were very forthcoming with detailed accounts of their hookup experiences. Focus group conversations were each 2 to 3 hours long. Information about campus counseling resources was made available to focus group participants.

The intent of these issue-defining focus groups was to gather student "intelligence" with the aim of yielding emergent theory about what makes some hookup experiences difficult. Students were first asked to discuss definitions of the term *hookup* and talk about characteristics of and motivations for hookups. Students were then asked to contrast good and bad hookup experiences and to discuss what made hookup experiences difficult. We then discussed how students respond to or cope with difficult hookup experiences and concluded with discussion of how hookup experiences were associated with one's sense of oneself as a future relationship partner. While it was made explicit that hookups could be same- or mixed-sex interactions, the focus of most of the students' comments was on hookups between women and men. While research has revealed that students often choose not to talk with one another about bad hookup experiences, when given an opportunity to talk more abstractly about the challenges of hookups, they are garrulous and insightful.

Using an emergent grounded theory approach (Glaser, 1998), key themes were identified in extensive written notes following each focus group. A striking feature of each focus group was the consistency in students' thoughts about the challenges or difficulties of hookups. Key categories, properties, and linkages emerged, leading to identification of relevant social scientific literature. The final focus group clearly substantiated the emergent theory.

Theory and research on the self system is a useful framework for understanding difficulty in youths' hookup experiences. The self is a dynamic system of self-concepts, including current and possible selves, desired and undesired selves, socially accepted and unaccepted selves (e.g., Cross & Madson, 1997; Markus & Nurius, 1986). The self system organizes and directs our behavior and perceptions such that individuals are motivated to approach wanted or desired selves and avoid dreaded or unwanted selves (Cross & Markus, 1991). Discrepancies or conflicts between current and possible selves, or between wanted and unwanted selves trigger emotional responses aimed to be self-protective and self-preservative. Instead, they are often painful and unproductive (Ferguson, Eyre, & Ashbaker, 2000; Markus & Nurius, 1986). Moreover, social and cultural influences often interfere, creating elusive and unattainable possible selves, and heightening difficult emotional responses to failure so as to reactivate the pursuit of the desired self (Markus &

Wurf, 1987). In difficult hookup experiences, there is a collision between contrasting real and possible *selves* as well as real and possible notions of *relationship* when youths' hookup myths are challenged by experiential reality.

THE COLLISION OF UNWANTED AND WANTED SELVES IN HOOKUPS

Difficult hookups result from contradictions between the perceived personal and social benefits of hooking up and the unexpected painful emotional and social reality of many hookup experiences. Hooking up is seen as a normative part of college student culture, driving many students to seek out hookup opportunities so they can feel like they "fit in." The social norm paints a rosy picture of hookup experiences—*anonymous* sexual and social experiences that are exciting in the moment and free from emotional and relational aftermath (Paul & Hayes, 2002).

Present-day youths live in a culture that is rife with sexual models and stimuli. The desired identity promulgated in popular media is one of nonchalance about sex and easy sexual prowess. The ideal of close love relationships is met with skepticism and doubt. Thus, youths seek to develop a sexual identity based on models that emphasize unattached sexual competence—sex outside of the context of close relationships. Quick sexual encounters are viewed as the vehicle to establishing one's sexual prowess. Yet the complicated experiential reality during and after hookup interactions thwarts the pursuit of this desired self and leaves youths with challenging emotions and self-loathing. Pitted against each other are wanted and unwanted selves. The elusiveness of the wanted or ideal self, and the predominance of the unwanted self leads to difficult emotions such as shame, rejection, alienation, and loneliness.

Further alienating the wanted self is the persistent self-referent power of the perceived social norm that most college students hook up as a fun and emotion-free pastime (Lambert et al., 2003; Paul & Hayes, 2002). When students have a difficult hookup experience or when they *feel* a negative emotional response to a hookup, they compare it with their rosy and inflated perceptions of the college norm. They conclude that something must be wrong with them because they failed to have a good or unemotional hookup like everyone else. Internalization, shame, and repression are likely to follow.

THE POWER OF GENDER SOCIALIZATION IN DEFINING WANTED AND UNWANTED SELVES

Wanted or desired selves reflect societal values and expectations; as gender is arguably the dominant social category, gender stereotypes and pressures play a central role in ideal self-definition (Cross &

Madson, 1997). A "Good Woman" is one who peaceably maintains close relationships, putting others' needs above her own; a "Good Man" is one who is socially dominant and sexually virile (e.g., Brigman & Knox, 1992; DeLamater, 1987). These societal expectations powerfully influence youth socialization and both the wanted selves toward which youths strive and the unwanted selves to which they fall prey. Popular gendered stereotypes hold that women are motivated to hook up as a strategy for starting a love relationship and that men are the primary determinant of women's worth, whereas men hook up for sexual interest and for social dominance among their peers.

While a few females described hooking up as a strategy for starting a romantic relationship, more females spoke emotionally about hooking up out of desperation to catch a male's interest and attention, quelling their lack of confidence as an attractive or desirable woman. One female explained:

> Hookups are confidence boosters. This person wants to hook up with me. That makes me feel attractive and accepted—that's good enough for the moment. But when it's over, I don't know what he really thought about me, about the hookup. Not knowing is very hard.

Some females assertively denounced feminine stereotypes: "Women don't go to a party thinking 'I'm going to get into a relationship with someone' ... they look for sex!" The relationship of gender to wanted and unwanted sexual selves, though still strong, appears to be growing more complicated. There has been some expansion of desired "gendered" sexual selves particularly for women. Perhaps oxymoronically, both the power of the women's movement and the pervasiveness of sexuality in contemporary culture urge women to claim their sexuality, permitting women to desire a sexual self. Yet women's sexuality still incurs societal condemnation marked by the ascription of disparaging labels such as "slut" to sexually experienced women. One woman explained:

> Girls have to be careful. When they have a lot to drink they are seen as a slut with little self-control. You need to watch out for other drugs and being manipulated by guys. This is especially the case when you are at a party. 'Oh, she's a slut' ... people expect and assume things, rumors get started, a lot of people you don't know make a lot of jokes, judgments, and exaggerations.

Such social condemnation undermines women's desired sense of themselves as alluring and competent sexual beings (Crozier, 1998) and leaves them feeling dirty, regretful, and confused: "I'm not good enough," "I feel inferior," "I lost respect for myself."

Women also face a double bind between what men consider to be "girlfriend" material and what they consider to be "hookup" material. A male student explained, "Guys no longer consider a long-term relationship to be a possibility once they hook up with that person. They don't want a girl who gives it up the first night." A female student added: "Guys want to hookup with a really pretty girl but then they will think she is a slut for having sex the first time." Indeed, relatively few hookups develop into longer-term romantic relationships; if a relationship continues after a hookup, it is typically short-lived (Paul & Hayes, 2002). One female described the self-questioning she does following a hookup:

> Did I move too fast? I may have jeopardized a future relationship. I'll use this hookup experience for him to get to know me. I put myself on the line so the guy will get the hint. But he usually doesn't get the hint. Then I'm stuck because guys don't want a girl who gives it up the first night. It feels good that a guy was attracted to me, but now what?

The sexual double standard and perceived societal contradiction regarding gendered notions of sexual prowess appear to contribute significantly to difficulty in college students' hookups. There has been some convergence in men's and women's sexual attitudes and behaviors (Oliver & Hyde, 1993). But men and women are still influenced by the sexual double standard (Leigh, Aramburu, & Norris, 1992; Oliver & Hyde, 1993). Western sociocultural expectations reinforce sexual experience as a celebrated aspect of masculinity but denigrate women for sexual activity (e.g., O'Sullivan & Byers, 1992). As a result of internalization of such societal standards, women emphasize relational elements of sexual interactions and experience more negative reactions to sexual experience (e.g., DeLamater, 1987; Oliver & Hyde, 1993; Sprecher & Barbee, 1995). Men are more motivated sexually by feelings of sexual desire, social status, and societal support, and experience sexual interaction as positive and gratifying (e.g., Oliver & Hyde, 1993; Regan & Dreyer, 1999).

Many young men seek a socially dominant and sexually proficient self through hookups. Many males defined good hookups as those that earn you "bragging rights," especially when the hookup partner was perceived as physically attractive by the male's peers: a "trophy." Bragging rights are intensified when there was a "good chase" before the hookup, in which two males were competing for the same female. "Sometimes the chase is better than the actual hookup."

But the flip side of these cavalier experiences is when you disappoint your social network; for example, when "beer goggles lead you to hookup with a dog of a girl and the guys come in the next morning and find you in bed with her." One young man explained, "Afterwards guys are looking for social approval. Do you think she was hot?" Men also felt regret when they learned after the fact about a network connection with the hookup partner thereby threatening their social dominance; for example, their good friend hooked up with her the night before, or her boyfriend was someone they knew.

THE WANTED SELF AS ABSTRACTION

The wanted self to which many youth strive through hookups seems to be vague and incompletely defined—a romanticized and abstract notion of self as conforming, sexual, and belonging. Youths seem to protect this abstract self, but in so doing maintain its remoteness to becoming an actual self. The very fact that a prototypical characteristic of hookups is anonymity confirms the remoteness of achieving an authentic desired self. One young woman explained, "I don't have an identity with the person I did it with, so I have to look to myself for the blame."

Moreover, the behavioral interaction characteristic of hookups prevents interpersonal permeability and connection. Nonverbal communication is predominant in the initiation and experience of a hookup. Verbal communication is rare and is viewed by many students as "breaking the moment." One student remarked about talking during a hookup, "then you have to think about what you are doing." It is ironic that an impersonal and distant strategy is chosen to meet a personal need for connection and closeness. It appears that the notion of *relationship* desired by youth is also unspecified.

Noteworthy is the infrequent mention of sexual gratification as a benefit of hooking up. This underscores the need to examine the psychological functions and social motives served by such sexual behaviors (Cooper, Shapiro, & Powers, 1998; Miller, Bettencourt, DeBro, & Hoffman, 1993). Sexual interests and needs seem to be tertiary to identity definition and affirmation as well as social attractiveness and approval.

Further complicating the pursuit of the wanted self, the act of hooking up also seems to contain varying behavioral connotations. College students have differing perspectives—and therefore mismatched expectations—on the degree of sexual interaction connoted by the term *hookup*. Some college students view hookups as involving only kissing and petting whereas other college students define hookups as "going all the way," including some form of penetrative sexual interaction. Unarticulated expectations and unchecked assumptions about partners' expectations often prompt difficult experiences. One student explained:

> A good hookup is when my expectations about how far it will go are in line with the other person's expectations; we have the same understanding. But there is little communication about this, so there is often a lot of ambiguity and it would break the moment to make sure the person wants to do what you want to do.

The precariousness of the wanted self in tandem with the unarticulated expectations (unarticulated to both self and partner) for the hookup is indicative of ill-defined sexual and emotional boundaries. Many females, but also a few males told of hookup experiences in which they "went too far" because they felt pressured by their partner's greater sexual expectations. One female commented, "I felt so disgusted the next day because I went too far."

SEXUAL VIOLATION

Some youths' worst hookup experiences appear to be sexual violations (Paul & Hayes, 2002). Mostly women, but some men too, described instances in which sexual interaction escalated to a level with which they were uncomfortable, they tried unsuccessfully to stop the interaction, and they were sexually violated. Some women described interactions which they felt "went too far," engaging in sexual behaviors that they "didn't want to do in the first place." Some described being too intoxicated to have control over what was happening. Some described being forced to engage in sexual acts despite saying "no." Some described willingness in the moment to do anything because they liked having someone find them attractive. Some described succumbing to males' pressure because it was pointless to resist: "I figured it was going to happen whether I wanted it to or not, so I just gave in to it and got it over with. I felt dirty and used after."

Of even greater concern is the tendency to avoid reflecting on the hookup itself and identifying these interactions as violations by their partner; rather, self-blame is the norm:

> I hold myself responsible for what I allowed to happen. When you blame it on the other person, it sounds *rapish*. That's not the way it is most of the time. It takes two people; it's not one person's relationship more than the other. But you question yourself, not the other person. That's for the other person to think about.

By blaming the self, youths seem able to maintain the perception of control over what happened.

Clearly, being sexually violated is very difficult for both women *and* men. Stereotypes that cast women as victims and men as perpetrators keep male victims closeted, as one male described:

> My only choice was to internalize the bad experience. I can't tell anyone else because I can't lose power. What are people going to think of me? Once you tell someone, everyone knows. You lose a lot of control; it's my life, I can't lose that control.

Some women and men describe going along with sexual behaviors with which they are uncomfortable. They keep their discomfort silent and "allow" it to happen (Impett & Peplau, 2002; O'Sullivan & Allgeier, 1998; Sprecher et al., 1994). Though most research focuses on unwanted sex in the context of a longer-term love relationship, women's reasons for consenting to unwanted sex with a love partner may shed light on unwanted hookup experiences. Research has found that women consent to unwanted sex because of (a) beliefs that men's stronger sexual drive is "uncontrollable" and therefore it is useless or unreasonable for them to refuse (Miller & Marshall, 1987; Moore & Rosenthal, 1993; Walker, 1997), (b) compliance to their felt responsibility for relationship maintenance and success (Cross & Madson, 1997), and (c) anxiety about rejection that prompts consenting to unwanted sex to keep partner's interest and to foster intimacy (Fraley & Waller, 1998). Internal working models of attachment guide such behaviors (Impett & Peplau, 2002). Anxiously attached individuals are plagued by worries about acceptance and rejection. To avoid this tension, they are more likely to consent to unwanted sex with the hopes of keeping the partner from losing interest and abandoning them.

There is some evidence that women are more willing to consent to unwanted sex in interaction with partners with whom sexual activity has been less frequent (Impett & Peplau, 2002). Evidence also suggests that insecure individuals' sexual interactions with a partner who is unknown or newly known might be less threatening to self-concept (Cooper et al., 1998). Cooper and colleagues (1998) hypothesized, for example, that "the insecure individual who uses sex to affirm his or her attractiveness may find having sex with (or seducing) a new partner more validating than having sex with a long-standing one" (p. 1535).

THE EMOTIONAL PAIN OF AN UNWANTED SELF

A wanted self thwarted and replaced by an unwanted self leaves youths feeling shameful (e.g., Crozier, 1998; Ferguson et al., 2000; Markus & Nurius, 1986). Shame is a global self-attribution as flawed; an act of self-injury at having revealed a dreaded or unwanted self. Comparisons to the inflated social norm add further insult as students feel abnormal in comparison to the perceived unfettered sexual and social accomplishments of their peers (Gilbert & Miles, 2000; Paul & Hayes, 2002). This felt insult to the self leads them to further internalize their feelings of failure, hoping to avoid further injury from social ridicule and rejection (Tangney & Dearing, 2002). Burying the difficult emotions and avoiding self-questioning obfuscates constructive reflection and meaning-making, making likely repeated—though likely unsuccessful—efforts to approach their wanted self and banish their unwanted self (Markus & Wurf, 1987). Students are also less likely to discuss their negative hookup experiences with others because they internalize their concerns and worries rather than seek support in a time of difficulty (Paul & Hayes, 2002):

> If I had a tough hookup, I try to forget it, repress it, pretend it's not there. If I'm regretful ... the more personally harmful to my self-esteem, the less likely I am to talk about it. If I have a series of bad hookups, that leads to big questions about myself, and an exaggeration of bad thoughts about myself. And if I am feeling bad about myself, I hook up.

Global, internal attributions for failure and feelings of shame are more prototypical of females' than of males' descriptions of dissatisfying hookup experiences. This is congruent with theory and research on gender and emotion (e.g., Brody, 1999; Ferguson et al., 2000). Women's continued lesser social status and socialized tendencies to behave with less agency and power contribute to women's greater tendency to respond intropunitively (Ferguson & Eyre, 2000; Williams & Best, 1990). One young woman explained, "You can't see the person again, so you have to blame yourself. Women are always told, 'it is your personal responsibility, protect yourself', so you blame yourself."

While the social ascription of "slut" renders women's sexual self a "dreaded self" or anti–ideal self–image (Ferguson et al., 2000; Lindsay-Hartz, deRivera, & Mascolo, 1995; Markus & Nurius, 1986), for men, the demasculinizing impact of unexpected emotion during hookup experiences and insecurity about sexual performance and/or social dominance form a dreaded self. Some men feel shame at not being "prince charming" or for acting like a "cad." For example, "When you know someone else wants her and you go ahead and get one over on the other person, this can cause problems afterwards. I feel bad about it." This negative self-feedback, coupled with the continuing societal obsession with sex, can motivate individuals to seek out experiences that they think could verify or confirm the ideal self-concept or disconfirm the dreaded self (Swann & Hill, 1982; Tesser & Campbell, 1984), leading to a repeated pattern of unfulfilling and perhaps even damaging sexual experiences.

Several women described how negative hookup experiences catapulted them into a pattern of serial hookups; one woman explained:

> When I had a bad hookup, it threw me into a cycle of continuous hookups. Maybe this time it will be different. It's easy to fall into that cycle. I need the ego boost of trying another hookup to prove that I can be better at it.

Another woman added,

> More women, but also men, prove something about themselves by repeating hookups. Sexuality is part of it, but for women it's more about proving a holistic sense of self …. And once you have a hookup, however far you have gone, next time you have to go that far or farther.

Males also react to bad hookups by seeking more hookup interactions to "hone their skills." "If the girl wants to stop, I'll accept it and get out fast. Then I'll go back downstairs and find another girl to get rid of that bad feeling." Another male explained, "If I have had a bad hookup, I'll hook up with someone else to seek redemption. It makes you forget. The best way to get over a girl is to get on top of another one." "You want to erase the bad by doing it again—doing it good this time." Repeat hookups may be motivated by frustrated physiological arousal in search of physical relief achieved by sexual climax. Yet youths rarely discuss physiological arousal, frustration, or satisfaction in the experience of repeat hookups; rather, they emphasize seeking psychological relief from feelings of failure.

Aversive emotional states left in the wake of dissatisfying hookup experiences make especially attractive the promise of immediate relief believed to be characteristic of quick and easy casual sex (Baumeister & Scher, 1988). The perceived immediate benefits overshadow any possible long-term costs associated with such risky behaviors, explaining the striking absence of mention of the physical risks of casual sexual behavior in students' accounts of difficult hookups (e.g., negotiating sexually transmitted disease [STD]/pregnancy prevention). Students also rely on other short-term palliative strategies, such as alcohol and drug use.

ALCOHOL AS SELF-STRATEGY

Alcohol and drug use may serve self-protective functions for individuals whose unwanted selves threaten their wanted selves. Intoxication from alcohol use commonly co-occurs with casual sexual interaction (e.g., Desiderato & Crawford, 1995; Gold, Karmiloff-Smith, Skinner, & Morton, 1992; for a review, see Leigh & Stall, 1993). Alcohol intoxication is a primary correlate of hookups, particularly those involving sexual intercourse (including times when the sexual interaction "went further than you wanted it to"; Paul & Hayes, 2000). Students described alcohol as a potentially useful trigger for hookups, reducing inhibitions so that connections were made more easily and less self-consciously (Leigh, 1990, 1996): "Alcohol is a great disinhibitor, especially if you are feeling bad about yourself." Alcohol reduces self-awareness and dulls negative affect associated with self-concept threat (Cooper, Frone, Russell, & Mudar, 1995; Hull, 1987).

Alcohol may also serve an anticipatory excuse function: alcohol use before a hookup experience gives the individual a ready-made excuse for failure (Berglas & Jones, 1978; Lang, 1985). For example, students describe the "beer goggles" created by intoxication—clouding of perception, reduction of partner standards, and fuzzy short-term memory. One student explained, "When alcohol is involved guys will take any girl who shows any interest; same for girls." Afterwards, they may feel that "I wouldn't have done that if I wasn't drunk," regarding the sexual behaviors in which they engaged, or the type of partner (based on looks or reputation) with whom they hooked up.

Sometimes, however, the excuse of intoxication is not enough to protect the self and prevent shameful feelings:

> Alcohol is a great excuse. You can do anything with this excuse. You can say you don't remember so you don't have to be embarrassed about what you did. You can make a joke of it—I was drunk! But if you are

drunk enough and you are an idiot, you have to account for that when you are sober. The *walk of shame* back to your room the next morning is so humiliating.

Students also described how the continued progression of the hookup with increasing intoxication contributed to difficult hookup experiences. One female explained:

> Alcohol brings out feelings that are bottled up; it brings them to the surface—loneliness, sadness. It makes you more vulnerable to a hookup. You may find yourself being a person you don't want to be. You wake up and you don't know what happened. You feel frustrated with yourself. You may say to a friend, "Why did you let me do that?" You may realize you were just a *tool* [sexual object]. You are mad at yourself. You can't blame the other person.

Men and women shared a host of other potentially self-destructive behavioral responses to bad hookup experiences, including working out excessively and over eating. Some women also reported crying, feeling terrified, and staying away from people for a while, and three women talked about resorting to cutting themselves. Such self-injuring behavioral responses show the depth and difficulty of internalized negative emotions, as well as the lack of direct mechanisms for expression. Favazza (1998) views self-cutting as a "self-help effort providing rapid but temporary relief from feelings of depersonalization, guilt, rejection, boredom, hallucinations, sexual preoccupations, and chaotic thoughts" (p. 259). Self-injury aims to avoid problems and numb emotional pain; however, such relief is temporary, only to give way to the return of emotional angst and repeated—perhaps even worsened—self-destructive behavior (Gratz, 2003; Greenspan & Samuel, 1989).

THE PRESS OF SOCIAL NETWORKS ON WANTED SELVES AND WANTED RELATIONSHIPS

Self-conceptions are a social creation, developed and tested through interpersonal interaction and social comparison (e.g., Stryker, 1980). Thus, social networks serve as source, audience, and arbiter of wanted and unwanted selves. Many youths desire the wanted self who excels at carefree sexual interaction and belongingness. Therefore, many college students' social networks are densely focused on this accomplishment. While youths keep their unwanted selves buried and private, the pursuit of their wanted self is a "cool" social project.

Students described feeling "social pressure to hook up so I'll maintain my reputation with my friends." Moreover, some students reported feeling external social pressure to hook up—sometimes very direct pressure. Friends "cheer them on": "If guys observe a male friend hooking up and it looks like it is going well, they put pressure on the friend and urge him on." Group goals may be set, including sanctions for not contributing to the group goals: "We have a 'pre-game toast' before a party: 'everyone is going to hook up at this party and if you don't you will have to do X.'" Competitions are created: "Me and my friends from home had a competition. We had all broken up with boyfriends recently. We wanted to get back at our boyfriends—I can do that too! So we would have contests: How many people can you HU with in one night?" A group of first-year women described "Hookup Weekend": "The goal was to see how much ass you could get. It was really set up for people who didn't ever get ass, to give them a goal. Tonight you are going to get ass!"

Pushing friends to realize the desired self is a vicarious thrill—perhaps because it adds hope to one's own ascension to this coveted status, or because it is a distraction from focusing on one's own remoteness from the desired self. Exerting pressure on peers might also be an impression management strategy in which self-presentation is manipulated so as to emphasize certain self-conceptions in the mind of an important audience (Markus & Wurf, 1987).

Peer pressure heightens felt discrepancy between current and desired selves, often motivating behavioral attempts to close this gap (Carver & Scheier, 1982). Some students said they coped with direct peer pressure by experiencing one hookup so they could say "I hooked up" to their peers. For some, this was enough to quell their angst about fitting in; for others, direct and indirect external and continued internal pressure continued to weigh heavily on them.

Some hookups are difficult because of reactions from one's social network or ramifications within the social network. A preeminent aspect of students' stories about hookup experiences is the aftermath or *fallout*. For some students, hookups are about the drama that occurs afterward: "Seeing the person again can be very awkward, especially when social groups mix." One student explained: "'Seven degrees of separation.' Depending on the size of the school, there are bound to be interconnections between people you have hooked up with."

In the Greek social organization community, social network ramifications are heightened; for example:

> In the network of sorority girls, they are all friends. So if you have a bad experience, you might have to pay for that later. You could burn bridges to hooking up with another girl you have wanted because of that. Especially when a girl is dragged away by her friends because of the 'No girl left behind rule' [a social pact that the women with whom you attend a party will all leave together], that is very awkward.

Sometimes the social network's response to the hookup determines one's post-hookup feelings. One student explained, "The hookup could be good—but if someone else says something, that could ruin it, even if you liked it. For example, say your friend told you that the guy you were hooking up with has a girlfriend." A male added, "Or if you find that your friend also hooked up with her—or that you know her boy-friend." Such experiences cast shadows on the glorified ideal of easy and unfettered hookup and thereby threaten the glorified desired self as sexual conquistador.

IMPLICATIONS OF DIFFICULT HOOKUP EXPERIENCES FOR FUTURE SELVES

Difficult hookup experiences can prompt intense self-questioning about youths' sense of themselves as a present and future relationship partner. But common responses of shame and self-recrimination inter-fere with self-reflection. The tendency to internalize blame for bad hookup experiences does not bode well for growth and recovery (Tashiro & Frazier, 2003).

The internalization of the sexual double standard influences women's intense self-interrogation: "If you feel like you went too far, you have to question your character. Am I a slut? Am I a bad person?" But a male "player" also struggles with social valuation and thereby his sense of himself as a future relationship partner. A player prides himself (and is lauded socially) as a coveted sex partner. His reputation precedes him as a stoic, self-assured man with many sexual conquests under his belt. Sometimes a player goes too far, earning the term "male slut" and becoming "black-balled" by women. "When girls call you a male slut, you've burned all bridges. You don't have any more chances to hook up. Girls are very cautious around you."

An older male student commented:

> It is really hard to walk around campus and see all these people I have had sex with. They won't talk to you. There is nothing you can do about it. If you are a player and you want to move on to another period in your life, it is very awkward. You're labeled a player for a long time. This comes back to burn you later. Say you find someone you want to build a relationship with and they learn you are a player—she might know someone who knows someone—it makes building that relationship really hard, if not impossible.

They described the difficulty of seeing a person with whom they ex-perienced a bad hookup on campus at a later time, "because it brought back all of those bad feelings about myself." One student tearfully explained:

> A bad hookup will tell me what I don't want in a relationship, what to avoid the next time. It influences the long-term, but not necessarily the short-term. It won't necessarily change what I do next week. Oh, I'll take it easy for a while after a bad hookup, I'll take a couple of days off. It just rein-forces the notion that a "real" relationship won't build from a hookup. It reinforces the stereotypes of slut and player.

The desired self to whom students aspire is one that thrives on short-term relationships; yet, the unwanted self from whom they are struggling to break free is lonely and disconnected. Many students report that a common motivation for hooking up is to feel an intense sense of interpersonal connection without the perceived emotional baggage of a long-term relationship. Often prompting this need are feelings of loneliness, social isolation, and/or lack of belongingness, or the perceived lack of relational alternatives. For some, hookups are used for healing from a relationship breakup, albeit ineffectually. Their feelings of loneliness or lack of belongingness are only temporarily abated, returning and sometimes even intensifying after the hookup has ended. One student exclaimed, "A hookup gives you a thrill of connection, but it's only temporary. Afterwards, you are still lonely. You are still trying to find something." For these students, the "hookup high" they felt during the experience often promotes further hookup experience: "It is very difficult to take time off from hookups or relationships. It is very hard to be alone. There is no support for being alone. In society, it is very hard to be separate ... alone."

One student explained:

> College students don't know what they want. They are busy, but they still want to go out and have fun. They don't want a serious relationship but they want a quick fix of connection, so they hook up. It would be cool to have a long-term relationship sometime, but they know they don't want it now. So they choose the McDonald's Drive-Through rather than the extended dinner at Le Cirque.

Emotional connection during hookups is an anathema for students. Students perceive "catching feelings" (feeling romantic interest in your hookup partner) as a particular hazard of hookups, leading to difficulty in various ways. Some college students define a good hookup as one in which "no one catches feelings" or where both partners come to the hookup with the same short-term agenda: "Both know you aren't going to get attached so there won't be any drama after." "It is someone I don't have to think about the next day, there are no strings attached." Especially difficult is when one person "catches feelings" during the hookup and the other does not. Also difficult is when one person catches feelings for someone and they never get to hook up with them. Imbalanced feelings can result in feelings of rejection, regret, and self-blame.

Interestingly, as many men as women discussed the difficulties of *catching feelings* when the other person did not.

> If you catch feelings and she rejects you because you are not good enough for her, that hurts. Next time I don't want to reveal if I feel something too early. If it's one-sided and I felt the connection, it's very hard.

Although one male observed, "Guys are less willing to admit they care so they will show a front." However, other men concurred with this male perspective:

> Guys like to be jerky after a hookup and make girls feel used, so nothing
> else will develop. Sometimes after a hookup I feel like now I have to deal
> with this girl who is in love with me now. Girls get needy and clingy so guys
> need to draw a boundary.

Catching *friendship* feelings may be acceptable, however. A few males
and females defined a good hookup as something that develops into a
friendship or even just a social connection in which you can comfort-
ably acknowledge each other when you see each other again; they further noted how rare this is.

CONCLUSION

The term *casual sex* connotes noncommittal and unemotional sexual
interaction (prototypically sexual intercourse). As such, casual sexual
intercourse is considered a physically risky behavior, putting individuals at risk for an array of STDs and unintended pregnancy. It is important to recognize that for many youths, hookup experiences pose
emotional and social as well as physical risks.

It appears that the social context is posing a no-win situation for
youth—sexual propaganda is rife in popular media (albeit the sexual
double standard for women persists), there is an increasing trend toward later ages for "coupling," dating has become passé, and yet youths
crave interpersonal connection and belongingness and seem at a loss as
to how to achieve it. Yet another layer is youths' ineffective interpersonal negotiation of sexual and social interactions, exacerbated by the
persistent social taboo against open and direct communication about
sexuality.

Most apparent in students' reflections on hookups is lack of self-
worth and self-confidence, as well as an insecure or unformed sense of
themselves as relational and sexual beings. Surely, traditional-aged college students' normative developmental preoccupations with sexual interest and experimentation, as well as autonomy and self-definition
contribute to this angst (Buzwell & Rosenthal, 1996; Paul & White,
1990). But this drama seems to be further complicated by the context of
a changing social milieu in which students feel confused about social-
and self-expectations for interpersonal relating; indeed, it seems that
youths increasingly perceive this drama to be unsolvable.

Moreover, it is apparent that students grapple internally with these
challenges, avoiding direct communication about troubling experiences. This internalization thereby prevents possibilities for "perspec-
tive-checking," social support, understanding, and even social progress.
Many students described feeling isolated and alone, yet they were
caught up in social and sexual behaviors that offered only temporary
appeasement.

Youths' need for connection and belongingness seems at once both to motivate and to be thwarted by hookup interactions. They appear to struggle with how to seek connection in a way that is healthy—physically, psychologically, and socially—and fulfilling. Rather, they focus on hookups that are sexually and perhaps even emotionally intense, albeit temporary and finite.

It is important to note that some hookup experiences appear to be positive and constructive for some youths. Yet, even in descriptions of students' best hookup experiences, they report feeling a panoply of emotions—from excitement to confusion to pride to anxiety (Paul & Hayes, 2002). Indeed, in the focus groups, students were most stymied by being asked to define a good hookup experience. One student remarked, "What an interesting question! I never thought about that before." Perhaps with more open discussion about the complex and often challenging experiential realities of hookups, as well as deeper understanding about factors contributing to such difficult experiences, students can choose more positive sexual and social interactions facilitative of healthy psychological, sexual, and social development.

REFERENCES

Baumeister, R. F., & Scher, S. J. (1988). Self-defeating behavior patterns among normal individuals: Review and analysis of common self-destructive tendencies. *Psychological Bulletin, 104,* 3–22.

Berglas, S., & Jones, E. E. (1978). Drug choice as a self-handicapping strategy in response to noncontingent success. *Journal of Personal and Social Psychology, 36,* 405–417.

Brigman, B., & Knox, D. (1992). University students' motivations to have intercourse. *College Student Journal, 26,* 406–408.

Brody, L. R. (1999). *Gender, emotion, and the family.* Cambridge, MA: Harvard University Press.

Buzwell, S., & Rosenthal, D. (1996). Constructing a sexual self: Adolescents' sexual self-perceptions and sexual risk-taking. *Journal of Research on Adolescence, 6,* 489–513.

Carver, C. S., & Scheier, M. F. (1982). Control theory: A useful conceptual framework for personality-social, clinical, and health psychology. *Psychological Bulletin, 92,* 111–135.

Cooper, M. L., Frone, M. R., Russell, M., & Mudar, P. (1995). Drinking to regulate positive and negative emotions: A motivational model of alcohol use. *Journal of Personality and Social Psychology, 69,* 990–1005.

Cooper, M. L., Shapiro, C. M., & Powers, A. M. (1998). Motivations for sex and risky sexual behavior among adolescents and young adults: A functional perspective. *Journal of Personality and Social Psychology, 74,* 1380–1397.

Cross, S. E., & Madson, L. (1997). Models of the self: Self-construals and gender. *Psychological Bulletin, 122,* 5–37.

Crozier, W. R. (1998). Self-consciousness in shame: The role of the 'other'. *Journal for the Theory of Social Behavior, 28,* 273–286.

DeLamater, J. (1987). Gender differences in sexual scenarios. In K. Kelley (Ed.), *Females, males and sexuality* (pp. 127–139). Albany, NY: State University of New York Press.

Desiderato, L. L., & Crawford, H. J. (1995). Risky sexual behavior in college students: Relationship between number of sexual partners, disclosure of previous risky behavior, and alcohol use. *Journal of Youth and Adolescence, 24,* 55–67.

Favazza, A. R. (1998). The coming of age of self-mutilation. *Journal of Nervous and Mental Disorders, 186,* 259–268.

Ferguson, T. J., & Eyre, H. L. (2000). Engendering gender differences in shame and guilt: Stereotypes, socialization, and situational pressures. In A. H. Fischer (Ed.), *Gender and emotion: Social psychological perspectives* (pp. 254–276). Cambridge, UK: Cambridge University Press.

Ferguson, T. J., Eyre, H. L., & Ashbaker, M. (2000). Unwanted identities: A key variable in shame-anger links and gender differences in shame. *Sex Roles, 42,* 133–157.

Fraley, R. C., & Waller, N. G. (1998). Adult attachment patterns: A test of the typological model. In J. A. Simpson & W. S. Rholes (Eds.), *Attachment theory and close relationships* (pp. 77–114). New York: Guilford Press.

Gilbert, P., & Miles, J. N. V. (2000). Sensitivity to social put-down: Its relationship to perceptions of social rank, shame, social anxiety, depression, anger and self-other blame. *Personality and Individual Differences, 29,* 757–774.

Glaser, B. (1998). *Doing grounded theory: Issues and discussions.* Mill Valley, CA: Sociology Press.

Gold, R. S., Karmiloff-Smith, A., Skinner, M. J., & Morton, J. (1992). Situational factors and thought processes associated with unprotected intercourse in heterosexual students. *AIDS Care, 4,* 305–323.

Gratz, K. L. (2003). Risk factors for and functions of deliberate self-harm: An empirical and conceptual review. *Clinical Psychology, 10*(2), 192–205.

Greenspan, G. S., & Samuel, S. E. (1989). Self-cutting after rape. *American Journal of Psychiatry, 146,* 789–790.

Hull, J. G. (1987). Self-awareness model. In H. T. Blane & K. E. Leonard (Eds.), *Psychological theories of drinking and alcoholism* (pp. 272–301). New York: Guilford Press.

Impett, E. A., & Peplau, L. A. (2002). Why some women consent to unwanted sex with a dating partner: Insights from attachment theory. *Psychology of Women Quarterly, 26,* 360–370.

Lambert, T. A., Kahn, A. S., & Apple, K. J. (2003). Pluralistic ignorance and hooking up. *The Journal of Sex Research, 40,* 129–133.

Lang, P. J. (1985). Cognition in emotion: Concept and action. In J. Kagan & C. E. Izard (Eds.), *Emotions, cognition, and behavior* (pp. 192–226). New York: Cambridge University Press.

Leigh, B. C. (1990). The relationship of sex-related alcohol expectancies to alcohol consumption and sexual behavior. *British Journal of Addiction, 85,* 919–928.

Leigh, B. C. (1996). The role of alcohol and gender in choices and judgments about hypothetical sexual encounters. *Journal of Applied Social Psychology, 26,* 20–30.

Leigh, B. C., & Aramburu, B., & Norris, J. (1992). The morning after: Gender differences in attributions about alcohol-related sexual encounters. *Journal of Applied Social Psychology, 22,* 343–357.

Leigh, B. C., & Stall, R. (1993). Substance use and risky sexual behavior for exposure to HIV: Issues in methodology, interpretation, and prevention. *American Psychologist, 48,* 1035–1045.

Lindsay-Hartz, J., deRivera, J., & Mascolo, M. F. (1995). Differentiating guilt and shame and their effects on motivation. In J. P. Tangney & K. W. Fischer (Eds.), *Self-conscious emotions: The psychology of shame, guilt, embarrassment, and pride* (pp. 274–300). New York: Guilford Press.

Markus, H. R., & Nurius, P. (1986). Possible selves. *American Psychologists, 41,* 954–969.

Markus, H. R., & Wurf, E. (1987). The dynamic self-concept: A social psychological perspective. *Annual Review of Psychology, 38,* 299–337.

Miller, B., & Marshall, J. C. (1987). Coercive sex on the university campus. *Journal of College Student Personnel, 28,* 38–47.

Miller, L. C., Bettencourt, B. A., DeBro, S. C., & Hoffman, V. (1993). Negotiating safer sex: Interpersonal dynamics. In J. B. Pryor & G. D. Reeder (Eds.), *The social psychology of HIV infection* (pp. 85–123). Hillsdale, NJ: Lawrence Erlbaum Associates.

Moore, S., & Rosenthal, D. (1993). *Sexuality in adolescence.* New York: Routledge.

Oliver, M. B., & Hyde, J. S. (1993). Gender differences in sexuality: A meta-analysis. *Psychological Bulletin, 114,* 29–51.

O'Sullivan, L. F., & Allgeier, E. R. (1998). Feigning sexual desire: Consenting to unwanted sexual activity in heterosexual dating relationships. *Journal of Sex Research, 35,* 234–243.

O'Sullivan, L. F., & Byers, E. S. (1992). College students' incorporation of initiator and restrictor roles in sexual dating interactions. *The Journal of Sex Research, 29,* 435–446.

Paul, E. L., & White, K. M. (1990). The development of intimate relationships in late adolescence. *Adolescence, 25,* 375–401.

Paul, E. L., & Hayes, K. A. (2002). The casualties of 'casual' sex: A qualitative exploration of the phenomenology of college students' hookups. *Journal of Social and Personal Relationships, 19,* 639–661.

Paul, E. L., McManus, B., & Hayes, A. (2000). "Hookups": Characteristics and correlates of college students' spontaneous and anonymous sexual experiences. *The Journal of Sex Research, 37,* 76–88.

Regan, P. C., & Dreyer, C. S. (1999). Lust? Love? Status? Young adults' motives for engaging in casual sex. *Journal of Psychology and Human Sexuality, 11,* 1–24.

Sprecher, S., & Barbee, A. (1995). "Was it good for you, too?": Gender differences in first sexual intercourse experiences. *Journal of Sex Research, 32,* 3–16.

Sprecher, S., Hatfield, E., Cortese, A., Potapova, E., & Levitskaya, A. (1994). Token resistance to sexual intercourse and consent to unwanted intercourse: College students' dating experiences in three countries. *The Journal of Sex Research, 31,* 125–132.

Stryker, S. (1980). *Symbolic interactionism.* Menlo Park, CA: Benjamin/Cummings.

Swann, W. B., Jr. (1985). The self as architect of social reality. In B. Schlenker (Ed.), *The self and social life.* New York: McGraw-Hill.

Swann, W. B., Jr., & Hill, C. A. (1982). When our identities are mistaken: Reaffirming self-conceptions through social interaction. *Journal of Personality and Social Psychology, 43,* 59–66.

Tangney, J. P., & Dearing, R. L. (2002). *Shame and guilt.* New York: Guilford Press.

Tashiro, T., & Frazier, P. (2003). "I'll never be in a relationship like that again": Personal growth following romantic relationship breakups. *Personal Relationships, 10*, 113–128.

Tesser, A., & Campbell, J. (1984). Friendship choice and performance: Self-evaluation maintenance in children. *Journal of Personality and Social Psychology, 46*, 561–574.

Walker, S. J. (1997). When "no" becomes "yes": Why girls and women consent to unwanted sex. *Applied and Preventive Psychology, 6*, 157–166.

Williams, J. E., & Best, D. L. (1990). *Measuring sex stereotypes: A multination study*. Newbury Park, CA: Sage.

Chapter 9

Gossip and Network Relationships

Eric K. Foster
Institute for Survey Research, Temple University
Ralph L. Rosnow
Emeritus, Temple University

Colloquially, gossip is typically thought of as a destructive or mischievous social phenomenon. The motive to gossip has been categorized as a form of indirect aggression. Stewart and Strathern (2004), for instance, call it "a covert form of witchcraft against persons" (p. ix), and Stirling (1956) also observed that, in literate society, gossip is a descendent of witchcraft and sorcery in that it is an anonymous outlet for aggression that avoids open conflict. It is presumed to create a variety of institutional and interpersonal difficulties: poisoning reputations, wasting time, impairing reasoning abilities, causing guilt, corroding power bases, and generally stirring up trouble. The Victorian novelist George Eliot (1878/1960) called gossip "a sort of smoke that comes from the dirty tobacco-pipes of those who diffuse it; it proves nothing but the bad taste of the smoker" (p. 102). It is discouraged or condemned by parents, teachers, managers, philosophers, writers, clerics, and social authorities.

Yet, in spite of the admonitions, gossip is imperviously persistent in everyday affairs. It is an enormous cultural and economic enterprise at the level of mass media. Not only have philosophers, poets, novelists, and social critics commented on gossip for centuries, but many of them produced volumes of it themselves. Readers look to these gossipy writers not only for passing entertainment, but as vital sources of social knowledge and of proper ways to live and behave. Compelling arguments have been made that gossip also played a role in the social and biological evolution of our species (Barkow, 1992; Dunbar, 1993a, 1993b, 1994; Enquist & Leimar, 1993).

161

Gossip, then, should not be blithely dismissed to the bin of deplorable social behaviors. It is useful and fundamental to the construction and expression of our social selves. The common negative connotations of the term are simply insufficient to encompass its variegated forms and effects. While it is certainly true that gossip can harm, it may also enable people to pursue their daily affairs in a more effective manner. From the grapevine, we can learn how to behave, what to believe, and how to communicate in ways that smooth out some of the bumps one is likely to encounter otherwise in the trials and errors of everyday life. In complex societies, gossip can be an efficient means of disseminating useful information about how things operate (Baumeister, Zhang, & Vohs, 2004).

So gossip can serve both positive and negative purposes in social affairs. In a recent literature review, one of us concluded that a common characterization of gossip among many researchers may be summarized as follows: "In a context of congeniality, gossip is the exchange of personal information (positive or negative) in an evaluative way (positive or negative) about absent third parties" (Foster, 2004, p. 83). In this chapter, we explore the implications of this inclusive definition to see how gossip can bring society and individuals both benefits and difficulties, from minor advantages and annoyances to matters of life and death. On the content side, we will distinguish gossip from rumor, showing how they affect relationships primarily by their content and the context in which they occur. Then we will move into the realm of social network analysis to explore the ways in which the structure of the gossip network can affect relationships both favorably and unfavorably.

GOSSIP AND RUMOR IN THE SOCIAL COMMUNICATIONS MATRIX

Gossip and rumor are often confused in everyday usage, and while there are some common features of the two, there are very important differences as well. Both forms of communications are Janus-like in their manifestations in that they can be positive and negative in their content and effects. A brief compare-and-contrast approach will help to identify the ways in which rumor and gossip operate.

Under conditions of generalized anxiety and uncertainty, rumors, though unconfirmed, tend to circulate because of their capacity to explain ambiguous or unclear events, and thus provide a rationale for behavior (Allport & Postman, 1947; Fine & Turner, 2001; Kapferer, 1990; Rosnow, 1980, 1991). Kimmel (2004) describes organizational rumors (the "grapevine") as a healthy sign that people seek information that typically does not come through formal channels. For this reason, writes Kimmel, it is rarely in the best interests of a company to stop the internal grapevine entirely, although during times of stressful organizational change, it may be prudent to take formal steps to address unfettered allegations based on hearsay.

But it is also possible for rumors to exacerbate fear. This is likely to occur when they express collective anxieties under conditions of low control and high stakes (Fine & Turner, 2001). As propagandists know, rumors among combatants and civilian populations in times of war may be deleterious to morale and effective in altering the behavior of thousands of people (Kelly & Rossman, 1944; Pratkanis & Aronson, 1991; Watkins, 1943). Another example of how rumors can plant and amplify mass fear to disturbing levels was the aftermath of the famous radio broadcast in 1938 of Orson Welles' *The War of the Worlds*, dramatizing H. G. Wells's novel of the same name (Cantril, Gaudet, & Herzog, 1940). The broadcast came within a month of the Munich Crisis, and for weeks the American people had been listening to their radios. This, combined with the sheer technical realism of the broadcast, created an atmosphere of apprehension and contagious suggestibility that swept across the United States.

These examples do not preclude the possibility of rumors building and circulating largely for entertainment value. This appears to have been the case in late 1969, in an absurd rumor extensively documented and analyzed by Rosnow and Fine (1974), that Paul McCartney of the Beatles had been killed in an automobile accident and replaced by a double. A plethora of "evidence" of McCartney's demise, purportedly hidden in multiple clues in various media, stoked and embellished the rumor for many months in what became a kind of collective game of inventive one-upmanship.

Rumors may thus involve events, organizations, or people, and this fact separates rumor from gossip, which targets only people—typically, persons known to the conversants so that the content may affect interpersonal encounters. More than rumor, gossip is usually presumed to be true (although in the realm of mass media, intermediary agendas may encumber it otherwise). In everyday interpersonal contexts, gossip's quotidian, bric-a-brac content makes it easily absorbed and repeated. Contrasting the condition of generalized anxiety that may accompany rumor, many writers have remarked on the idle, casual, and frequently trivial nature of gossip, pointing to the atmosphere of congeniality or easy exchange in which much gossip is generated (Rosnow, 1977, 2001; Spacks, 1982; Yerkovitch, 1977). Rumors are often sought deliberately and openly. However, motives to acquire gossip frequently are camouflaged in what Bergmann (1993) refers to as "neutralizing behaviors" (p. 77)—ways to hear or even transmit gossip that are contrived to appear unintended or accidental, such as when people pretend to be absorbed in "serious" thought or activity while actually attending closely to the gossip around them. As the British writer H. H. Munro (a.k.a. Saki; 1921) wryly observed: "Hating anything in the way of ill-natured gossip ourselves, we are always grateful to those who do it for us and do it well" (p. 152).

Indeed, perhaps more important than the content of an exchange, the situation and context of a communication may definitively distinguish gossip from rumor (Abrahams, 1970; Hannerz, 1967; Rosnow, 2001; Spacks, 1982). In addition to the ostensibly superfluous and evasive nature of gossipy exchanges, there are other earmarks of gossip in this regard. Hannerz (1967) and Schoeman (1994) maintain that informality and privacy are important conditions for its transmission. Privacy further implies that the participants jointly hold a set of shared social meanings, in other words, that they are likely to be more than mere acquaintances (Abrahams, 1970; Blumberg, 1972; Noon & Delbridge, 1993; Yerkovich, 1977). These meanings are typically rooted in long and complicated histories and frequently expressed in a kind of jargon, of which only close participants can divine the subtleties (Gluckman, 1963; Noon & Delbridge, 1993; Roy, 1958). This sort of "inner circleness" is not characteristic of rumor, which is suited for less specific (or at least, less personally connected) audiences.

Another distinction between gossip and rumor may be found in the social functions that each serves. One of the most common observations about gossip is that it creates and maintains social norms (Bergmann, 1993). Culture in general depends on repetition of norms and mores in many forms, and gossip is certainly a common one. Many forms of social comparison—and therefore, social understanding—are expressed as gossip (Suls, 1977; Wert & Salovey, 2004). Baumeister et al. (2004) present evidence that a primary function of gossip is cultural learning.

No doubt, rumors that involve people's behavior, insofar as the latter is upholding or breaching cultural norms, might be called gossip, as long as the exchange takes place in an atmosphere of passing time or relative idleness among friends. On the other hand, as a number of writers have observed, gossip, like rumor, may have a psychological utility for the gossiper and gossipee in that it can sometimes discharge certain anxieties, fear, hostility, or guilt (Bergmann, 1993; Eckert, 1990; Gilmore, 1978; Levin & Arluke, 1985, 1987; Rosenbaum & Subrin 1963; Spacks, 1992; Stirling, 1956). Chit-chat about newly hired employees or about authority figures in the workplace, for instance, may be rumor or gossip, depending partly on the situation in which the information is exchanged and the relationships of the conversants.

Distinctions, then, between gossip and rumor are important and necessary, but perfect separation of these constructs is sometimes impossible. There are instances of rumor that would seem to fall under the category of gossip, and vice versa. There are many that are not so interchangeable.

CHARACTERIZING THE GOSSIP ENVIRONMENT USING THE PRISONER'S DILEMMA

So far, we have characterized gossip in the social communications matrix as Janus-like, in that it is full of contradictions and oblique faces. In spite of its reputation and the social sanctions against it, it is a useful social strategy. It is pursued and eschewed. It is valuable and trivial. It may be true, or it may be false.

A number of interesting questions arise about how certain relationships may be affected by gossip. Rather than scrutinizing the content of gossip, we choose to examine certain variables that characterize the gossip environment. Though there are a multitude of such variables, we will concentrate on a subset of environmental variables using the graphic and quantitative methodologies collectively known as social network analysis (SNA). SNA comprises a standardized set of tools to measure and analyze the structure of a network (Wasserman & Faust, 1994). Employing SNA concepts, we propose a theory and model of how gossip influences individuals and relationships based on the structure of the gossip network.

To understand how the structure of a gossip network may influence the experience of members' relationships, let us first posit and examine a network in which there is no possibility for the exchange of third-party information. In other words, we imagine a world where no one has a way to obtain information about anyone else's likely behavior ahead of time in, say, a performance task of some kind. In this baseline hypothetical world, a single direct contact is the only avenue of information exchange. People are randomly paired for the task and must decide in the dark whether it is better to cooperate or not with their partner.

This situation is captured in the famous Prisoner's Dilemma game (Table 9.1, Axelrod, 1980b, p. 381; Burt, 1999, p. 315), which has been the subject of countless articles in social psychology, economics, marketing, evolutionary biology, management, political science, criminal justice, and other fields. Table 9.1 shows the typical two–by–two matrix form of the game. If both partners decide to cooperate with one another, there will be a fair and the highest mutual payoff, although not the highest possible individual payoff. If one partner decides to betray the other and the other cooperates, then the defector will receive all benefits and the "sucker" will receive none. But if both betray each other, there will be the smallest mutual payoff.

If there were only one iteration of the game, then there is the greatest incentive to defect, because no matter what the partner's choice, the payoff to the individual is higher with defection. Of course, both partners can perceive this choice and outcome. If they both defect, they will be mutually worse off than if they both cooperate, yet the incentive to defect is still greater for the individual. This is the crux of the dilemma.

Now let us complexify the game. Introduce to the situation the opportunity for randomly *repeated* games with partners. Third-party information is still not available. The only way to know how anyone will behave is by *direct* previous experience with that person. Retain the restriction that there is a finite set of partners, a closed box. The strategies available to each person are necessarily more complex with repeated play. One may decide, for instance, to follow the rule to always cooperate, never cooperate, randomly cooperate, or retaliate according to how

TABLE 9.1
Payoffs in The Prisoner's Dilemma

		Column player	
		Cooperate	Defect
Row player	Cooperate	3, 3	0, 5
	Defect	5, 0	1, 1

Note: The pairs of numbers indicate the payoff to the row and column player, respectively. For example, in one variant of this game, two suspected "prisoners" are separated by police and unable to communicate with one another. The police have evidence to prosecute for a lesser crime, but need cooperation from at least one prisoner to convict on a greater crime. The police promise not to convict for the lesser crime if the prisoner confesses to the larger crime. If both prisoners stick to their story, they both avoid conviction for the greater crime, yielding an incentive of 3 points awarded to each and a total payout incentive of 6 points. But if only one prisoner betrays the other, the defector gets off for both the greater and the lesser crime (5 points), and the "sucker" pays the cost for both crimes (0 points). Total payout incentive is less than optimum, but it is the highest outcome for the defector. If both betray each other, they both are convicted for the greater crime but not for the smaller one, thus the incentive of 1 point each.

one's partner just played the previous game, and so on. Thus, in this situation, people can alter their play according to some predetermined heuristic depending, through trial and error, on how their partner behaves or without regard to that feedback.

In SNA terms, when everyone plays many repeated games with everyone else in this finite universe, *maximum density* occurs. All possible pairings happen equally (allowing for random variations that cancel out over a large number of plays). If only half the possible pairings were allowed, we would say that the density of the network was .50 and the network is more sparse. If only 10% of the possible pairings were allowed, the density would be even more sparse, only .10, and so on. Table 9.1 shows what outcomes are possible with one play of the game, but what would be the best approach for the individual (i.e., the winning strategy) under conditions of maximum density and repeated play? Note that the opportunity to gather third-party information (gossip) is still not present in this universe; only directly gathered information is available.

A common way to determine the outcome, used by numerous researchers under many strategy conditions, is via computer simulation. Through a series of such simulations, Axelrod (1980a, 1980b, 1984), and later Burt (1999), showed that one strategy is most robustly the winner in the long run. This strategy is to play the first game cooperatively and then to do whatever the other player has done on the previous move. Called "Tit-for-tat" by these authors,[1] this strategy is likened to the philosophy of an "eye for an eye" (Axelrod, 1980a, p. 21). Its success is believed to be due to its unique combination of "altruism" (never the first to defect), immediate retaliation (giving unequivocal feedback to the partner for defection), and flexibility or forgiveness (cooperating following cooperation, regardless of prior defections from the partner; Axelrod, 1980b; Burt, 1999).

In the closed box simulation with maximum density above, the simulated participants play a predetermined strategy with everyone in the network. Now suppose that players can choose to move on to new partners depending on the outcome of the game—a situation more like the real world. Burt also simulated this. He found that players with the most aggressive strategies came out ahead. Players who always defected no matter what (Hostile) and those who defected half the time (Pushy) were winners when allowed to move on to other, "naïve" players. This situation is analogous to the "con man in the big city" (Burt, 1999), because a deceiver can take advantage of naïve players over and over again, until the supply is exhausted. "Defection is the optimum prisoner's dilemma move against a partner you won't meet again," writes Burt (1999, p. 322). The greater the supply of new players, the sparser the network will be, because there will be a smaller and smaller proportion of possible games played repeatedly. In this situation, players can choose to have only an initial exchange with someone and then limit their repeated games to preferred (i.e., naïve) players. In other words, by moving on they can pre-empt others from learning about their strategy. *The sparser the network, the more advantage the aggressive players have.* In Burt's simulations that supplied naïve players at densities of about .60 or lower, and where no third-party information was available, hostile players totally dominated repeated games.

Various network densities and a set number of predetermined strategies comprise the limit of current computer simulations. What cannot be easily programmed beyond these conditions is the introduction of third-party information. That is, what if players had at their disposal not just a fixed strategy for dealing with information from a direct encounter with another player, but also information about their counterparts *ahead of time*, learned from third parties (i.e., gossip)? This new condition better resembles the complexity of the real world and should alter the balance of play considerably. There are no examples in the simulation literature of how such a complex network would function over the long term, because players' strategies would be fluid, not predetermined, and it is not clear how participants would use gossip to adjust their behavior. Nevertheless, there are some important details of networks that have implications for how people will behave in the presence of gossip. We next describe these details and also discuss evidence that is consistent with our conjectures.

TWO NETWORK DIMENSIONS THAT AFFECT
THE IMPACT OF GOSSIP

Density

Figure 9.1 is a schematic representation of the links in a group of five people. The lines indicate a *pattern* of exchanges among these people. Suppose the figure represents a pattern of repeated conversations of board members. Member A has spoken frequently to D, who has spoken to both B and C, neither of whom has been in much direct contact with A. Member E has had little or no contact with anyone on the board—in network terms, E is effectively an isolate. The density of this simple network, the ratio of links to total possible links, is $4 / [(5^2 - 5) / 2] = .40$, relatively low in terms of the Prisoner's Dilemma simulations run by Burt discussed earlier. Were these individuals not allowed to exchange information about one another freely regarding how each was likely to maneuver on the task at hand, Burt's simulations predict that members practicing deception with others would likely prevail over time.

However, allowing for third-party exchanges about how others are likely to behave (based on previous experience), all members except E theoretically possess approximately the same information about their social environment. Under this condition, it is vastly more difficult to deceive anyone about one's own intentions, and nearly everyone has at least some advance information predicting the others' behavior. Conformity is not necessarily assured, but transparency virtually is. It is easy to see why gossip, as Enquist and Leimar (1993) and Dunbar (2004) maintain, functions like an informal policing device for controlling free-riders and social cheats. Thus, any member's plan for deception will not get much leverage. Conversely, a plan to forge a consensus will at least have the advantage of avoiding unproductive and deceptive

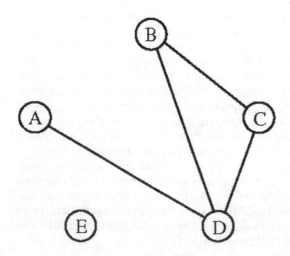

FIG. 9.1.   A simple network.

relations before beginning. "Nasty players [Hostile and Pushy]," notes Burt (1999), are kept at bay by "friends and colleagues who warn managers away from people known to exploit their partners" (p. 332). This may be why, once eccentricities are identified, there is a tendency of group members to focus on these extremes and reign them in for the sake of consensus (Brehm & Festinger, 1957; Festinger & Thibaut, 1951). Gossip, and perhaps even the threat of gossip, is an effective and accessible means of accomplishing just this.

If gossip is how "the individual gets a map of his social environment" (Hannerz, 1967, p. 57), then it follows that the density of the gossip network will be positively related to the individual's ability to gather information that could make the individual more influential, or at least more cognizant of the group's norms and goals. Suls (1977) argued that gossip is an excellent source of social comparison information, particularly if the information sought is of an unfavorable kind. Knowing who is aggressive or deceitful, who has resources, who is reliable and truthful, and who is politically aligned should improve the knower's chances for successful influence in the group. With such knowledge, a player can more efficiently align himself or herself with like-minded partners. Conversely, not knowing about such information could result in wasted time and effort in, say, finding political or personal support. To be sure, there are individual differences in the ability to read other people's intentions and actions (Aditya & Rosnow, 2002), but the gossip network, if active and inclusive, generally tends to level these differences among individuals.

Density therefore has two implications for network members. First, because higher density means more information flow to more people, members whose intentions are better aligned with the average of the group's norms should be more influential in a higher density network. Groups with incoherent norms and sparse ties put little pressure on members to conform. Individual resistance is easier and influence is less likely. Second, members of a high-density network with coherent norms should find it more difficult to exercise resistance and remain eccentric, and so on. These relationships are summarized in Table 9.2.

TABLE 9.2

Influence in and Resistance to the Group in a Gossip Network

		Network density	
		High	Low
Network norm coherence	High	Influence: easy Resistance: difficult	Influence: sporadic Resistance: factional
	Low	Influence: factional Resistance: sporadic	Influence: difficult Resistance: easy

The literature on gossip is consistent with these two conjectures about density. A common observation of the social effect of gossip is that it creates and maintains shared behavioral expectations and norms (Bergmann, 1993; Dunbar, 2004; Eckert, 1990; Gluckman, 1963; Loudon, 1961; Noon & Delbridge, 1993). However, from the perspective of people aligned with the group, gossip is inclusive. From the perspective of those outside the group, or wishing to change the norms, gossip is divisive. Denser gossip networks allow for more efficient dissemination of social expectations (Pfeffer & Salancik, 1978), assisting those whose values better match the group's expectations and hindering those less aligned. Thus, gossip may either propel or impede one's sense of contentment within the group, depending on whether one wishes to be in accord with or independent of the mean group opinions. There will be more efficiency in the process if density is high.

Betweenness

Another important aspect of network structure that may interact with density is implied in Fig. 9.1. This SNA measure, called *betweenness*, may alter the network dynamic and the challenge of achieving influence and satisfaction for the individual and group.

Betweenness is often referred to as *gatekeeping*, a term popularized by White (1950) in a classic article on news dissemination through the press. This usage may be more intuitively evident if Fig. 9.1 is redrawn as Fig. 9.2. The relationships are the same in both figures, but the spatial representation has been changed. In Fig. 9.2, member D can be readily seen to have a special status in the flow of third-party information. Because this person is along the shortest distance, or *geodesic*, between members A and B and between A and C, member D has more power in that D can control, manipulate, and alter any gossip (or information of any kind) passed along to other members. This power is strongest with reference to A, who must traverse D to get information about any network member, and it is reduced with reference to B and C, who must tra-

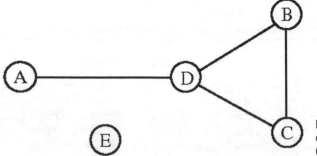

FIG. 9.2. An example of high betweenness (D).

verse D to get information only about A, but who can share information directly about themselves and about D between themselves without any intercession from D.

Density is a feature of the whole network and belongs to no one individual. Betweenness, on the other hand, refers to a particular kind of prominence or status of an individual, attributable to the position of the individual in the network structure. The quantification of betweenness is more complex than density and beyond the scope of this chapter. What is of interest is how betweenness can affect the outcome of the exchanges and, therefore, the satisfaction of network members. If there are people with high betweenness in the network, then others' influence and relational satisfaction will tend to be more dependent on the motives and attitudes of the gatekeeper. Density can also interact with betweenness, as summarized in Table 9.3.

REAL-WORLD EXAMPLES OF NETWORK EFFECTS ON GOSSIP

The power of network members with high betweenness can be seen in examples of extreme interpersonal and organizational influence. Nearly all cult leaders, for example, depend on near-absolute gatekeeping to maintain control of every aspect of their followers' activities, communications, and presumably even thoughts (Bearak, 1997; Joseph, 1997). By means of physical separation, and especially coercion, leaders make gossip among the cult members nearly impossible to generate (Kisser, 1997), thus reducing density, as well. Such leaders instinctively arrange a network structure that eliminates or skews gossip about them among the people inside and outside the group and even within the group (see Fig. 9.3). Consequently, members do not have a chance to acquire or apply third-party information about social interactions or members in the group, and the ability to analyze what is going on is greatly diminished (Waters, 1980). By the same token, the member with high betweenness can create gossip or otherwise manipulate information that is difficult to check, thus augmenting its effectiveness.

TABLE 9.3
Network Interaction of Density (Connections) and Betweenness (Gatekeeping) on Member Influence

| | | Network density | |
		High	Low
Network betweenness	High	Shared, possibly contentious influence	Controlling influence
	Low	Subordinate, occasional influence	Isolated and uninfluential

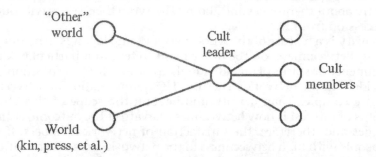

"Other" world

Cult leader

Cult members

World
(kin, press, et al.)

FIG. 9.3.   Cult network: Leader has absolute betweenness.

In parallel (if less pathological) fashion, personally forceful top executives sometimes occupy both the CEO position and the chair of their company's board (Fig. 9.4). Executives holding both positions have a special status in that they can control the information flow to each of the constituent groups shown in the figure. While this network structure provides certain advantages in a competitive environment, occasionally negative (and accurate) evaluative statements do not flow to important decision makers between the different constituencies. If the executive, for instance, is mistreating employees, the board may not learn of this in a timely way. Similarly, if the board's decisions and recommendations are not being executed operationally at the company level, board members may not know about this because the CEO/Chair is controlling the information flow. And if there is strife among the board members, the CEO/Chair can control the shareholders' perception of such misalignments to his advantage. It was not coincidental that in two corporate makeovers in 2004, the CEO and board chair positions of The Walt Disney Company and the New York Stock Exchange were separated. Vested constituencies perceived that power had grown too centralized within the respective organizations, the network structure having contributed to and exacerbated this state of affairs.

The simple networks shown in Figs. 9.1 and 9.2 have relatively low density and, for member D, high betweenness. We have illustrated how higher density facilitates overcoming potential aggressiveness of members, but high betweenness may moderate this effect. Some specifications from a social network gathered by Foster (2003) further illustrate these relationships. In a study of 48 residence assistants (RAs) at an eastern university, the gossip network's overall density was .27. At this density level, were this group to function without gossip as in Burt's model, then hostile players who only deceive others would dominate the group. Gos-

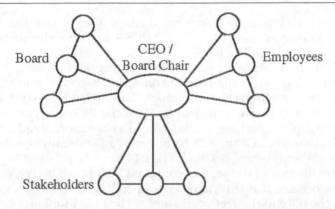

FIG. 9.4. Company chief executive/board chairman with high betweenness.

sip, however, was ubiquitous: the average number of gossip partners reported was about 20 per person. Hostile players were evidently scarce: The average number of close friendships reported by these RAs was about 24 per person. Betweenness was also difficult to achieve for individuals in this group. Eighty-six percent of the network members were within an average of just 1.8 links to everyone else in the gossip network, so the flow of third-party information encountered few obstacles.

Finally, network analysis of a literary masterpiece provides still another illustration of how social network structure can affect the potency of gossiping behavior. The key figure in William Shakespeare's *Othello* (1604/1975), the villain Iago, epitomizes the kind of gossip that colloquially comes to mind: false and negative gossip that is ultimately destructive of the target (and, as it happens in this play, others in the orbit of the target).

A brief summary of the plot: Iago is the manservant to the accomplished military commander Othello, a Moor, who has recently married Desdemona. Cassio is an honorable lieutenant who has served Othello on the battlefield. Iago plots to bring down the Moor by gossiping to him that Desdemona and Cassio have been adulterous. Iago separately manipulates Cassio's and Desdemona's behavior in such a way that further insinuations to Othello about their intentions can be interpreted as dishonorable. Othello takes the bait, and in a clouded, jealous rage, he murders Desdemona. In the dénouement, Iago's treachery is revealed, and Othello stabs himself from grief.

We defined and coded each scene of the play in terms of which characters are onstage. Scenes were demarcated by an entrance or exit of a character or characters (excluding only minor actors without dialog, such as "attendants," "officers," and so forth, as indicated in the stage directions). The play thus has 89 such scenes, which may be thought of as discrete, successive networks. The resulting database is a record of the amount of each character's presence onstage and the number of dyadic contacts among all the characters. Table 9.4 shows the summary of such stage activity in the play.

The first observation we can make from the data in Table 9.4 is that Iago clearly dominates the play (a common observation in *Othello* reviews). Even more than the eponymous character, it is Iago who is at the center of the action. He is present in 59 of the 89 scenes, or about two thirds of the play. Further, he has considerably more dyadic ties than any other character. Of the 638 total dyadic relationships onstage, Iago has 20% of them, whereas Othello has 14%.

Of most interest in the present context is how much betweenness Iago manages, because it is this network property we posit to be essential in altering the potential effect of gossip for the individual and the group. Iago is with *either* Othello or Cassio in 25 scenes, but he is with *both* in only 12 scenes. Thus, he can manipulate information and spread falsehoods to one or the other with relative impunity. More specifically, an analysis of the social links across scenes among all the characters reveals Iago to have the most betweenness. This is shown in Table 9.5, which is the valued adjacency matrix of all the characters based on the 89 scenes of the play (the sums form the right-hand portion of Table 9.4). One

TABLE 9.4

Stage Presence and Contacts of Actors in *Othello*

Character	Number of scenes character is present	Character	Dyadic contacts between characters
Iago	59	Iago	127
Othello	38	Othello	91
Cassio	35	Cassio	87
Desdemona	27	Desdemona	71
Emilia	26	Roderigo	63
Roderigo	22	Emilia	61
Montano	12	Lodovico	30
Lodovico	9	Montano	28
Grantiano	7	Grantiano	27
Brabantio	6	Brabantio	22
Bianca	5	Bianca	16
Duke of Venice	4	Duke of Venice	12
Clown	2	Clown	3
Total number of scenes	89	Sum of dyadic contacts	638

TABLE 9.5

Valued Adjacency Matrix of Characters in *Othello*

	Othello	Brabantio	Cassio	Iago	Roderigo	Duke	Montano	Clown	Desdemona	Emilia	Bianca	Lodovico	Grantiano	Sum
Othello	—	5	14	25	7	3	3	0	16	12	1	3	2	91
Brabantio	5	—	1	5	6	3	0	0	2	0	0	0	0	22
Cassio	14	1	—	25	10	0	7	1	10	8	3	4	4	87
Iago	25	5	25	—	19	2	10	0	13	11	4	7	6	127
Roderigo	7	6	10	19	—	3	3	0	5	3	1	3	3	63
Duke	3	3	0	2	3	—	0	0	1	0	0	0	0	12
Montano	3	0	7	10	3	0	—	0	2	2	0	2	1	28
Clown	0	0	1	0	0	0	0	—	1	1	0	0	0	3
Desdemona	16	2	10	13	5	1	2	1	—	19	0	2	0	71
Emilia	12	0	8	11	3	0	2	1	19	—	1	2	2	61
Bianca	1	0	3	4	1	0	0	0	0	1	—	3	3	16
Lodovico	3	0	4	7	3	0	2	0	2	2	3	—	6	30
Grantiano	2	0	4	6	3	0	1	0	0	2	3	6	—	27

Note. This table shows the number of dyadic contacts between all pairs of actors in the play *Othello*. The character Othello is in five scenes with Brabantio, 14 scenes with Cassio, 25 with Iago, etc. (with "scene" defined as "on stage with" as described in the text). The matrix is nondirectional, that is, the relationship "on stage with" is necessarily reciprocal between pairs of characters. Thus, the table is symmetric above and below the diagonal. By convention, the diagonal cells are undefined.

way of conceptualizing the numbers in the body of this table is that they represent the amount of dramatic information flowing from one character to another. The row sums capture the total dyadic flow of information for each character. Indicative of high betweenness on Iago's part, much information about Othello, Desdemona, and Cassio is flowing through Iago, who thereby has the opportunity to skew both truths and falsehoods to his own ends. It is this structure that enables Iago to successfully manipulate the characters (most profoundly and tragically, Othello, in spite of the Moor's demonstrated worldliness at the beginning of the play). Table 9.6 shows betweenness scores (using an algorithm in the SNA software Ucinet; Borgatti, 2002), with Iago easily outpacing all others. Thus, Shakespeare's tragedy offers engaging evidence that high betweenness can accentuate the influence of a single gossiper—should that be his motive—over the network.

CONCLUSION

In this chapter, we have outlined a theoretical model of gossip and influence in a network of interpersonal relations. The logical foundation of our model consists of an amalgamation of theoretical insights and intuition with some computer simulation data, observational findings, and even a literary example. The thread of commonality is that gossip is not a static entity of social knowledge available at a public trough. Rather, its flow and location are constantly changing, reforming, and

TABLE 9.6
Betweenness of *Othello* Characters

Character	Betweenness
Iago	26.2
Cassio	20.9
Othello	16.6
Desdemona	15.9
Roderigo	15.8
Emilia	13.9
Lodovico	7.7
Grantiano	7.4
Brabantio	6.2
Bianca	3.5
Duke of Venice	3.0
Montano	1.8
Clown	.3

reaggregating in ways that are affected by the structure of connections with and around network members.

We have illustrated how social groups can benefit from a dense gossip network. Prisoner's Dilemma simulations imply that the lack of third-party information puts individuals at risk of the "con man in the big city." But even in dense networks with available third-party information, members with high betweenness—gatekeepers—can reduce information efficiency and endanger the status quo. Whether this is for better or worse depends on the perspective of the observer and the motives of the gatekeeper. Beyond computer simulations, empirical data from actual gossip networks support the hypothesis that dense gossip networks improve the flow of information and the ease of individual influence. Other network examples show how high betweenness can concentrate power and information, thus altering the effects of gossip, potentially with very undesirable outcomes.

Perhaps the best way to curtail malevolent gossip is to disintermediate the gatekeepers, that is, by forming social links around them so that the information they pass is naturally checked and verified. If the information is negative and true, the target will hardly have an incentive to increase the number of independent verifications, and the network as a whole should benefit from having such information disseminated. If the information is negative and false, then everyone but the gatekeeper will benefit from more density around the gossiper, which in turn should isolate the gossiper socially. Like cult leaders, controlling corporate executives, and the villain Iago, such gatekeepers may act to keep network members around them ignorant of certain information that could expose the gatekeeper's ulterior motives and source of social power.

We have also alluded to the Janus-like nature of gossip. Despite its reputation and the ostensible social sanctions against it, gossip is undeniably a major social strategy used to determine and convey views of the social world. "Good" gossip from the individual target's perspective is positive information; yet if false, it is bad gossip. "Bad" gossip from the group's perspective is negative information; yet if true, it is good gossip. The structure of the network through which gossip passes offers clues as to how good "good" gossip will be and how bad "bad" gossip will be. The network, as much as the content of gossip, has the potential for creating collegiality and understanding between and within groups. However, it may also create inequality, misunderstanding, and conflict. Insiders relish the exchange of gossip; outsiders fear it and wait for initiation into the gossip cabal. To no insignificant degree, we learn how to behave, think, and communicate from and with gossip, but groups may also fracture irremediably along gossip's structural lines. Thus, there are wide real-world implications for a better understanding of the networks of gossiping behavior, and strengthening the proposed model in this area may better inform the way we—managers, administrators, peers, and colleagues—view gossip in context.

NOTE

The eight heuristics used in the simulations by Axelrod and Burt are as follows:

Happy ························· always cooperates
Hostile ······················· always defects
Erratic ······················· random moves
Tit-for-tat ·················· matches partner's previous play
Other cheek ················ Tit-for-two-tats
Righteous ··················· never forgives, i.e., always defects after first betrayal by partner
Sneaky ····················· up to 10% defections
Pushy ······················· up to 50% defections

REFERENCES

Abrahams, R. D. (1970). A performance-centered approach to gossip. *Man, 5,* 290–301.

Aditya, R. N., & Rosnow, R. L. (2002). Executive intelligence and interpersonal acumen: A conceptual framework. In B. Pattanayak & V. Gupta (Eds.), *Creating performing organizations* (pp. 225–246). New Delhi: Response/Sage.

Allport, G. W., & Postman, L. (1947). *The psychology of rumor.* New York: Holt, Rinehart & Winston.

Axelrod, R. (1980a). Effective choice in the Prisoner's Dilemma. *Journal of Conflict Resolution, 24,* 3–25.

Axelrod, R. (1980b). More effective choice in the Prisoner's Dilemma. *Journal of Conflict Resolution, 24,* 379–403.

Axelrod, R. (1984). *The evolution of cooperation.* New York: Basic Books.

Barkow, J. H. (1992). Beneath new culture is old psychology: Gossip and social stratification. In J. H. Barkow, L. Cosmides, & J. Tooby (Eds.), *The adapted mind* (pp. 627–637). Oxford, UK: Oxford University Press.

Baumeister, R., Zhang, L., & Vohs, K. D. (2004). Gossip as cultural learning. *Review of General Psychology, 8,* 111–121.

Bearak, B. (1997, April 28). Odyssey to suicide; A special report; Eyes on glory: Pied pipers of Heaven's Gate. *The New York Times,* p. A1.

Bergmann, J. R. (1993). *Discreet indiscretions: The social organization of gossip.* New York: Aldine de Gruyter.

Blumberg, H. H. (1972). Communication of interpersonal evaluations. *Journal of Personality and Social Psychology, 23,* 157–162.

Borgatti, S. P., Everett, M. G., & Freeman, L. C. (2002). Ucinet for Windows: Software for social network analysis [Computer software] (Version 6.15). Harvard, MA: Analytic Technologies.

Brehm, J., & Festinger, L. (1957). *Pressures toward uniformity of performance in groups.* London: Sage.

Burt, R. (1999). Private games are too dangerous. *Computational & Mathematical Organization Theory, 5*(4), 311–341.

Cantril, H., Gaudet, H., & Herzog, H. (1940). *The invasion from Mars.* Princeton, NJ: Princeton University Press.

Dunbar, R. I. M. (1993a). Coevolution of neocortical size, group size and language in humans. *Behavioral and Brain Sciences, 16,* 681 694.

Dunbar, R. I. M. (1993b). On the origins of language: A history of constraints and windows of opportunity. *Behavioral and Brain Sciences, 16,* 721–735.

Dunbar, R. I. M. (1994). *Grooming, gossip, and the evolution of language.* London: Faber & Faber.

Dunbar, R. I. M. (2004). Gossip in an evolutionary perspective. *Review of General Psychology, 8,* 100–110.

Eckert, P. (1990). Cooperative competition in adolescent "girl talk." *Discourse Processes, 13,* 91–122.

Eliot, G. (1960). *Daniel Deronda.* New York: Harper. (Original work published 1878)

Enquist, M., & Leimar, O. (1993). The evolution of cooperation in mobile organisms. *Animal Behaviour, 45,* 747–757.

Festinger, L., & Thibaut, J. (1951). Interpersonal communication in small groups. *Journal of Abnormal & Social Psychology, 46,* 92–99.

Fine, G. A., & Turner, P. A. (2001). *Whispers on the color line: Rumor and race in America.* Berkeley: University of California Press.

Foster, E. K. (2003). *Researching gossip with social network analysis.* Unpublished dissertation, Temple University, Philadelphia.

Foster, E. K. (2004). Research on gossip: Taxonomy, methods, and future directions. *Review of General Psychology, 8,* 78–99.

Gilmore, D. (1978). Varieties of gossip in a Spanish rural community. *Ethnology, 17,* 89–99.

Gluckman, M. (1963). Gossip and scandal. *Current Anthropology, 4,* 307–316.

Hannerz, U. (1967). Gossip networks and culture in a Black American ghetto. *Ethnos, 32,* 35–59.

Joseph, J. (1997, August 7). Willingly brainwashed, despicably betrayed. *The Times,* p. 16.

Kapferer, J.-N. (1990). *Rumors: Uses, interpretations, and images.* New Brunswick, NJ: Transaction.

Kelly, F. K., & Rossman, M. (1944). The "GI" and the rumor. *Infantry Journal, 54*(2), 37–38.

Kimmel, A. J. (2004). *Rumors and rumor control: A manager's guide to understanding and combating rumors.* Mahwah, NJ: Lawrence Erlbaum Associates.

Kisser, C. (1997, April 1). The road to Heaven's Gate-gate. *The Wall Street Journal,* p. A18.

Levin, J., & Arluke, A. (1985). An exploratory analysis of sex differences in gossip. *Sex Roles, 12,* 281–286.

Levin, J., & Arluke, A. (1987). *Gossip: The inside scoop.* New York: Plenum Press.

Loudon, J. (1961). Kinship and crisis in South Wales. *British Journal of Sociology, 12,* 333–350.

Munro, H. H. (Saki). (1921). *"The soul of Laplashka" in Reginald and Reginald in Russia with an introduction by Hugh Walpole* (p. 209). New York: Viking.

Noon, M., & Delbridge, R. (1993). News from behind my hand: Gossip in organizations. *Organization Studies, 14,* 23–36.

Pfeffer, J., & Salancik, G. R. (1978). *The external control of organizations.* New York: Harper & Row.

Pratkanis, A. R., & Aronson, E. (1991). *Age of propaganda: The everyday use and abuse of persuasion.* New York: Freeman.

Rosenbaum, J. B., & Subrin, M. (1963). The psychology of gossip. *Journal of American Psychoanalytic Association, 11,* 817–831.

Rosnow, R. L. (1977). Gossip and marketplace psychology. *Journal of Communication, 27,* 158–163.

Rosnow, R. L. (1980). Psychology of rumor reconsidered. *Psychological Bulletin, 87,* 578–591.

Rosnow, R. L. (1991). Inside rumor: A personal journey. *American Psychologist, 46,* 484–496.

Rosnow, R. L. (2001). Rumor and gossip in interpersonal interaction and beyond: A social exchange perspective. In R. M. Kowalski (Ed.), *Behaving badly: Aversive behaviors in interpersonal relationships* (pp. 203–232). Washington, DC: American Psychological Association.

Rosnow, R. L., & Fine, G. A. (1974). Inside rumors. *Human Behavior, 3,* 64–68.

Roy, D. F. (1958). Banana time: Job satisfaction and informal interaction. *Human Organization, 18,* 158–168.

Schoeman, F. (1994). Gossip and privacy. In R. F. Goodman & A. Ben-Ze'ev (Eds.), *Good gossip* (pp. 72–82). Lawrence: University Press of Kansas.

Shakespeare, W. (1604/1975). *Othello.* In A. Harbage (Ed.), *William Shakespeare: The complete works* (pp. 1018–1059). New York: Viking.

Spacks, P. M. (1982). In praise of gossip. *Hudson Review, 35,* 19–38.

Stewart, P. J., & Strathern, A. (2004). *Witchcraft, sorcery, rumors, and gossip.* Cambridge, UK: Cambridge University Press.

Stirling, R. B. (1956). Some psychological mechanisms operative in gossip. *Social Forces, 34,* 262–267.

Suls, J. M. (1977). Gossip as social comparison. *Journal of Communication, 27,* 164–168.

Wasserman, S., & Faust, K. (1994). *Social network analysis: Methods and applications.* New York: Cambridge University Press.

Waters, H. F. (1980, April 21). CBS's Jonestown: Making of a 'Savior'. *Newsweek,* 88.

Watkins, J. G. (1943). Further opportunities for applied psychologists in offensive warfare. *Journal of Consulting Psychology, 7,* 135–141.

Wert, S. R., & Salovey, P. (2004). A social comparison account of gossip. *Review of General Psychology, 8,* 122–137.

White, D. M. (1950). The "gate keeper": A case study in the selection of news. *Journalism Quarterly, 27,* 383–390.

Yerkovitch, S. (1977). Gossip as a way of speaking. *Journal of Communication, 26,* 192–196.

Chapter 10

Nonresidential Parent–Child Relationships: Overcoming the Challenges of Absence

Stephanie S. Rollie
University of Iowa

This chapter is a consideration of nonresidential parent–child relationships and the challenges and barriers associated with maintaining those relationships. The chapter covers a particularly urgent but neglected topic as the prevalence of nonresidential parents (NRPs) continues to grow. With approximately half of all marriages ending in divorce, it is estimated that almost a million children in the United States each year become members of single-parent households for at least some time (Wallerstein, Lewis, & Blakeslee, 2000). At the same time, the birth rate to unmarried parents continues to rise while the marriage rate declines. From 1980 to 1995, the number of Caucasian births occurring outside of marriage increased from 14.5% to about 25%, with even greater increases for Hispanic and African American births (Teachman, Tedrow, & Crowder, 2000). As a result, about half of White children and two thirds of African American children spend at least part of their childhood in a single-parent home, away from the other biological parent (Teachman et al., 2000). While it is difficult to determine the effects of this increase in single and nonresidential parenting, research suggests that these changes have negative effects on parents and children, especially for the NRP–child relationship.

Although parenthood is typically perceived to be a lifelong commitment, popular media and current research on NRPs indicate that this is not always the case. Following parental separation, the NRP–child relationship is particularly vulnerable (Fox & Bruce, 1999). A number of factors cause parental involvement to decrease significantly, and many NRP–child relationships end or are never established. Following divorce, the frequency and quality of interaction with children drops dramati-

181

cally for NRPs (Furstenberg & Nord, 1985; Marsiglio, Amato, Day, & Lamb, 2000). Stewart (1999b) reports that 20% of NRPs have had no contact with their children in the previous year. Another 27% see their children several times a year or less. Contact with children is even less likely for never-married NRPs (Cooksey & Craig, 1998; Marsiglio et al., 2000; Seltzer, 1991). Unlike divorced NRPs, many never-married NRPs have not had opportunities to establish close bonds with their children through daily contact and engagement in rituals and routines associated with cohabitation. Once parents no longer live in the same house as their children, opportunities for contact generally, and face-to-face communication specifically, are greatly diminished.

A number of factors are correlated with reduced involvement by NRPs. First, contact with their biological children decreases as the amount of time since separation increases. Thus, relationships that initially continue following separation may eventually fade away (Seltzer, 1991; Stewart, 1999b). NRP–child involvement is also associated with the NRP's geographic distance from the child (Stewart, 1999b). Cooksey and Craig (1998) found that fathers who live more than 100 miles from their children are less likely to talk and interact with those children. When the distance is between 11 and 100 miles, fathers have more interaction, but are more likely to call than to visit their children regularly. Involvement is greatest for NRPs who live short distances from their children. Fathers are also more likely to see their children regularly when multiple biological children live in the same household (Cooksey & Craig, 1998), when socioeconomic status before separation is high (Seltzer, 1998), and when they have more education (Cooksey & Craig, 1998, Seltzer, 1998). Levels of custody are also important. Fathers with joint legal custody not only spend time with children more frequently than other nonresidential fathers, they also see their children for greater lengths of time (i.e. more overnight visits; Seltzer, 1998). NRPs are more likely to reduce contact with their biological children when minor children (e.g., stepchildren) reside in their current household (Cooksey & Craig, 1998). Finally, NRPs' attitudes about parenthood have an impact on involvement with absent children. Fathers who value parenthood and who believe children are important to life satisfaction are more likely to have frequent contact with their children (Cooksey & Craig, 1998).

These trends suggest that maintaining the NRP–child relationship is particularly difficult. While many NRPs successfully engage in fulfilling and lasting relationships with their nonresidential children, for others, the barriers to maintaining a "normal" parental relationship are insurmountable, leading to reduced or discontinued contact with children. Thus, it is clear that the legal status of being a parent guarantees neither a lasting nor a close relationship with biological children, particularly if that parent lives in a separate household. Consequently, this chapter is an exploration of the challenges and barriers to maintaining the NRP–child relationship. This chapter begins with an acknowledgment of some of the constraints of research on NRP–child relationships; followed by a discussion of the value of NRPs to their children; then an illustration of the many obstacles that NRPs face in maintaining this relationship; concluding with a brief discussion of the general sources of relationship difficulty. Because the great majority of NRPs are men, most research on the NRP–child relationship has focused primarily on divorced fathers. Very little research has focused on nonresidential mothers or on unmarried NRPs. Accordingly, much of the research described here is limited, in some degree, to the experiences of fathers whose nonresidential status was created by a divorce. Even so, research that has examined nonresidential mothers has found their experiences to be similar to those of nonresidential fathers (Stewart, 1999a, 1999b). Similarly, while the experiences for never-married nonresidential and divorced parents may be quite different, particularly when the never-married NRP has not lived with the child, many of the challenges and the barriers to the relationship are the same. Research suggests that the experiences of divorced parents and never-married parents who cohabited and then separated are quite similar (Cooksey & Craig, 1998).

THE VALUE OF THE NRP–CHILD RELATIONSHIP

As divorce rates climbed in the 1970s and 1980s, researchers were particularly concerned about the effects on children's well-being. Policymakers have known that the mother's role is particularly important, but they were uncertain about the effects of the nonresidential father's influence on child outcomes. In response to this need, researchers began to conduct studies that examined whether interaction with the nonresidential father had any impact on the child's adjustment and well-being. In general, this research has been fairly inconsistent and inconclusive. A number of studies have found that involvement of nonresidential fathers has almost no effect on their child's well-being (e.g., Furstenberg, Morgan, & Allison, 1987; King, 1994). Furstenberg et al. (1987) examined the relationship between frequency of paternal contact and measures of child well-being such as problem behavior, distress, and academic difficulty. They noted, "On the basis of our study, we see no strong evidence that children will benefit from the judicial or legislative interventions that have been designed to promote paternal participation, apart from providing economic support" (pp. 699–700). However, on the basis of their meta-analysis, Amato and Gilbreth (1999) suggest that no clear associations exist between frequency of NRP–child contact and child outcomes and that frequency of contact is a poor predictor of child outcomes. Still other research has found some important links between NRP–child interaction and positive child outcomes (Lamb, 1999).

Lamb (1999) asserts that the relationship between NRP absence and negative child outcomes is actually fairly weak. He argues that a large number of factors associated with divorce have consequences for child adjustment, including marital conflict, stress, disruption of parent–child relationships, undersupervision, and economic hardship. As a result, it is impossible to fully determine the specific outcomes associated with maintaining the NRP–child relationship. Other research illustrates that contact with the NRP actually benefits children (Simons, Whitbeck, Beaman, & Conger, 1994). Simons et al. found that interaction between nonresidential fathers and their children is associated with a reduction in risk for behavior conduct problems. In assessing the value of NRPs for the lives of their children, researchers have focused on three specific aspects: payment of child support, frequency of contact, and relationship quality.

Payment of Child Support

More than any other factor, the link between economic support and child outcomes such as academic achievement has been consistently well supported (Furstenberg et al., 1987; King, 1994). This finding is intuitively plausible given the well–established connection between poverty and negative child outcomes such as academic achievement and health. To the extent that NRPs (particularly fathers) can improve the financial status of the residential parent, children will generally benefit. Unfortunately, a majority of nonresidential fathers do not pay any child support (King, 1994). One of the primary reasons given is they are unable (or perceive that they are unable) to pay the amount ordered (Meyer, 1999). Compliance is strongly associated with the ordered amount of support and the NRP's income. As the ordered amount increases, noncompliance increases.

For NRPs who do regularly pay child support, the payments are typically small, sometimes below the assigned amount. Some research indicates that nonresidential fathers could be paying more child support than is currently being paid (Meyer, 1999; Sorensen, 1997). Nonresidential mothers are even less likely to pay child support, even when the incomes of mothers are similar to those of nonresidential fathers (Greif, 1986). The NRP's level of cooperation in payment of child support is also relevant. The voluntary payment of child support is associated with more positive family experiences than when NRPs are forced to pay child support through court orders or wage garnishment (Argys, Peters, Brooks–Gunn, & Smith, 1998). In short, children benefit psychologically when NRPs voluntarily support their children economically.

Frequency of Contact

Understanding how often parents interact with their children and the effects on child outcomes has been particularly important to scholars interested in influencing policy. Many scholars have emphasized visitation based on the assumption that the more often a nonresidential parent visits his or her biological children, the stronger the relationship between the parent and child (Amato & Gilbreth, 1999; Seltzer & Bianchi, 1988). Overall, researchers have found little or no correlation between the frequency of contact with parents and child well-being (Furstenberg et al., 1987; King, 1994). Many researchers are skeptical about the counterintuitive nature of these findings, particularly since both parental roles have been found to be important in intact families (Amato & Gilbreth, 1999). Researchers began to recognize that the quantity and quality of interaction between parents might differentially affect child well-being (Furstenberg et al., 1987). Simply visiting a child regularly does not necessarily benefit the child. It is the nature of the interaction that influences the relationship.

Relationship Quality

Some scholars argue that current literature has not adequately captured the factors of NRP–child interaction that actually influence child well-being. For example, Amato and Gilbreth (1999) found that feelings of closeness and, more importantly, engagement in authoritative parenting positively affect child outcomes such as academic achievement (i.e., test scores, grades, years of school completed), internalizing problems (i.e., low self-esteem, depression, and anxiety) and externalizing problems (i.e., aggression, misbehavior at home or school, and delinquency). However, instead of engaging in authoritative parenting, which includes behaviors like helping children with homework, talking over personal problems, setting rules, and disciplining children, many NRPs engage primarily in leisure activities with their children. While these recreational relationships may be fun and can contribute to feelings of closeness, they place most of the responsibilities associated with parenting (e.g., discipline, helping with homework) on the residential parent.

Despite inconclusive evidence about the link between NRP involvement and child outcomes, most researchers agree that NRPs can play an important role in their children's lives. Yet, as noted earlier in the chapter, NRP–child relationships can be quite fragile. A number of factors act as barriers to the establishment and maintenance of the NRP–child relationship. The remainder of this chapter examines those barriers and the effects on the NRP–child relationship.

BARRIERS TO MAINTAINING THE NRP–CHILD RELATIONSHIP

While challenges certainly exist for any relationship, the NRP–child relationship faces a number of particular barriers and constraints that make it difficult to maintain. These barriers emerge from a number of sources: household structure, the social network, social and cultural norms, and individual circumstances. Although many of the barriers are interconnected, each influences the relationship in different ways. This section discusses the primary obstacles to establishing and maintaining the NRP–child relationship and the consequences for relational functioning.

Nonresident Structure

Microstructural theory suggests that different parental experiences can be explained by examining the types of opportunities and social expectations associated with a person's position or situation such as marital status or living arrangement (Shapiro & Lambert, 1999). That is, married or cohabiting individuals have opportunities different from those available to separated or divorced individuals. More specifically, residential fathers have opportunities different from those available to nonresidential fathers, and these different "opportunities" directly affect both the nature and experience of the parent–child relationship. Accordingly, most of the difficulties associated with maintaining NRP–child relationships are directly associated with the nonresident structure. Since the parent and child do not live in the same household, it is virtually impossible to engage in a "normal" parent–child relationship associated with traditional coresident parenting. The reality of living in a separate household presents a number of challenges for NRPs.

First, custody arrangements are an important structural constraint, and access to one's child is not automatically guaranteed. In almost all cases, children live with the mother rather than the father (Doherty, Kouneski, & Erickson, 1998), even though social norms about the role of the father have changed, and men are obtaining custody of their children more frequently (Meyer & Garasky, 1993; Stewart, 1999b). One researcher estimates that up to 14% of custodial parents in the United States are men, meaning that approximately one million U.S. mothers are NRPs (Stewart, 1999b). As noted earlier, custody arrangements make a difference for parental involvement and interaction. Parents with joint legal custody are more likely to be involved in their children's lives than those without joint legal custody (Seltzer, 1998). Fathers who have not verified paternity may find that they have no custodial rights to see their children.

Even under conditions of joint custody, where children may spend considerable time in both households, one parent typically assumes more responsibility (e.g., providing housing) than another. This means that NRPs must work with custodial parents to make arrangements to see their children. Sometimes parents engage in lengthy court battles in an effort to establish custody and rules concerning how often, where, and under what circumstances NRPs are able to spend time with their children. Even the term *visitation* suggests the NRP's status under this structure (Lamb, 1999). NRPs must often invest considerable time and energy in arranging and coordinating opportunities to interact with their children. Consequently, custody decisions and arrangements can have an enormous influence on opportunities for NRPs to have access to (and form relationships with) their children.

Geographic distance is another structural factor that influences the NRP–child relationship. Because it is often emotionally easier for separated parents to live in different areas, the NRP may live a considerable distance from the child (Lund, 1987, found that on average, NRPs lived 42 miles away). As a result, it may be very difficult for the parent to engage in frequent face-to-face interaction with the children or to establish regular routines and rituals that are part of many parenting practices. Additionally, because NRPs must assume the financial and time costs associated with obtaining and transporting children during visits, those who live farther away from their children are less likely to visit and to be involved in their children's lives (Cooksey & Craig, 1998; Seltzer, 1991; Stewart, 1999a). In short, the nonresidential status automatically puts NRPs at a disadvantage in establishing and maintaining a strong relationship with their children. They often have fewer opportunities for parent–child interaction and must assume the burden of arranging visitation. Some NRPs find it easier to simply terminate the relationship than expend the energy necessary to parent from a distance (Lund, 1987).

Feelings of Loss

Many NRPs feel a general sense of loss associated with living in a separate household from their children (Wilbur & Wilbur, 1988). This sense of loss can be particularly strong for divorced and separated parents. Hagestad and Smyer (1982) discuss the loss of three bonds associated with marriage dissolution that can have profound effects on the individuals. These bonds could apply equally well to NRPs. First, NRPs experience the *loss of emotional attachments* to both the spouse and the family unit. This process of separation is often very painful. Individuals have typically invested considerable emotional energy in both the marriage relationship and as a parent in the family. Through the process of separation and relational dissolution, individuals lose opportunities for certain types of emotional expression. Some fathers struggle so much with the emotional turmoil associated with the breakup that they are ill-equipped to deal with issues of visitation (Lund, 1987). Intense feelings of guilt, anger, sadness, and concern all interfere with the establishment of a long-term relationship with the children. Some NRPs decide to terminate the parent–child relationship rather than deal with emotional pain of visiting their children (Lund, 1987).

Hagestad and Smyer describe the *inability to perform valued roles* as a second loss experienced by divorcing individuals. The performance of roles greatly influences one's sense of self. With the dissolution of the marriage, individuals can no longer assume the role of "husband" or "wife." As a result, they may feel that they have lost a part of the self. Divorce or separation also necessitates a change in the role of "parent," particularly for NRPs. For many, the parent role has meaning only in relation to the spouse's parent role such that the parent identity is linked to the spousal role (Stueve & Pleck, 2001). This means that NRPs may not be able to enact the parent role as a single parent in the same way as they did before the divorce. Specifically, because they live in a different household, NRPs often have limited opportunities to enact the full range of behaviors and expressions that normally make up the parent identity. Although they are still *legally* "parents," they may only get to enact that "full" role occasionally. As a result, some NRPs feel that they have "lost" the parent role.

NRPs may also view themselves as a secondary parent. The process of having to "visit" children acts to reinforce the "subparent" status. Lamb (1999) explains this situation well:

> Although it has not yet been demonstrated empirically, critics argue that many fathers drift away from their children after divorce because they are deprived of the opportunity to be parents rather than visitors. Most non-custodial parents are awarded *visitation* and they function as visitors, taking their children to the zoo, to movies, to dinner, and to other special activities in much the same way that grandparents or uncles and aunts behave. Children may well enjoy these excursions, and may not regret the respite from arguments about completing homework, cleaning up their rooms, behaving politely, having their hair cut (or *not* having their hair cut!), going to bed on time, getting ready for school, and respecting their parents' limited resources, but the exclusion of fathers from these everyday tribulations is crucial, ultimately transforming the fathers' roles and making these men increasingly irrelevant to their children's lives, socialization, and development. (p. 116)

Lamb notes that most custody and visitation arrangements do not allow NRPs the opportunity to engage in the types of activities and interactions that allow them to function as parents rather than visitors. NRPs may feel unnecessary and unneeded when children are doing well without them and yet may feel sad and guilty when children are not adapting (Wilbur & Wilbur, 1988; Greif, 1997). In both cases, parents are plagued with feelings of loss and blame.

The third deficiency according to Hagestad and Smyer (1982) is the *loss of routines*. Over time, families develop routines and patterns of interaction that become a fundamental way of experiencing the world. These processes and ways of interacting are often taken for granted. Their value is not fully recognized until they can no longer be enacted. These routines function both to make the world predictable and to maintain and confirm valued relationships. The nonresident parent no longer participates in the daily routines of parenthood even though many of the routines may continue in some form with the residential family (Lund, 1987). Thus, NRPs not only experience the loss of valued routines but also recognize that the routines continue in a form that excludes them.

In sum, the loss of valued roles, routines, and emotional bonds tend to lead to lower levels of psychological well-being for separated and divorced individuals (Shapiro & Lambert, 1999). This in turn can negatively affect the abilities of NRPs to establish patterns of visitation and strong relationships with their children (Lund, 1987).

Role Ambiguity

A related challenge that NRPs face is role ambiguity (Minton & Pasley, 1996; Seltzer, 1991). This is particularly true for nonresidential fathers whose role as father is often perceived as ambiguous (Atkinson & Blackwelder, 1993; Lupton & Barclay, 1997). In the past, the mother and father roles were based on different "gendered" tasks. While mothers are still recognized as the nurturer responsible for child care tasks (as evidenced by their greater likelihood of being granted custody), the father role has changed considerably. The image of the ideal father has moved from the stern patriarch in colonial times to the distant breadwinner from 1830 to 1900, to the agreeable dad and sex-role model from 1900 to 1970, to father as co-parent in recent decades (Pleck & Pleck, 1997). In reviewing popular magazine articles from 1900 to 1989, Atkinson and Blackwelder (1993) found that during the 20th century, the definition of fathering fluctuated considerably, moving between fathers as providers and fathers as nurturers. Thus, one current model of fatherhood asserts that fathers share equally in child care and housework. In this sense, the role of parent has become more gender neutral, where "mothers" and "fathers" are no longer completely separable roles (Atkinson & Blackwelder, 1993; Lupton & Barclay, 1997). Daly (1995) argues that modern fathers suffer from generational changes in family structure which have altered current perceptions of fatherhood. Thus, fathers must "creatively forge new rules" about what it means to be a modern father because previous models of fathering (e.g., father as provider) are no longer applicable in today's society. As a result, enacting the father role can be particularly challenging as men try to determine and enact what it means to be a "good" father (Daly, 1995).

Seltzer (1991) explains that parents fulfill three different roles: (a) supporting the child economically, (b) making decisions about how the child should be raised, and (c) spending time with the child. These roles are easily filled when parents live with their children, but opportunities are greatly reduced when parents live in separate households. Similarly, the parent role includes a number of associated roles such as teacher, breadwinner, caretaker, moral developer, planner, protector, and disciplinarian (Lupton & Barclay, 1997; Minton & Pasley, 1996; Stueve &

Pleck, 2001). While some of these roles, such as breadwinner, are not necessarily affected by the nonresidential status, it is particularly difficult to communicate caregiving, teaching, protection, or moral development in absence. NRPs may not have the opportunity to calm their child following nightmares, to help with homework, or to provide discipline and guidance following a child's wayward behavior. In short, NRPs are unable to enact some aspects of the parent role in the traditional, culturally prescribed and immediate manner.

Consequently, the problem of role ambiguity is even greater for NRPs because there are few rules and norms for engaging in a NRP–child relationship. The relatively clear societal guidelines associated with the "parent" role when the family lives in the same household are no longer applicable when the parent lives in a separate location. Again, there are few models on which to base behavior. As a result, parents may experience anxiety about how to be an effective NRP (Shapiro & Lambert, 1999). NRPs may also experience a form of role loss. NRPs retain the status of parent while living in a separate household, but they are unable to perform many of the activities, duties, and ways of interacting associated with being a parent (Ihinger-Tallman, Pasley, & Buehler, 1995).

Role ambiguity or inability to fully enact the parental role has several consequences for the NRP–child relationship. First, it affects the *form* of the NRP–child relationship. Because NRPs are unable to fully enact the socially prescribed parent role, they must redefine or modify the traditional parent role to better fit within the structural and social constraints of their nonresidential status. As a result, postdivorce parenting styles differ greatly (Seltzer, 1991). The NRP may find that he or she may not act as a parent at all, but may define the relationship more as a friend or peer relationship (Furstenberg & Nord, 1985; Seltzer, 1991).

This, in turn, affects how NRPs interact with their children. As noted earlier, research indicates that authoritative parenting involving reasoning, monitoring, and consistent discipline is associated with better child outcomes (Amato & Gilbreth, 1999; Simons et al., 1994). However, degrees of structural constraints affect levels of difficulty for NRPs to engage in authoritative parenting. That is, the less often parents see their children, the more difficult it is to provide discipline, or help with homework, and to engage in other authoritative parenting practices. As a result, both nonresidential mothers and fathers are more likely to engage in leisure activities than routine day-to-day behaviors such as helping with homework, thus promoting the stereotype of "Disneyland Dad" (Furstenberg & Nord, 1985; Stewart, 1999a; Wilbur & Wilbur, 1988). Some NRPs fear that they may do something that will cause their children to not want to spend time with them. Thus, engaging in fun activities and avoiding discipline is a method of trying to preserve a fragile relationship (Lund, 1987).

NRPs' perceptions of and investment in the parent role also influence *involvement* with their children. Ihinger-Tallman et al. (1995) draw on identity theory to account for NRPs' reduced levels of involvement following separation. They argue that "the change in identity that accompanies the loss of daily interaction with a child is responsible for the extent to which an absent father stays involved (or becomes more or less involved) with his child" (p. 76). Consequently, if the parent role continues to be particularly salient and the NRP remains invested and committed in the role, the NRP is more likely to continue to be involved with the children. A key element to continued interaction is the NRPs' continued identification with the parent role. This may be particularly difficult for NRPs who may feel anxiety about not residing in the home or who feel they have essentially lost their parent role.

Finally, role ambiguity influences NRPs' perceptions of self and overall mental well-being as well. The benefits of fatherhood diminish significantly when fathers do not live with their biological children. Eggebeen and Knoester (2001) found that "once men step away from coresidence, the transforming power of father dissipates" (p. 391). Specifically, because the NRP role is ambiguous, many NRPs perceive lowered levels of competence and self-efficacy in enacting the parent role (Minton & Pasley, 1996; Nomaguchi & Milkie, 2003). They also report less satisfaction with being a parent than coresident parents do (Minton & Pasley, 1996). Negative feelings about being a NRP can further reduce NRPs' sense of competence and satisfaction. Because competence, satisfaction, and investment in the father role are positively related to interaction with their children, NRPs' feelings of inadequacy may lead to reduced or discontinued involvement with their children. For example, Greif (1997) found that feelings of inadequacy are sufficient to lead parents to completely terminate contact with their children. He explains that many NRPs believe that they are no longer important in the lives of their children. He notes, "Some fathers who drop out feel unneeded and ashamed if their role as breadwinner has been overemphasized to the diminution of their role as nurturer" (p. 38).

The Parental Relationship

The nature of the relationship between parents can have a direct impact on the parent–child relationship in a number of ways (Hetherington & Stanley-Hagan, 1997). Many postseparation parents engage in parallel parenting, that is, engaging in parenting practices without coordination with or regard for the other parent's practices. However, parents' ability (or inability) to work together, share information, put the needs of the child before their own, manage conflict, and coordinate schedules has a significant impact on both NRP–child involvement and child outcomes. For example, Argys et al. (1998) found that when parents have cooperative relationships, the NRP is more likely to pay child support voluntarily (i.e., without a court order). In cooperative situations, fathers may even make payments and offer other forms of financial support when they are not legally obligated to do so. The voluntary payment of child support and the presence of a cooperative relationship between parents are associated with positive cognitive outcomes for children, such as improved test scores (Argys et al., 1998).

The postseparation parental relationship can take many forms. Ahrons (1994) identified five different types of postdivorce relationships that have implications for both parents and children. In the first two categories, *Perfect Pals* and *Cooperative Colleagues*, parents continue relationships following the divorce that facilitate positive parent–child relations. These postdivorce parental relationships focus on building a functional binuclear family, a family that exists across two households in which both parents actively continue to engage in parenting practices (e.g., providing financial, emotional, and psychological support; discipline; and moral guidance). *Perfect Pals* remain good friends following the divorce. Ahrons notes that these uncoupled parents continue to be interested in each other's lives and communicate weekly. They function well as a binuclear family and typically continue to be involved in each other's extended families. They work well together as parents, sharing custody and decision making equally. Unlike *Perfect Pals*, *Cooperative Colleagues* do not consider themselves good friends, yet they cooperate on issues relating to the children. These ex-spouses are able to separate their failed marriage from their responsibilities as parents. Although the custody agreements and amount of contact between these parents differ, both parents see the children regularly and view maintaining the parent–child relationship as a priority.

In contrast, *Angry Associates* and *Fiery Foes* engage in troubled, conflictual relationships that often have negative consequences for the children. Although *Cooperative Colleagues* are able to compartmentalize their feelings about the failed relationship, *Angry Associates* are unable to contain their anger and frustration with the other parent. As a result, although these ex-spouses communicate regularly, often about the children, the communication typically deteriorates quickly into conflict. Customarily, mothers have sole custody of the children, leaving fathers to negotiate visitation. For *Fiery Foes*, hostility directly interferes with individuals' abilities to parent. These ex-spouses rarely communicate and are often unable to negotiate satisfactory living or visitation arrangements, sometimes leading to sequential custody battles. However, some *Fiery Foes* are able to formalize visitation despite their inability to communicate civilly.

The final category, *Dissolved Duos*, represents the stereotypical "absent" parent arrangement. Rather than moving to a binuclear family, these ex-spouses discontinue contact completely. Often one of the parents separates geographically from the other and one parent, typically the father, completely withdraws from interaction with both the former spouse and the child(ren).

Postdivorce relationships have also been categorized based on levels of commitment between the former spouses. In drawing on Ahrons' (1994) work and her research on postdivorce relationships, Masheter

(1999) discusses five different commitment levels between ex-spouses, each of which affects parenting in different ways. When individuals have *no commitment*, the spouses have little or no interaction. The divorce leads to a complete termination of the relationship in which individuals have no need or desire to continue interaction following divorce. Masheter notes that frequently this lack of commitment to the former spouse translates into lack of commitment to one's children, particularly for fathers. This may be a product of lack of commitment prior to divorce, alienation following divorce due to difficulties associated with maintaining the relationship, or for some other reason. In some cases, parents experience "confusion" between commitments to the ex-spouse and commitments to their children. When this occurs, the parent may or may not continue commitment to children based on the relationship with the former spouse. For example, visitation or child support may depend on the relationship with the ex-spouse rather than on the desired level of commitment to the children.

Some ex-spouses engage in what Masheter (1999) calls *negative commitment*. Here individuals continue to engage in and promote dysfunctional involvement with the ex-spouse. Often this interaction is in the form of conflict, hostility, or power struggles. Children may be "triangulated" and so placed as the center of this involvement as when parents engage in repeated battles over custody. Children may also suffer when parents are unable to separate their feelings about their former spouse from their parental relationship with the child. This may lead to demonization of the other parent and can complicate efforts to negotiate parenting. Occasionally negative commitment emerges in the form of dependence on the ex-spouse. Here individuals are unable to fully establish themselves as independent parents.

As with Ahrons' Cooperative Colleagues, ex-spouses with *coparental commitment* are able to effectively separate their commitment as parents from their lack of commitment to each other as individuals. Both parents recognize that it is important that each is actively involved in parenting and each works to create an environment in which this is possible. Similarly, ex-spouses may redefine their relationship following divorce as friends or extended family members. Here ex-spouses have commitment to both the children and each other. They communicate regularly to fulfill both individual and parental needs.

Finally, unlike Ahrons, Masheter recognizes that ex-spouses do not always agree about their postdivorce relationships. *Discrepant commitment* occurs when ex-spouses desire different types of relationships or levels of involvement with each other. Ex-spouses may also differ in their definitions or meanings associated with commitment as a friend or co-parent. Masheter notes that inability to establish or negotiate a satisfactory relationship often leads to no commitment by one or both parents and to an eventual termination of the relationship as a whole. As noted earlier, this often leads to termination of the NRP–child relationship as well.

As is apparent in the above relational types, conflict, in some form, is present in many postseparation parental relationships. For example, payment of child support is often a source of conflict between the NRP and the residential parent, even when the relationship is good (Wright & Price, 1986). Often both residential parents and NRPs are dissatisfied with child support arrangements. Residential parents find the amount inadequate; NRPs find it financially burdensome (Lund 1987). Another point of conflict is custody and visitation. In general, mothers tend to be satisfied with the nonresidential father's involvement with the children (King & Heard, 1999). However, in some cases residential parents do not want the NRP to be involved in the children's lives. This can pose a problem when NRPs express a desire to see their children regularly. Many NRPs are at least somewhat dissatisfied with custody and visitation arrangements (Wright & Price, 1986).

Yet, it is not the presence of conflict that is problematic. Instead, it is the way that parents manage the conflict that affects child outcomes. When parents are able to cooperate and work together despite occasional conflict, children adjust well (Ihinger-Tallman et al., 1995; Lund, 1987). Conversely, negative forms of conflict involving competition or hostility can have adverse effects on child adjustment and well-being. Direct or indirect coparental competition can create a negative environment for children (Ihinger-Tallman et al., 1995). Children may feel frustrated or upset with parental conflict, especially when they feel caught in the middle (Simons et al., 1994). Sometimes anger, frustration, or resentment associated with the relational breakup emerges as overt hostility in parental interactions. When this is the case, the NRP may actively avoid interaction with the children's custodial parent, contributing to decreased visitation. In some cases, parents may find it easier to terminate visits to children than to continue the relationship under highly negative emotional circumstances (Lund, 1987).

Gatekeeping is another relational process that can have an impact on the NRP–child relationship. The marital partnership has been identified as a "port of entry" for fathers (Fox & Bruce, 1999). Some researchers argue that men's roles as fathers are greatly facilitated or hampered by the mother, particularly when the children are young. The quality of the relationship has an even greater impact on the father role when the parents are separated. When mothers act as gatekeepers, they can greatly influence the frequency and nature of contact between NRPs and their children (Minton & Pasley, 1996). Seltzer & Brandreth (1994) found that residential parents tend to orchestrate the NRP–child relationship by controlling schedules and constructing guidelines for NRP–child involvement. They often have the ability to manage the frequency, length, and conditions of NRP visits. Efforts to coordinate contact may be "circumscribed by mothers who prefer to avoid their former spouse or who are busy juggling the demands of paid employment and family responsibilities" (Seltzer & Brandreth, 1994, p. 73). Greif (1997) found that in some cases, residential parents actively blocked NRP involvement by accusing (sometimes correctly, sometimes falsely) the NRP of violence and/or abuse. In some cases, the accusations were (at least in the NRP's eyes) either completely false or very exaggerated. In other cases, NRPs admitted they had a problem, for example, with alcohol, but felt that the problem was used as a means to keep the parent from the child (rather than working with the problem).

The residential parent can also act as an information gatekeeper. Custodial parents are empowered to make the majority of decisions regarding children (Meyer & Garasky, 1993). Even when parents share custody, they do not always share equally in making decisions about the children. NRPs often have few opportunities for involvement in this capacity (Furstenberg & Nord, 1985; Wilbur & Wilbur, 1988). As a result, NRPs must rely on the custodial parent for information about their children's lives (Furstenberg & Nord, 1985). However, resident parents report that they have few discussions about childrearing with the NRP. Lack of information also makes it difficult for the NRP to maintain a relationship with the child. Additionally, to the extent that they are not given this information, NRPs cannot participate in decisions about the child (Wilbur & Wilbur, 1988). NRPs may actively disagree with decisions that have been made and may become angry and frustrated at their lack of input and influence.

Other Constraints

The constraints just described have received considerable attention in the literature. Structural changes, role loss, role ambiguity, and parental relationships all have a significant impact on the construction and maintenance of the NRP–child relationship. However, several other factors also influence the NRP–child relationship but have received less attention by researchers.

Financial Constraints.   The nonresidential status is associated with financial barriers as well. NRPs typically assume the financial and time costs associated with obtaining and transporting children during visits. As a result, NRPs who struggle financially and are unable to finance the cost of seeing their children are less likely to be involved in their children's lives (Cooksey & Craig, 1998; Seltzer, 1991; Stewart, 1999b). NRPs may also experience difficulties associated with paying child support (Meyer, 1999; Seltzer, 1991; Wilbur & Wilbur, 1988). Like single mothers, many NRPs, especially those who were never married, struggle to survive financially on their own. As a result, they may be unable to pay the amount of child support ordered (Meyer, 1999). In some cases, NRPs are not able to see their children if they are not paying child support. The payment of child support may be used as leverage by the custodial parent to control and shape the NRP–child relationship

(Pasely & Minton, 1997; Wilbur & Wilbur, 1988). This is particularly problematic for parents who either are unable to support two households or disagree with the way in which the custodial parent uses the money (Seltzer, 1991).

Social Network.   Network members can also have an influence on the NRP–child relationship. For those who become NRPs through divorce or relationship breakup, there is often a change in network structure. Most individuals' social networks decrease as a result of divorce (Terhell, Broese van Groenou, & van Tilburg, 2004). As a result, NRPs may not have the same financial, psychological, and emotional support they had before the divorce or breakup.

Network members' attitudes and beliefs are also important. Because identities are developed and presented through interaction with others, members of the social network can affect how an individual perceives a particular identity and the way that he or she enacts it (Ihinger-Tallman et al., 1995). Nonresident parents are more likely to maintain the NRP–child relationship when network members support and encourage their involvement in the relationship. Conversely, network members can negatively affect the NRP–child relationship if they are unsupportive or if they discourage NRP involvement. As a result, NRPs may feel less motivated to maintain active relationships with their children.

NRP–Child Relationship.   Although the burden to maintain the NRP–child relationship may fall primarily on the NRP, the child also influences the interaction. NRPs who have poor relationships with their children before separation are less likely to maintain a relationship with their child afterward in absence (Lamb, 1999). Greif (1997) reports that some NRPs who have discontinued contact with their biological children have done so because their children have either refused to see them or because the relationship between the NRP and child is so weak that it proves difficult to maintain. In some cases, the NRP asserts that the residential parent has in essence brainwashed or "poisoned" the child against him or her (Greif, 1997; Johnston, 1993). In these cases, residential parents essentially secure their relationship with their children by focusing on the negative aspects of the NRP (e.g., drinking, hostility). This is more likely to occur when there is overt hostility between the parents. The children, who feel caught in the middle, generally align with one parent (Johnston, 1993). When NRPs feel rejected or are particularly insecure about the NRP–child relationship, they may further stress the NRP–child relationship by countering the residential parent's attacks and/or actively pursuing the child through phone calls and unexpected visits (Johnston, 1993).

Individual Factors.   Finally, it is essential to recognize that NRPs can play an active role in maintaining the relationship. Because they face a number of barriers, NRPs have to be motivated to maintain the NRP–child relationship. Overcoming the constraints of distance takes work and commitment (Lund, 1987). Greif (1997) estimates that 10% to 15% of NRPs lack either the capacity or the desire to maintain a relationship with their children. Elements such as the NRP's emotional stability, financial stability, attitude toward parenthood, desire to maintain the relationship, and commitment to the parent role all have an impact on the NRP's ability and likelihood of maintaining the NRP–child relationship (Ihinger-Tallman et al., 1995). In general, NRPs with more education and higher incomes are more likely to maintain the NRP–child relationship.

DISCUSSION

As this book clearly illustrates, difficulty comes in many forms and from many sources. This chapter is partly an effort to define difficulty in terms of barriers and challenges that must be overcome. In this sense, what is particularly interesting about the NRP–child relationship is the overwhelming abundance and complexity of difficulty present. These barriers and challenges emerge at a number of different levels from a variety of sources—structural, individual, and social—and are interconnected in many ways.

At the most basic level, the NRP–child relationship faces a number of challenges as a result of its structure. In fact, all other barriers to maintaining the NRP–child relationship emerge to some extent as a result of the material structure of daily life. This structure influences both the form of the relationship and the nature of the interaction between NRPs and their children. When parents live in two different households, each parent's time with his or her children is limited. However, fully enacting the parent role requires day-to-day presence. It is very difficult to be an effective moral developer, disciplinarian, teacher, caretaker, or protector when interacting with a child two weekends a month. Even when time with the child is split evenly between the two parents, time spent by either parent with the child is always constrained to some extent by (expectations of) absence. Parents must find ways to pick up where they left off the previous week and be prepared to discontinue interaction at the designated "cut-off" time.

Consequently, many NRPs are forced to modify the parent role into something that accommodates the structural constraints, such as friendship. When this occurs, NRPs often face criticism for being "Disneyland Dads/Moms," who are focused on entertaining rather than disciplining and guiding children. Role loss associated with change in the parent status is particularly prevalent for NRPs. Other forms of loss also emerge, including emotional loss connected with seeing loved ones less often and loss of routines and rituals that form the basis of life where a parent lives with one's children.

In addition to splitting time, the structure of the NRP–child relationship brings with it other difficulties. Regardless of the extent to which they are able to see their children, NRPs are typically responsible for parenting financially. Because many NRPs are fathers, this should seem to be a natural extension of the provider role. Yet NRPs have little to no control of how the money is spent or whether it is used for the child. Some parents refuse to pay, and many others feel that they are simply unable to do so. NRPs are also often responsible for time and costs associated with visitation arrangements. When NRPs live far away from their children, the distance becomes prohibitive.

The NRP–child relationship also faces both broad and localized social constraints. At the social-cultural level, the NRP–child relationship suffers from ambiguity. No clear rules and norms for being a successful NRP exist. More often than not, media focus on the images of absent parents and "Disneyland" dads, neither of which is a positive role model for struggling fathers. NRPs' social networks may also lack models of nonresidential parenting, or parenting at all. It may be particularly difficult for young, never-married NRPs to prioritize the father relationship when few members of the social network share in that role. Conversely, when NRPs have a supportive social network, it becomes easier for parents to remain committed to maintaining a supportive relationship with their children.

Most immediately, NRPs may face social and structural constraints at the hands of the residential parent. Custodial parents often act as gatekeepers to the children. They frequently control the flow of information between NRPs and their children when they are apart. They may or may not share information about important events such as parent-teacher conferences or include the NRP in important decisions about the child. Custodial parents also have opportunities to influence the frequency and nature of contact between NRPs and their children. Consequently, NRPs must successfully negotiate their relationships with their children through their relationship to the residential parent. When NRPs have a positive or cooperative relationship with the residential parent, this task is relatively easy. However, when NRPs experience anger, hurt, guilt, or hostility toward (or from) the other parent, the barrier can become almost insurmountable.

Finally, difficulty comes from within. Individual circumstances, background, education, income, and emotional well-being all influence the NRP's ability to maintain the relationship over time. Individual motivation, attitudes, determination, and commitment to parent are all necessary to overcome structural and social obstacles. Individual constraints may emerge from the child as well. Although it occurs infrequently, some children refuse visitation. This is often the result of alignment with one parent against the NRP. Circumstances have made it such that the NRP is viewed as a negative or unhealthy influence.

Particularly troublesome for NRP–child relationships is that all of these barriers and constraints are interconnected. The pragmatic difficulties of maintaining the NRP–child relationship associated with the structural issues of visitation, separate households, and child support are intimately connected with the individual psychological difficulties of being an NRP. Taken together, they affect the shape of the NRP–child relationship in both content and form. As in all relationships, communication is central to the vitality of the NRP–child relationship. The nature, content, form, and frequency of interaction between custodial parents, NRPs, and their children function to shape the NRP–child relationship.

Unfortunately, in focusing on relationship difficulty, it is easy to get lost in negativity and to concentrate only on the dark side of these relationships. Yet, the encouraging thing about difficulty, as opposed to impossibility, is that it can be overcome. It urges readers to look for success stories, find what works, and to promote those aspects of relationships. Many NRPs are successfully maintaining strong, positive, rich relationships with their children. Consequently, this chapter speaks to the resiliency of the human spirit and the strength and importance of the parent–child bond.

REFERENCES

Ahrons, C. (1994). *The good divorce.* New York: HarperCollins.

Amato, P. R., & Gilbreth, J. G. (1999). Nonresident fathers and children's well-being: A meta-analysis. *Journal of Marriage and the Family, 61*, 557–573.

Argys, L. M., Peters, H. E., Brooks–Gunn, J., & Smith, J. R. (1998). The impact of child support on cognitive outcomes of young children. *Demography, 35*, 159–173.

Atkinson, M. P., & Blackwelder, S. P. (1993). Fathering in the 20th century. *Journal of Marriage and the Family, 55*, 975–986.

Cooksey, E. C., & Craig, P. H. (1998). Parenting from a distance: The effect of paternal characteristics on contact between nonresidential fathers and their children. *Demography, 35*, 187–200.

Daly, K. J. (1995). Reshaping fatherhood. In W. Marsiglio (Ed.), *Fatherhood: Contemporary theory, research, and social policy* (pp. 21–40). Thousand Oaks, CA: Sage.

Doherty, W. J., Kouneski, E. F., & Erickson, M. F. (1998). Responsible fathering: An overview and conceptual framework. *Journal of Marriage and the Family, 60*, 277–292.

Eggebeen, D. J., & Knoester, C. (2001). Does fatherhood matter for men? *Journal of Marriage and Family, 63*, 381–393.

Fox, G. L., & Bruce, C. (1999). The anticipation of single parenthood: A profile of men's concerns. *Journal of Family Issues, 20*(4), 485–506.

Furstenberg, F. F., Jr., Morgan, S. P., & Allison, P. D. (1987). Paternal participation and children's well-being after marital dissolution. *American Sociological Review, 52*, 695–701.

Furstenberg, F. F., Jr., & Nord, C. W. (1985). Parenting apart: Patterns of child rearing after marital disruption. *Journal of Marriage and the Family, 47*, 893–905.

Greif, G. L. (1986). Mothers without custody and child support. *Family Relations, 35*, 87–93.

Greif, G. L. (1997). *Out of touch*. New York: Oxford University Press.

Hagestad, G. O., & Smyer, M. A. (1982). Dissolving long-term relationships: Patterns of divorcing in middle age. In S. Duck (Ed.), *Dissolving personal relationships* (pp. 155–187). London: Academic Press.

Hetherington, E. M., & Stanley-Hagan, M. M. (1997). The effects of divorce on fathers and their children. In M. E. Lamb (Ed.), *The role of the father in child development* (3rd ed., pp. 33–48). New York: Wiley.

Ihinger-Tallman, M., Pasley, P., & Buehler, C. (1995). Developing a middle-range theory of father involvement postdivorce. In W. Marsiglio (Ed.), *Fatherhood: Contemporary theory, research, and social policy* (pp. 57–77). Thousand Oaks, CA: Sage.

Johnston, J. R. (1993). Children of divorce who refuse visitation. In C. E. Depner & J. H. Bray (Eds.), *Nonresidential parenting: New vistas in family living* (pp. 109–135). Newbury Park, CA: Sage.

King, V. (1994). Nonresident father involvement and child well-being: Can dads make a difference? *Journal of Family Issues, 15,* 78–96.

King, V., & Heard, H. E. (1999). Nonresident father visitation, parental conflict, and mother's satisfaction: What's best for child well-being? *Journal of Marriage and the Family, 61,* 358–396.

Lamb, M. E. (1999). Noncustodial fathers and their impact on the children of divorce. In R. A. Thompson & P. R. Amato (Eds.), *The postdivorce family: Children, parenting, & society* (pp. 105–126). Thousand Oaks, CA: Sage.

Lund, M. (1987). The noncustodial father: Common challenges in parenting after divorce. In C. Lewis & M. O'Brien (Eds.), *Reassessing fatherhood* (pp. 212–224). London: Sage.

Lupton, D., & Barclay, L. (1997). *Constructing fatherhood: Discourses and experiences*. London: Sage.

Marsiglio, W., Amato, P., Day, R. D., & Lamb, M. E. (2000). Scholarship on fatherhood in the 1990s and beyond. *Journal of Marriage and the Family, 62,* 1173–1191.

Masheter, C. (1999). Examples of commitment in postdivorce relationships between ex-spouses. In J. M. Adams & S. H. Jones (Eds.), *Handbook of interpersonal commitment & relationship stability* (pp. 293–306). New York: Kluwer Academics/Plenum.

Meyer, D. R. (1999). Compliance with child support orders in paternity and divorce cases. In R. A. Thompson & P. R. Amato (Eds.), *The postdivorce family: Children, parenting, & society* (pp. 127–158). Thousand Oaks, CA: Sage.

Meyer, D. R., & Garasky, S. (1993). Custodial fathers: Myths, realities, and child support policy. *Journal of Marriage and the Family, 55,* 73–89.

Minton, C., & Pasley, K. (1996). Fathers' parenting role identity and father involvement: A comparison of nondivorced and divorced, nonresident fathers. *Journal of Family Issues, 17,* 26–45.

Nomaguchi, K. M., & Milkie, M. A. (2003). Costs and rewards of children: The effects of becoming a parent on adults' lives. *Journal of Marriage and Family, 65,* 356–374.

Pasley, K., & Minton, C. (1997). Generative fathering after divorce and remarriage: Beyond the "disappearing dad." In A. J. Hawkins & D. C. Dollahite (Eds.), *Generative fathering: Beyond deficit perspectives* (pp. 118–133). Thousand Oaks, CA: Sage.

Pleck, E. H., & Pleck, J. H. (1997). Fatherhood ideals in the United States: Historical dimensions. In M. E. Lamb (Ed.), *The role of the father in child development* (3rd ed., pp. 191–211). New York: Wiley.

Seltzer, J. A. (1991). Relationships between fathers and children who live apart: The father's role after separation. *Journal of Marriage and the Family, 53,* 79–101.

Seltzer, J. A. (1998). Father by law: Effects of joint legal custody on nonresident fathers' involvement with children. *Demography, 35,* 135–146.

Seltzer, J. A., & Bianchi, S. M. (1988). Children's contact with absent parents. *Journal of Marriage and the Family, 50,* 663–677.

Seltzer, J. A., & Brandreth, Y. (1994). What fathers say about involvement with children after separation. *Journal of Family Issues, 15,* 49–77.

Shapiro, A., & Lambert, J. D. (1999). Longitudinal effects of divorce on the quality of the father-child relationship and on fathers' psychological well-being. *Journal of Marriage and the Family, 61,* 397–408.

Simons, R. L., Whitbeck, L. B., Beaman, J., & Conger, R. D. (1994). The impact of mothers' parenting, involvement by nonresidential fathers, and parental conflict on the adjustment of adolescent children. *Journal of Marriage and the Family, 56,* 356–374.

Sorensen, E. (1997). A national profile of nonresident fathers and their ability to pay child support. *Journal of Marriage and the Family, 59,* 785–797.

Stewart, S. D. (1999a). Disneyland dads, Disneyland moms? How nonresidential parents spend time with absent children. *Journal of Family Issues, 20*(4), 539–556.

Stewart, S. D. (1999b). Nonresident mothers' and fathers' social contact with children. *Journal of Marriage and the Family, 61,* 894–907.

Stueve, J. L., & Pleck, J. H. (2001). "Parenting voices": Solo parent identity and co-parent identities in married parents' narratives of meaningful parenting experiences. *Journal of Social and Personal Relationships, 18,* 691–708.

Teachman, J. D., Tedrow, L. M., & Crowder, K. D. (2000). The changing demography of America's families. *Journal of Marriage and the Family,62,* 1234–1246.

Terhell, E. L., Broese van Groenou, M. I., & van Tilburg, T. (2004). Network dynamics in the long-term period after divorce. *Journal of Social and Personal Relationships, 21,* 719–738.

Wallerstein, J., Lewis, J., & Blakeslee, S. (2000). *The unexpected legacy of divorce: A 25 year landmark study.* New York: Hyperion.

Wilbur, J., & Wilbur, M. (1988). The noncustodial parent: Dilemmas and interventions. *Journal of Counseling and Development, 66,* 434–437.

Wright, D. W., & Price, S. J. (1986). Court ordered child support payment: The effect of the former-spouse relationship on compliance. *Journal of Marriage and the Family, 48,* 869–874.

Chapter 11

Difficult Relationships and Relationship Difficulties: Relationship Adaptation and Chronic Health Problems

Renee Lyons
Lynn Langille
Dalhousie University

Steve Duck
University of Iowa

> I thought, well, this is pretty scary, like, who the hell am I and who is my wife and what is our relationship? Who are my children and what is our relationship?
>
> (Toronto Prostate Cancer Focus Group)

For the past 25 years there has been considerable research conducted on the importance of good relations and social support in dealing with traumatic life events such as serious illness, as well as the role of relationships in health and illness (Schmaling, 1997). However, acquiring a serious health problem, in itself, poses considerable difficulties in sustaining quality relationships–difficulties in relationship adaptation that few of us expect or are skilled in addressing. For many years, we have studied the difficulties in dealing with relationships where one person has a chronic illness, and how people confront them (Lyons, Sullivan, Ritvo, & Coyne, 1995). This chapter describes our conclusions based on the results of a recent Canada-U.S. study that has helped to clarify relationship issues in the context of chronic health problems.

Although the difficulties of managing such relationships are somewhat specific to the illness, they nevertheless illustrate this book's broad purpose in clarifying the nature of relational difficulty more

generally. Accordingly we provide a short description of the study purpose and approach, and then spend the rest of the chapter focusing on
conclusions that identify and synthesize the menu of illness-related relationship difficulties and determinants. Our main focus will be to
identify the general features of relationship difficulties which are created for relationships, citing findings but also providing accounts from
our respondents.

WHY STUDY ILLNESS AND RELATIONSHIPS?

The World Health Organization defines chronic conditions as "health
problems that require ongoing management over a period of years or
decades" and reports that "the disease burden will increase to 60% by
the year 2020" (World Health Organization, 2004). Heart disease,
stroke, cancer, and mental illness are major contributors, although the
illnesses that affect the proper functioning of relationships take many
different forms, and the consequences of illness may be subtle as well as
obvious. Somewhat paradoxically, medical advances are a contributor
to relationship difficulties. As medical advances increase life expec-
tancy, our relational worlds are increasingly impacted by living longer
with chronic illness and disability. The probability that one partner in a
long-term relationship will develop a chronic illness is correspondingly
quite high. An aging population demographic also exacerbates the likelihood of illness affecting a relationship.

In their book, *Relationships in Chronic Illness and Disability*, Lyons et
al. (1995) provide a comprehensive review of studies on the relationship
impacts of illness. They indicate that the difficulties do not just arise
within couples and families, but also stem from relationships with
health professionals, coworkers, and in the community—one's social
world. In fact, many people with health problems often leave work (and
financial independence) as a function of being unable to negotiate workplace relationships. Poor psychosocial and functional outcomes of illness and disability have been tied to relational difficulties, including
chronic loneliness, social isolation, and a lack of social support (Gottlieb,
1981; Schreurs & deRidder, 1997). Thus, the impacts of illness have
many ramifications.

As suggested in chapter 1 of this book, relationships with people can
be difficult irrespective of the characteristics of individuals or the type of
relationship, the *situation* being the prime contributor. How does illness
function as a situational factor in relationships? The perspective given
at the beginning of the chapter by a man with prostate cancer echoes the
fact that serious health problems constitute one of life's most difficult
adaptive challenges, often forcing individuals to redefine themselves
and their relationships: In short, illness affects personal identity as well
as the functioning of an intimate relationship between two people. Although findings from studies of chronic illness and relationships are im-

portant in and of themselves, relational difficulties or adaptive challenges exist for other life–altering circumstances as well, such as divorce, war, or natural disasters. In the social sciences, these studies are typically classified as the study of "negative life events." Taken together, researchers who study life events and relationship difficulties can provide important theoretical and practical insights into how people cope with, repair, or exacerbate any kind of relationship difficulties. This research can also contribute to constructing the role that health and social service systems could play in softening the relational and personal impacts of illness (Fisher & Weihs, 2000).

INTRODUCTION TO THE STUDY "SOCIAL INTEGRATION, ILLNESS AND DISABILITY: CLARIFICATION OF RELATIONSHIP ISSUES IN FAMILY, WORK AND COMMUNITY"

In order to provide a context for our discussion, it is necessary for the reader to have a general understanding of the manner in which our results were derived. However, since this chapter is not appearing in an empirical journal, our description of the work will be somewhat cursory.

The purpose of this 2–year study, funded by the Social Sciences and Humanities Research Council of Canada, was to identify relationship difficulties that occur because of chronic illness and disability and to consider potential strategies that would ease the burden of these difficulties. The research team was composed of relationship researchers, psychology researcher/clinicians who study relationships difficulties, people with health problems, and hospital and community agency partners.[1] Findings from the study cast considerable light on the complexity of factors involved in defining and addressing relationship issues in disability and illness. Findings also provided the basis for the development of a "Relationships Menu," which lists key words and phrases describing the impacts of illness and disability on people and their social worlds.

In contrast to quantitative measures (e.g., attachment and loneliness scales), which provide scores on predetermined items, the qualitative structure of the Relationships Menu permitted individuals and groups to select relevant issues, define relevant social contexts and relationships, identify their preparedness to address them, and develop strategies if they wished to do so. The use of the Relationships Menu provided for several outcomes that potentially positively impact relationships: telling one's story, clarifying issues, communicating about issues, identifying strategies for addressing specific issues and sharing strategies with others. Outcomes included increased attention to relationship issues, selection and clarification of key issues, assessment of readiness to act on relationship problems, initiation of discussion with others, opportunities for receiving and providing support, selection of strategies to address identified issues, and potential actions formulated as a result of using the Relationships Menu.

Co-investigators provided content expertise and facilitated the recruitment process in each community. Focus groups were conducted in six locations in Canada (Halifax, Ottawa, and Toronto) and the United States (Cleveland, Iowa City, and Ann Arbor) with two types of participants: (1) researchers and clinicians who study personal relationships and who encounter relationship issues in their work and (2) people with a chronic health problem/disability.

Participants in the latter groups were selected by co-investigators in each study location, mainly from clinical contacts and associations with disability/illness-related organizations. The focus groups included adults with primarily acquired disabilities/illnesses. Specific target populations were persons with multiple sclerosis (MS), cancer, spinal injury, and stroke, which represented a range of physical illness and disability (e.g., stable, degenerate, various symptoms and treatments).

The illness/disability group was almost equally divided by sex/gender. About two thirds of the group members were married with the others being single, divorced, or widowed. The mean age of participants was 49 with a range from 28 to 82 years. The researcher/clinician group consisted of people from a variety of academic and clinical backgrounds, including psychology, communications, human development, leisure studies, social work, sociology, nursing, rehabilitation, geriatrics, counseling, social support, and mental health. About two thirds of the group had either a doctorate or a master's degree, and all were working in areas relevant to disability, chronic illness, or relationships.

The Relationships Menu (initial taxonomy of relationship issues and disability/illness contexts and challenges) was developed on the basis of both literature and research. The Menu was designed to facilitate thinking about the impact of the health condition on psychosocial and physical functioning, on lifestyle, and on relationships. It provided a preliminary framework for organizing relationship issues. It also translated concepts into a language that researchers, clinicians, and the lay public could mutually understand.

Discussions in the focus groups were initiated by asking the question, "When you think about the impact of illness or disability on relationships, what is the first thing that comes to mind?". Participants were invited to discuss relationship issues they had experienced in family, work, and community. Lively, reflective and insightful discussions took place in all the focus groups. A structured review of the Relationships Menu (e.g., inclusiveness, format, and terminology) was followed by general discussion.

The focus groups were tape recorded and transcribed. Content analysis of the transcripts was guided by the literature on relationships and chronic illness/disability, the Relationships Menu, and a conceptual framework developed for the study that included the illness and its impacts on self and relationships, and the specific relational issues being addressed. Sixteen focus groups were held involving 63 people with a chronic illness or disability and 32 researchers and clinicians.

The text of transcripts was coded for key themes. *Ethnograph*, a computer software package for the analysis of qualitative data, was used to organize the text. Following the data analysis, a 3-day meeting of the co-investigators was held to examine the analysis and to reach consensus on the findings and study conclusions.

FINDINGS RELATED TO ILLNESS AND RELATIONSHIP DIFFICULTIES

In the sections that follow, we examine some of the key findings from the "Social Integration" study on relationship difficulties in the context of illness, and their determinants. Findings are presented to demonstrate the similarity in relationship difficulties across a broad spectrum of illnesses and across the social contexts of family, friendships, work, and leisure. Six persistent factors related to relationships and relationship adaptation are presented, followed by suggestions for improving the responses of health professionals and health systems to help people address the impacts of illness and disability on relationships. Throughout the chapter, verbatim quotes from the study are included to highlight key themes and perspectives. Identifiers in brackets following the quotes indicate the location where the focus group took place and whether focus group participants were people with illnesses/disabilities or health researchers/clinicians.

Relationship Maintenance as a Primary Adaptive Task

> In terms of my practice, I guess one of the basic observations that I make is that once a family is touched significantly by illness and disability, their trajectories are altered perhaps for the full course of their family life. There is not really this question of being affected and then overcoming it, or adapting to it, and getting back to 'normal'. There isn't such a thing. (Toronto Researcher/Clinician Focus Group)

Both sets of focus groups (persons with illness/disability and researchers/clinicians) called attention to the increased pressures on relationships as a result of illness or disability. Indeed, one of the catastrophic effects of long-term illness or disability in a relationship is the need to adjust to its permanence. In those with illness or disability, the maintenance of quality relationships (family, friendships, work, and leisure) is a major challenge involving considerable resources to negotiate communication, activity adaptation, and support. This responsibility too often falls primarily on the shoulders of the people with the illness/disability. Neither they nor friends, family, or coworkers have sufficient resources (whether in the form of information, social skills, or support) or energy, it seems, to take on this task. All too often those people in the network of the person who is ill or disabled quite simply fail to recognize the comprehensive effects of a diagnosis on the personal and social life of the person involved.

> We all seem to take that guilt onto us. That we are responsible for this and we are the ones who have to find the solution. And lots of times we can't. And this, I think, makes us both angry and frustrated. (Toronto Breast Cancer Focus Group)

> There just comes a time when you say, 'Okay, I've seen enough of you people, go home'. Your fatigue has hit a point where you don't want to be sociable anymore. I don't want to put a strain on a relationship, but it (fatigue) will always affect a relationship with your family and spouse. (Cleveland MS Focus Group)

Although now there are somewhat greater resources for addressing these issues, many of the anticipated and actual relationship problems arising from disability/illness appear to be preventable. When they are not preventable, the stress of interaction could be substantially reduced.

Similarities Across a Broad Spectrum of Illnesses and Disabilities

At first glance, one might assume that different illnesses or disabilities create different stresses for the individuals involved. However, although this may be true in the physical domain, in the domain of relational difficulties, it appears that there are more similarities than differences. Our focus groups showed remarkable consistency despite the fact that they dealt with different disabilities and illnesses, although there were some differences by type and salience of specific relationship concerns across illnesses/disabilities. For example, the focus groups whose members had experienced cancer discussed sexual functioning and body image to a greater degree than did members of the other groups, but the particular issue of sexual functioning seems to be a major concern for almost everyone suffering from an illness or disability. Additionally, unpredictability of health status and invisible conditions created unique relationship challenges (Donoghue & Siegel, 2000) that are specific to individual illness (e.g., extreme fatigue in the case of a person with MS). Yet, commonalities between groups were more evident than differences. Common themes across the social contexts of family, friendships, work and leisure included (a) individual performance, role, and personal identity changes, (b) difficulties with communication, (c) challenges in adapting relationship expectations and activities, and (d) awkwardness in the activities of giving and receiving. Each of these themes is briefly elaborated below.

Individual Performance, Role, and Personal Identity Changes. These types of changes often lead to relationship changes (Noble Topf, 1995). For example, previous social network size and frequency of interaction with its members may be reduced. At the same time, health care personnel necessarily become newly incorporated into a person's social network, and relationships with other persons with illness/disabilities frequently develop. These changes constitute a transformation in the person's experience of relational networks in general and reinforce the identity of the person as fundamentally shaped and grounded by the illness rather than by the things that shape and ground identity for healthy persons. This situation necessitates a psychological shift that is one of the major sources of difficulty for the ill person and for his or her associates.

> You don't really know who you are. You are a different person. And you don't know how people out there will accept you. (Ottawa Composite Focus Group)

Perhaps we too often fail to recognize that in the evolution of personal identity, people develop behavior patterns that become typical, predictive, and demonstrative of a stable and describable character. This continuity of character, this steadiness of identity, promotes the development of the mutual trust central in relationships with others. The onset of chronic illness or disability threatens the perception of continuity of identity. Along with sudden changes in physical abilities and emotional states, serious challenges to maintaining typical behavior patterns arise. This can be tremendously disconcerting for individuals who acquire a disability or are diagnosed with an illness, and for those around them. Changing roles and identities can put extreme pressure on relationships.

Participants in the focus groups expressed a sense of loss or helplessness in relation to their ability to manage their relationships or provide a safe, secure environment for the people they care about. They were very sensitive to how they are being viewed by others, yet their condition often demanded that they become more assertive than they typically were about their own needs, as other people are usually unprepared to appreciate, notice, or respond to needs that have become extraordinary.

> I know my kids have been so shocked lately ... and they come home at 3:00 and I'm still sitting in the chair, flipping the channels, and watching the talk shows. And they are absolutely shocked that I could do this, because I have never done this. And they really have a problem with this because this is not what Mom does. (Toronto Breast Cancer Focus Group)

Difficulties With Communication.   These groups experienced difficulty communicating about the health problem and its emotional impact (Pistrang & Barker, 1995), performance abilities and expectations, the effect of illness/disability on relationships, and the negotiation of social support.

We avoid communication because of the misinterpretation and misunderstanding. (Ottawa Composite Focus Group)

It just gets frustrating sometimes because I don't know how to tell people that I am disabled. (Cleveland MS Focus Group)

Challenges in Adapting Relationship Expectations and Activities. Patience and flexibility were required to change traditional "ways of doing" in every social context, from work to sexual intimacy.

Within the whole work environment, it's very political .... The work environment is such that they don't want lame ducks. They want the movers and shakers and the people who can maintain high speeds for ongoing periods of time. (Toronto Prostate Cancer Focus Group)

My sex life is 'What is sex?' (Toronto Prostate Cancer Focus Group)

Awkwardness in the Act of Giving and Receiving.   Social support was not merely the process of receiving help, but tied to issues of reciprocity and equity (Lemaistre, 1995). Support often mis-fired. Although people may have good intentions, their approaches and responses may not be what the person who is disabled or ill needs at the time.

If I don't ask for help, let me do it. This was one of the first things that I projected to my husband when I was first diagnosed with MS because ... he was smothering me. (Cleveland MS Focus Group)

Relationships are not stagnant; nor are many health conditions. Relationship roles and adaptations are likely to change over time, as various stages of the illness/disability are encountered.

There's varying stages of the whole of the disease and with each stage, our needs certainly impact our relationships. Spousal, family, friends, business, whatever. There's the diagnosis stage, the treatment stage, there's the rehab stage and then there's the stage of the whole of survivorship. How do we function and how do we move forward beyond that point? With each of those stages, there is a whole different set of needs that present themselves. (Toronto Prostate Cancer Focus Group)

Context-Specific Relationship Difficulties

Four context areas were examined: (a) family, (b) friendships, (c) work, and (d) leisure. Each of these areas presented its own unique relationship challenges. Examples of context-specific relationship difficulties are presented next.

Families. Issues of intimacy, fear of divorce (being "dumped"), need for acceptance and support, social validation, role re-allocation, and social support were some of the major difficulties experienced. Major blockages to adaptation were created by denial of the illness/disability, resistance to adaptation or unwillingness to change expectations of performance, and the sense that the illness/disability was seen by other people as "tragic" or as an "inconvenience."

Denial is a very common response in the face of disability or illness. Since the person with the illness often has no choice but to acknowledge the problem and do what he or she can to address it, the lack of response represented by denial from family, in particular, can be frustrating and difficult to deal with.

> It was with my family that I had the worst problem. It was so hard to get a ride even down here for treatment. Because if they brought me for treatment, they would have to acknowledge that I had a problem. That there was something wrong with me. (Toronto Breast Cancer Focus Group)

> It's almost a matter of inconvenience .... People seem to be inconvenienced by you. And they take that ... quite personally. (Halifax Pilot Focus Group)

Many focus group participants who were part of a couple experienced changes in sexual activity and intimacy because of illness or disability. Communication was extremely important in this regard, as was a willingness to adapt to changing physical characteristics and needs.

> We all need to be loved and cared for. When I was discharged and went home, I couldn't believe that my wife didn't want to have anything physical to do with me. And that was a real shock. And you feel ... You're dying to be loved, and to love, and it isn't there. (Ottawa Composite Focus Group)

Many people in the focus groups who were parents talked extensively about their children's responses to their parent's changed health status. Teenagers were singled out in this regard. They often saw the illness or disability of a parent as a particular personal inconvenience for them.

> Teenagers are very selfish. So my cancer has been a total inconvenience to their lives. (Toronto Breast Cancer Focus Group)

Respondents suggested many approaches to reducing relationship difficulties within couples and families: They sought increased understanding about the condition itself and its emotional or functional impacts on family members; they wanted to know how to communicate effectively about their illness and how to develop activity adaptation strategies; they desired communication within the family about identity and role changes; and they needed to identify reasonable support expectations and how they could be shared more equitably within the

family. There was typically a desire by the participants for a family fo-
rum to discuss illness/disability and relationship issues in order to address family tensions and conflict. There was a need for more
community supports for families (e.g., family counseling, peer support,
or support groups). There was also a special need for spouses and children to have an opportunity to discuss relationship issues in a counseling or support group venue. Overall, it was stated repeatedly that the
health care system has an important role in facilitating healthy and
supportive family relationships. This role needed to be recognized by
health system planners and managers and addressed early on in the
"treatment" of illness or disability.

Friendships.   On the subject of friendships, focus group participants identified the following issues: loss of friendships; the need to
limit their friendship activities because of their own energy depletion;
the importance of support from friends who are not as obligated to provide support as family; and the development of new friendships with
other people with disabilities/illnesses. Key focal points in friendships
were the challenges presented by dating (e.g., mate/companion selection) and the consequent need for re-interpreting relationship expectations for intimacy or intensity.

Social expectations related to physical attractiveness, the nature of
the "dating and mating game," the types of activities that couples engage in together, and the prospects for marriage and family can weigh
heavily on one's perspectives about relationships.

> Our culture puts so much emphasis on having a relationship that I feel
> that in order to be self-fulfilled, I must have one. I should have one. And
> my disability compounds that problem in a very significant way. (Halifax
> Pilot Focus Group)

Many participants voiced a common sentiment: They had found out
who their "true" friends were. Unfortunately, friends are lost along the
way as allegiances and activities change following the onset of illness or
disability.

> [You learn] who your real friends are and you get some real shocks too.
> (Toronto Prostate Cancer Focus Group)

> I found with some of my relationships, or a good portion of them, most of
> them needed me a lot more than I needed them. And when they no longer
> had that, they were not interested. (Toronto Breast Cancer Focus Group)

> At first it was really tough getting used to what I could do physically and
> what I couldn't do. And I think my active lifestyle had a lot to do with that
> because I was involved in sports .... Like friends have asked me, 'Would
> you like to go snowmobiling?' Well, sure I would love to go snowmobiling.
> But I know if I hop on a snowmobile, that just the bumping, is going to

break my rear end. So I'm saying to myself, 'Well, I'm not going to do that because I'm not going to jeopardize my job and end up in bed for 3 months just for an hour's enjoyment going snowmobiling with some friends.' So these are some of the decisions that you make, that you have to make. (Halifax Work & Leisure Focus Group)

One suggestion for addressing friendship and dating issues was to identify strategies that might be shared in support groups. Where sexual relationships are concerned, many focus group participants argued that society has to get beyond seeing people who are ill or disabled as "asexual beings."

Work.   Work is an important source of personal identity, as well as the basis of individual and family livelihoods. Work gives people a sense of purpose, self-value, and self-reliance. When illness or disability prevents people from working, the financial difficulties are often compounded by psychological problems.

I just feel badly that my wife has to work in order to keep the roof over my head. (Iowa Stroke Focus Group)

I'm thinking too that we measure our self-worth in our productivity. What we give to our job or our volunteer work. It's society's expectation. (Halifax Family & Friends Focus Group)

There was a strong desire among many participants to continue to perform meaningful activity, but only if this could be accomplished with reasonably adjusted performance expectations. This did not seem possible in most work situations. Respondents noticed that difficulties consequent on their chronic illness were such things as disagreements about reasonable work performance in the changed circumstances; how to obtain support in the workplace; inflexible attitudes about disability or resistance to adaptation by supervisors or colleagues; perceived lack of competence related to disability; and distrust or disbelief that the disability/illness actually interfered with performance, and if so, to what extent. If work settings are to include persons whose method of work performance and productivity may be different from the norm, or may change over time, many ill or disabled people assumed—perhaps naively—that there would be existing policies and procedures to accommodate this. Otherwise, there is great potential for relationship tensions and conflicts to arise.

I think there was definitely a perception that a person with a disability was not as knowledgeable. (Ottawa Composite Focus Group)

At work, one of the most common problems was that experiences with one person who had health problems were "generalized" to others who had health problems. All illnesses and disability were essentially thought to be the same in the restrictions they created on work performance or the needs that they presented for accommodation. It was often frustrating and exasperating for people with disability or illness to address the resultant communication challenges to explaining the specific features of their own situation.

> They think, 'Well gee, we had Joe Blow working here 3 years ago, and he needed this, and therefore your needs must be the same.' (Halifax Work & Leisure Focus Group)

As indicated earlier, loss of the work role often appeared to be directly linked to unresolved relationship issues in the workplace, not just to decreases in functional ability.

> I worked in an extremely busy office where it's just go from the moment you step in the door until you walk out. And when you're not there, it puts stress on everyone else because everyone else has to fill your shoes. So you get guilt feelings as a result of not being there, and wanting to be there. And you get a bit of odd comments when you do return to work, such as 'Well, we were really busy while you were gone,' and that type of situation. So it did not help our relationships at work at all. I tended to withdraw from work more and more as time occurred. Talking less to my peers, interacting with them less. (Halifax Pilot Focus Group)

How can we encourage employers and employees to show more flexibility and adaptability in the workplace? It was suggested that accommodation and integration require education and awareness for coworkers as well as supervisors. Participants were aware of greater needs for opportunities to communicate directly about illness/disability and to address issues and attitudinal blocks. They often reported that many difficulties arose simply from ignorance and that such ignorance could readily be corrected if an opportunity for doing so was formally provided. Equally, people with an illness/disability would like to know what is expected as reasonable performance in their new circumstances, considering the demands or limitations of the illness/disability. Many further commented that their input could be useful to their employers in helping to address workplace issues by increasing the employer's knowledge of disability and coping in the workplace. In sum, then, the difficulties at work consequent on disability derive from or amount to differences in identity, self-worth, and relationships with others.

Leisure. Respondents accentuated the valuable role of leisure activities in reducing the tension and stress of relationship adaptation and illness. If ways could be found to make a new form of social interaction relaxing and enjoyable, then adaptation to the illness/disability could occur more readily and be more personally satisfactory. Enjoyment was indicated as a key factor in the maintenance of satisfying relationships with family, coworkers, and friends. Enjoyment for both the ill and the healthy clearly results from feeling included and valued, finding suitable activities, and the willingness and ability to make activity adaptations and substitutions in and for companionate activity.

If illness/disability changes the leisure activities that a person can perform, then some adaptation is also necessary so that enjoyment may still be achieved, even in some different or modified form. If leisure activities were previously shared with a spouse or partner, tensions often developed when it became difficult for these to be continued and both the difficulty in attempting them and their absence were played out as guilt and resentment.

> Particularly for people who have become disabled later in life, maybe the disabled partner can no longer do the things they used to be able to do. It begins to become a tug of war as to whether the non-disabled spouse is still able to enjoy the canoeing or the backpacking .... You can get into feelings of jealousy that the other person can still do these things and you can't. (Ottawa Composite Focus Group)

Physical access was an issue for people with a variety of mobility, sensory, and chemical-sensitivity problems. Despite considerable advances in increasing physical access for people who are disabled, in particular, many obstacles still need to be considered.

> In relationships, you become more dependent on the telephone, because there are a lot of places you can't go. (Halifax Work & Leisure Focus Group)

The notion of enjoyable activity extends to sexuality and intimacy, although some of the same general issues of adaptability and flexibility seen in other forms of companionate activity were applicable here as well. There was frequently a decrease in sexual activity at the same time as the person felt an increase in need to be attractive and loved.

> Our relationship has become different. There is more friendship. There is more intimacy. And it isn't strictly based on sex anymore. We have a lot better communication and are able to talk. And to feel comfortable just lying in each other's arms. (Toronto Breast Cancer Focus Group)

Strategies to improve enjoyable sexual relations included honest communication and redefining/valuing intimacy as a broader concept than sexuality.

Summary

In this section, we have provided an overview of themes in relationship change and maintenance that are common across a broad range of illnesses and disabilities. Dramatic changes often take place in individual identity and roles, along with challenges in communicating needs and expectations, and adapting relationship activities to accommodate changes related to the illness or disability. These challenges are present in a variety of contexts: in families and friendships, in workplaces, and in the community. Many relationship difficulties were clarified in the focus groups and strategies were identified to help address specific relationship difficulties.

FACTORS IN RELATIONSHIP DIFFICULTIES AS A RESULT OF ILLNESS OR DISABILITY

There were several persistent factors, arising from the illness/disability itself, that were repeatedly raised in the focus groups' discussions as significantly affecting relationships. These factors reduced or exacerbated relationship challenges and social integration. We examine six factors: four are relational (shared meaning, commitment, social support and equity, and relational competence) and two societal (stigma and health policy).

Relationship Factors

Shared Meaning. One of the main problems for people who become ill or disabled involves the redefinition of their relationships (what I/we have, desire, or expect). This need appears to strongly influence perceived relationship quality and the effort given to adapt relationships to illness/disability (Lyons, Mickelson, Sullivan, & Coyne, 1998). Illness and disability can contribute to a disharmony or lack of synchrony or agreement in all interactional contexts as people ask themselves questions such as Who am I now? Who are we now? What can I contribute to this relationship now? Can we, or how can we, still have a satisfactory relationship, given this illness/disability? What are the expectations of the relationship now? To what extent do things need to change, and how much am I (are we) willing to change?

Unfortunately people will make attributions for relationship issues personally (as their personal problem or another individual's "fault") instead of attributing problems to the situation or circumstance of illness/disability. If discrepancies in understanding and shared meaning are to be removed, then the resources required to facilitate this process include information about the condition and its effects on behavior and functioning, extensive communication about personal and interpersonal expectations, and the development of a set of strategies to ease tension.

Frequently, discrepancies between two partners (whether ill or well) exist, not only in terms of defining relationships, but in the allocation of responsibilities. In chronic illness, these discrepancies tend to grow. One key issue in the family or community relates to roles and the way in which each person's role is defined in facilitating communication, activity adaptation, and support. Of course once chronic illness or disability strikes, such definitions and responsibilities may need to be changed. Sometimes the best of intentions are shunned because the person who is ill or disabled wants to exercise independence in a certain area. Conversely, expectations made of an ill or disabled person can be greater than they can reasonably accomplish, and conflict can result when it is believed or suspected that the expectations exceed accomplishments. The "fine line" between dependence and independence must be negotiated in light of mutual support and reciprocity.

> You get that little edge because you get some people in your relationships that are overprotective. They won't let you grow. They won't let you learn your own capabilities. (Halifax Work & Leisure Focus Group)

Commitment in Relationships.   The normal expectations for the maintenance of relationships are disrupted, often in unexpected ways, once illness or disability is part of the scenario. The commitment to establish, maintain, and adapt relationships in the context of illness/disability plays a central role in the quality of life and the degree of familial or social integration of a person with a disability or illness. Types of adaptation include communication, social activities, and sexual attitudes and functioning. Contexts for adaptation include partnerships, families, friendships, and workplaces. In each relationship type and context, the degree to which people are willing to adapt and are committed to making necessary changes greatly influences the degree of integration for a person with an illness or disability.

> I thought that the least they could do was to try to learn sign language so that we can communicate. Even the basic signs, just to communicate. But there was no effort shown. (Halifax Family & Friends Focus Group)

Commitment is a complex concept involving social obligation, relationship rules and roles, relationship history, degree of attachment, other roles and commitments, and relationship expectancies. The extent to which illness/disability is perceived as an individual or communal issue evidently contributes in the minds of the relevant parties to the nature of the effort invested to address relationship issues. The more individualistic the people or culture, the greater the unwillingness to accommodate and change for others. With the relaxing of societal rules about commitment in relationships in general, people are left to sort out how they address these issues on their own.

Social Support and Equity.   In the cardiac area, I guess I see over-involvement or under-involvement. They are either doing too much for their spouse or not enough for their spouse. It's one of the primary areas of difficulty. (Toronto Researcher/Clinician Focus Group)

The balance of social support and equity is one that is carefully negotiated in the shaping of relationships, even when they are functioning well and both people are physically capable. A certain amount of give–and–take is characteristic of all relationships. How much is given and how much is taken will typically be established according to the comfort levels and social hierarchical positions of those involved, as well as resulting from the circumstances of particular situations and occasions (Hatfield, Traupmann, Sprecher, Utne, & Hay, 1984). The give–and–take balance between a mother and young child, for example, will be different from that established between coworkers or friends. The mother–young child relationship is typically characterized by the mother doing most of the giving, whereas the coworker or friend relationship is typically characterized by a much more equitable division. Balance is struck according to the norms of the particular relationship, and it is against such norms that performance is ultimately judged. Equally, it is true that in typical relationships people do not expect an immediate balance to be reestablished after the performance of every effort or favor; they merely expect that in the long term, a roughly equal balance between costs and rewards will be established for both parties.

Chronic illness or disability can drastically affect the balance of equity in a relationship, tipping the scales much more heavily to one side than the other without the prospect of return to status quo. With a reduction or change in one partner's capabilities, contributions of support in the relationship must now be reevaluated because the usually norms do not now apply. It is often difficult for people to ask for help, particularly if they strongly value their independence.

> I know there are things I can't do, but I don't let other people know that I can't do them. That includes my family members. (Cleveland MS Focus Group)

Illness forces people into the position of renegotiating their roles and reevaluating their worth. Misperceptions can have a profound effect on both the person with a health problem, who now confronts issues of dependence/independence, and the partner in the relationship who is faced with consciously evaluating and calculating a relationship's worth.

> There is such a vast difference between men with MS and women with MS. And especially dealing with any type of relationship, for the simple reason that men are supposed to be hunter-gatherers. We've got the muscle mass, all that kind of good stuff. But we don't have that now and our wives are now taking care of us in a little bit of a way …. You know, that's a very strange feeling for a man to know that really, to a potential mate out there, we have nothing to offer except intellect or a good sense of humor. (Cleveland MS Focus Group)

> We talked about it in the open and everything was fine. All the fears that I was conjuring up, and all the assumptions that I was making, were wrong. And it kind of brought us closer together as partners in the end. (Toronto Breast Cancer Support Group)

Relational Competence.   Relational skill or competence is understood in this context as the ability to effectively negotiate and adapt to the mutual benefit of the parties involved in a relationship. Relational competence greatly influences adaptation to the challenges and changes in relationships resulting from disability or illness. Relationships are generally improved when both parties can identify and agree on problem areas, which they can then set about correcting. This can be done by the individuals themselves or can be facilitated through such mechanisms as support groups, counseling, or self-analysis. A key aspect of relational competence is communication.

Communication is commonly identified as a central component of relational competence in the maintenance of relationships, whether they are affected by disability/illness or not. Good communication strategies enable us to share thoughts, feelings, and needs with friends, family members, and coworkers and to feel reaffirmed and reassured. Communication is essential in the sphere of social negotiation. Personality traits of both sender and receiver, content of message, social climate, and pressures are all factors that can affect whether or not communication of an idea, belief, or need is successful and well received. Unfortunately, chronic illness and disability can impose substantial barriers to these already complicated processes.

> I think I lost a lot of friends .... You know, they were friends, and they still are friends, but they really didn't know how to cope with a person who has a stroke. And they just stayed away because they didn't know what to say. (Iowa Stroke Focus Group)

Communication following an injury or illness depends to a large degree on the nature of communication prior to the illness or disability. Although communication actually improved in a few cases, most people in the focus groups reported that communication becomes more difficult and a great deal of time is spent "educating" others about the illness/disability and its impacts.

> I think that people with physical disabilities are more apt to be in a unique situation that requires more explanation. I wouldn't expect the rest of my family to appreciate wheelchair issues ... so it requires me to explain, and that is life. (Halifax Friends & Family Focus Group)

People who are facing an illness or disability may find themselves in a socially devalued position while trying to address issues that many people are uncomfortable confronting. They face both personal and societal

challenges in communicating their needs. These challenges are profoundly reflected in their relationships.

Although the focus of this chapter is difficult relationships, and
many difficulties have been identified, it is also important to note that
some relationships and perspectives on relationships actually improved
in some ways in the adaptation to illness or disability.

> This might sound a bit nuts. But I think it has to do with more spiritual in-
> sight or personal growth. But I'm a much softer person than I was before I
> was injured. And I can think of others much better than I used to. (Ottawa
> Composite Focus Group)

> I think family is so much more important to me today than it would have
> been if I had not had a stroke. (Iowa Stroke Focus Group)

Societal Factors

Stigma.   Illness and disability occur within relationships, and relationships take place within society. Ideas present in society about what
it means to be ill or well, or to be disabled or "abled," impact on how people with illness/disability and those around them perceive themselves in
the world and in their relationships (Royer, 1995). Beliefs about who is
valued in society, what they should look like, and how they should behave can lead to people with an illness or disability being assigned a
lower social status than someone who is not ill or disabled (Atlantic
Health Promotion Research Centre, 2002).

> The meanings, perceptions and attitudes surrounding (illness and) dis-
> ability and those with a disability are created by societies through a series
> of values and beliefs about illness of disability and the value of a person
> with an illness/disability and these beliefs are sustained by the people
> within those societies. (Devine, 1997)

Societal factors include insensitivity coupled with lack of relational
competence and a prevalence of negative interactions by societal members. In particular, there are well-established perceptions of illness/dis-
ability as inconvenient in our fast-paced, individualistic culture; an
assumed increase in loneliness and social isolation if someone has an illness or disability; and the perceived discomfort of others in interaction.
It was generally agreed in the focus groups that most people are not
comfortable with illness and disability and tend to avoid the topic, as
well as people who are ill or disabled.

> Somehow the feeling was that when one is in a wheelchair, your intelli-
> gence goes down by about 25 points. And you suddenly become … de-
> velopmentally delayed. And this was particularly apparent, I think, with
> the older generation. (Ottawa Composite Focus Group)

Public awareness and education about illness/disability and communication skills were repeatedly requested. There was a need for the public to learn more about specific conditions, which would ease the need to constantly inform and educate. People also need to know how to provide effective social support, and learn strategies to adapt activities; increased accessibility also is required in the community. People with illnesses/disabilities could play a larger part in these processes.

> I was never much of a talker. And my actions were louder than my words. I always rested on my laurels with that. It doesn't work any more. I have to explain so much and negotiate so much more. (Halifax Family & Friends Focus Group)

Health and Social Services Policy.   The quality of personal relationships is a key element in social integration no less in the case of illness or disability, although this area does not receive sufficient attention in the health care and social service sectors. There is a need for the health care system to address relationship issues through individual and family counseling, and better interactions with health professionals, in particular, doctors. This final section presents two sets of relationship issues: addressing the impact of illness/disability on relationships and improving relationships with health professionals.

ADDRESSING THE IMPACT OF ILLNESS AND DISABILITY ON RELATIONSHIPS

Whose role is it to facilitate good relationships? Whom does the person or family member consult with? Relationship problems often "fall between the cracks" in health and social services. People with illness/disabilities and family members often do not have an opportunity to discuss or address relationship issues. The model of acute health care is not set up to deal with the relationship stresses and strains produced by chronic health problems and disabilities. Health professionals need to be more aware of how relationships feature in their treatment and services, and that chronic illnesses and disabilities are relationship issues.

> The problem is that we've grown up [in] a medical model. And we've stuck with that medical model up to recent times. And that model does not include personal relationships. (Halifax Pilot Focus Group)

Family and marital counselors often do not have the background or clinical framework to deal with a disability in the family as a set of relationship issues, not as pathologies and/or dysfunctions. With the appropriate background, some health professionals could play a key role in directing discussion about relationships in support groups. Support groups can provide useful information to clinician groups regarding the

real–life issues of living with illness or disability although we noted earlier some of the more pressing issues concerning the distribution of information to a broader set of people and to the public at large. Clinicians
should be able to provide referral guidance to provide people with a
place to turn when there are relationship issues. In the focus groups, reports of poor communication, insensitivity, and discomfort on the part
of health professionals when treating people with disabilities were very
prevalent. There is obviously a need for curriculum development related
to disability issues and difficulties with relationships.

> Doctors do not open up lines of communication and provide information
> on support services. Many people talk about doctors and poor communi-
> cation with doctors. (Ottawa Composite Focus Group)

> A lot of the responsibility for changing the perceptions of health care pro-
> viders, particularly physicians, sometimes by design and sometimes by
> just being at the right place at the right time, falls on the consumers them-
> selves. (Toronto Prostate Cancer Focus Group)

The value of support groups for support and relationships was obvious in the focus groups. People with illness/disability need support
through opportunities to share relationship experiences and strategies
with others.

> The breast cancer support group has been my life line. (Toronto Breast
> Cancer Focus Group)

> When they came to their first self-help group and found that other people
> had problems like they did, it was like a reawakening. It was like finding
> that they weren't so different. (Ottawa MS Focus Group)

Although focus group participants talked about attending various
types of support groups, there still appeared to be a need for a greater
number of support groups, and for groups that feature the examination of relationship issues more systematically. Appropriately trained
health or social service professional could facilitate this process. Given
the salience of this issue, it is surprising that these difficulties have
been mostly left up to individuals directly involved to work out for
themselves. Health systems in most countries provide very little support for such difficulties. We posit that a method for repairing the lack
of health service that deals with the social side of illness is to decons-
truct relationships and then to clarify the types of challenges health issues bring to them.

CONCLUSIONS

Human beings are social creatures. We depend heavily on relationships
with others for companionship, empowerment, validation, support,

and a sense of who we are. Close relationships are established through constantly negotiated and renegotiated communication and companionate activity. With the onset of chronic illness or disability, patterns of behavior, hopes, and dreams, and even the sense of identity, are often seriously disrupted (e.g., fears about disability and death, health appointments, lost functioning, and social roles). Unpredictability and change can cause great stress not only within the person, but also within relationships, and can seriously test the mettle of even the most intimate and committed relationships.

These insights are not new. Numerous researchers have shown that the social side of a health problem may be more distressing than specific functional challenges (Kowal, Johnson, & Lee, 2003; Sprinzeles, 2000; Thompson & Braithwaite, 2000). Although it is intuitively obvious that characteristics of individuals and their relationships provide an important contextual backdrop within which these illness/disability challenges are played out, we suggest that simply increasing understanding of the illness–related relationship challenges can make an important contribution to examining the difficulties and decreasing them. It can provide the foundation for health and social advocacy as well as the development of evidence-based tools that health professionals and support groups can use to support people with these adaptational challenges. It is time that we "treat" the social manifestations of illness with the care and attention that the physical side receives.

ACKNOWLEDGMENT

Thanks are extended to Maureen Keough, Research Assistant at the Atlantic Health Promotion Research Centre, for her assistance with this chapter.

NOTE

1. Atlantic Health Promotion Research Centre (Dalhousie University), University of Michigan Medical School, Department of Communication Studies (University of Iowa), Toronto–Bayview Regional Cancer Centre, The Rehabilitation Centre (Ottawa), The Cleveland Clinic, Toronto General Hospital, Canadian Cancer Society, Disabled Individual's Alliance (Halifax), Institute for Rehabilitation Research and Development and the Rehabilitation Centre (Ottawa), Ottawa General Hospital.

REFERENCES

Atlantic Health Promotion Research Centre. (2002). *Picturing relationships: A workbook about relationships for people with an acquired illness or disability.* Halifax, Nova Scotia: Dalhousie University.

Devine, M. A. (1997). *The relationship between social acceptance and the leisure lifestyle of people with disabilities*. Doctoral dissertation, University of Georgia.

Donoghue, P., & Siegel, M. (2000). *Sick and tired of feeling sick and tired: Living with invisible chronic illness*. New York: Norton.

Fisher, L., & Weihs, K. L. (2000). Can addressing family relationships improve outcomes of chronic disease? Report of the National Working Group on family-based interventions in chronic disease. *Journal of Family Practice, 49*(6), 561–566.

Gottlieb, B. H. (Ed.). (1981). *Social networks and social support*. Beverly Hills, CA: Sage.

Hatfield, E., Traupmann, J., Sprecher, S., Utne, M., & Hay, J. (1984). Behavioral interdependence: Social exchange. In W. Ickes (Ed.), *Compatible and incompatible relationships* (pp. 1–27). New York: Springer-Verlag.

Kowal, J., Johnson, S. M., & Lee, A. (2003). Chronic illness in couples: A case for emotionally focused therapy. *Journal of Marital and Family Therapy, 29*(3), 299–310.

Lemaistre, J. (1995). *After the diagnosis: From crisis to personal renewal for patients with chronic illness*. Berkeley, CA: Ulysses Press.

Lyons, R. F., Mickelson, K. D., Sullivan, M. J. L., & Coyne, J. C. (1998). Coping as a communal process. *Journal of Social and Personal Relationships, 15*(5), 579–605.

Lyons, R., Sullivan, M., Ritvo, P., & Coyne, J. (1995) *Relationships in chronic illness and disability*. Thousand Oaks, CA: Sage.

Noble Topf, L. (1995). *You are not your illness*. New York: Simon & Schuster.

Pistrang, N., & Barker, C. (1995). The partner relationship in psychological response to breast cancer. *Social Science and Medicine, 40*(6), 789–797.

Royer, A. (1995). Living with chronic illness. *Research in the Sociology of Health Care, 12*, 25–48.

Schmaling, K. B., & Sher, T. G. (1997). Physical health and relationships. In W. K. Halford & H. J. Markman (Eds.), *Clinical handbook of marriage and couple relationships* (pp. 323–336). New York: Wiley.

Schreurs, K. M. G., & deRidder, D. T. D. (1997). Integration of coping and social support perspectives: Implications for the study of adaptation to chronic diseases. *Clinical Psychology Review, 17*(1), 89–112.

Sprinzeles, L. L. (2000). Effects of Parkinson's disease on family life. *Loss, Grief & Care, 8*(3/4), 135–142.

Thompson, T. L., & Braithwaite, D. O. (2000). "I'm still me": Communication and identity as a person with a disability. In D. O. Braithwaite & J. T. Wood (Eds.), *Case studies in interpersonal communication: Processes and problems* (pp. 26–35). Belmont, CA: Wadsworth.

World Health Organization. (2004). *Chronic conditions: The global burden*. Retrieved December 2004, from http://www.who.int/chronic_conditions/burden/en/print/html

Chapter 12

Relating Difficulty
in a Triangular World

Steve Duck
Megan K. Foley
D. Charles Kirkpatrick
University of Iowa

In the opening chapter of this volume, we outlined some possible theoretical concerns in defining and studying "difficulty" in relationships. We also considered some general issues pertaining to the nature of relational difficulty. Although our theoretical concerns were largely analytic and nonempirical, the subsequent chapters have offered some support for those claims. Although these chapters address specific contexts of difficulty, they have brought to light additional general issues regarding the nature of relating difficulty.

TRIANGULATION

In reviewing these chapters, we have discovered a principle underlying the nature of difficulty. We refer to this principle as *triangulation*: the juxtaposition between two people relating and some influence of social life. The influence may be another relationship, person, social activity, or set of expectations. Triangulation is an essential feature of all relating but becomes particularly important when relating is difficult. Several authors remarked in different ways that some of the "difficulty" of relationships is that they are not assessed only in and of themselves but instead are conducted in broader networks and social contexts (cf. Simmel, 1950). For example, Stephanie S. Rollie (chap. 10) discusses how a nonresidential parent and child can have a mutually satisfying relationship that only becomes difficult as a result of the influence of the residential parent. In essence, therefore, the relationship of the nonresidential parent with the child is driven not by internal factors, but by

225

triangulation—the influence of a third party. Another example is the divisive nature of gossip, which implies at least three parties: talker, listener, and absent third party. Still other examples include "shy" people, who would be satisfied with their friendships if it were not for the self-conscious awareness of others, and people with chronic illness, who indicate that one of their major concerns is that third parties will find them unattractive. Their self-image, and consequently, their relationships, are adversely affected by their expectations of others' reactions. In both of these cases, triangulation is represented by individuals' concerns about third parties' perceptions, as part of the way they feel about themselves and act in relationships is based on how they expect others will view them.

As the term *triangulation* specifies, a common feature of all these examples is that there are three terms to be considered: the first two are represented by the two relaters, whether it be a long-distance relationship, an intimate relationship, an acquaintanceship, or social interaction generally (as in the shyness case). The third term is the triangulator, which takes several different forms: the *Framer, Interferer, Linchpin*, or *Comparison Point* (see Fig. 12.1). The four different types of triangulation are based in, and differentiated by, the way in which the triangulation occurs. We will consider these each in turn.

Triangulator as Framer

Here, the essence of triangulation is that a particular relationship—perceived to be satisfactory by the relater—is now framed by an outside party as problematic. This leads the relater personally also to redefine

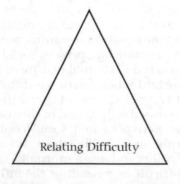

Triangulator

(Framer, Interferer, Linchpin, or Comparison Point)

Relating Difficulty

Relater 1
Target

Relater 2
Partner

FIG. 12.1. Locus of difficulty as triangulation. Note that in our discussion each **leg** of the triangle also represents a kind of relating although it is normally the **base** that is seen as representing the target "difficult" relationship.

the relationship as problematic. For example, when a victim-advocate frames a relationship as abusive, a friend frames a hookup as amoral, people view others with chronic illness as socially unacceptable, or a worker ascribes power or status imbalance to a boss or coworkers, then the target is forced to recognize that from some points of view, the relationship is viewed as difficult, and hence at some level that he or she is also viewed as a somewhat imperfect relater. An element of this form of triangulation therefore is that one of the individuals (see Fig. 12.1: Relater 1 "Target") is marked as incompetent or imperfect as a social being in a particular relationship.

This second element of the Framer triangulation, namely that there is a *Target* individual, requires that one of the relaters in particular is marked by the Framer as the source of the problem. For example, the Target could be the abuser (Foley, chap. 3), the person with a chronic illness (Lyons et al., chap. 11), the female hookup participant (Paul, chap. 8), or the co-worker (Lovaglia & Lucas, chap. 4). This relater (Target) is distinguished from the other one (Partner), who is absolved from being labeled as "difficult." An element of Framer Triangulation, therefore, is the identification and implicit accusation of one person as the source of the problem. However, as we indicated in chapter 1, and as Foley has discussed at length, things are not that simple, and the identification of an individual as "difficult" works only at a superficial level. While the Target is the person identified as difficult, that person may be understood as difficult only by the Partner based on the Framer's involvement in the triangle or by other Framers who also characterize the Target as difficult.

Another aspect of Framer Triangulation, therefore, is that the *Partner is implicated by association*: The Framer doesn't understand why the Partner would relate to the "difficult person." For example, some victim-advocates question why abused women stay in the relationship (Foley, chap. 3), people may wonder why the dominated worker doesn't quit (Lovaglia & Lucas, chap. 4), or why a "normal" person would befriend a person with a chronic illness (Lyons et al, chap. 11). The Partner is not seen as a problematic person (e.g., the male is not seen as "slutty" for having hooked up; Paul, chap. 8); only the choice of relationship partner is questioned (e.g., he hooked up with a "slutty" woman). In other words, behavior is not seen as identifying an inherent characteristic of the Partner, but rather some characteristic of the situation or process. On the other hand, the Target is identified as showing an inherent characteristic that is negative and difficult. What we have here, to paraphrase Strother Martin in *Cool Hand Luke*, is not only a failure to communicate, but also a double standard.

Triangulator as Interferer

In this second form of triangulation, the essence of the problem is that some third party intervenes or interferes with the conduct of the relationship marked as difficult. Examples are provided in chapter 10 by Rollie and chapter 9 by Foster and Rosnow. In these cases, the third party *Interferer* aims to separate the two relaters either physically (e.g., a residential parent's control over the nonresidential parent's visitation of the child) or symbolically (e.g., Foster and Rosnow's example from Shakespeare, where Iago uses gossip to create a symbolic and actual rift between the hearer and the subject of his report). This symbolic or actual rift disrupts the relationship between the parent (Target) and child (Partner) or the subjects (Target) and hearer (Partner) of gossip. The interferer creates this rift, in part, to strengthen her or his own relationship with the child or hearer of gossip. For example, relationship-building is one of the social functions of gossip; in this case, the gossiper intends to build a relationship with the listener rather than with the person described as the subject of the gossip. Similarly, Rollie (chap. 10) indicates how residential parents sometimes point out the other parent's absence or lack of financial support to children as a way of framing themselves as the "good" parent and the nonresidential parent as the difficult one. This interference serves an active blocking function. In this case, the interferer actively and intentionally blocks the Target from having an unproblematic relationship with the Partner.

A notable feature of this interferer triangulation is, therefore, that it imposes a forced choice on the Partner. Because the relational partner is desired both by the interferer and the Target, the interferer creates a situation where the Partner must choose between the interferer and the Target. When the relationship between the nonresidential parent and residential parent is fractious, for example, children are often required to form an allegiance to one parent or the other. Similarly, the hearer of gossip may feel forced to decide whether to believe the gossip and form a coalition with the gossiper against the object of gossip, or to reject the gossip and ally with the object of gossip against the gossiper.

Triangulator as Linchpin

In this form of triangulation, a linchpin creates an involuntary relationship between two relaters. For example, a marriage inevitably leads to an involuntary relationship between a mother-in-law and a daughter-in-law with the child/spouse as a linchpin (Morr Serewicz, chap. 6), or the interactions of an individual with others involuntarily brings together that person's shy and non-shy friends (Bradshaw, chap. 2). Relaters enter the involuntary relationship on the basis of their relationship with the linchpin and not as a result of their own preference. For example, a shy person may go to a party where he or she feels uncomfortable, but does so in order to spend time with a close friend. Often, for the sake of their child, parents work to get along with the spouses of their children, despite the difficulty. This is a particularly interesting case of relating difficulty because the linchpin, as the source of the involuntary relationship in the first place, often attempts to facilitate the relationship. For example, Morr Serewicz describes how individuals have a vested interest in promoting the relationship between their spouse and their parents. Bradshaw similarly shows how a shy person's close friends may act as "social lubricants" that make interaction with casual acquaintances easier for shy folk. It is clear in these cases, therefore, that third-party linchpins often recognize their contribution to the difficulty and try to do something about it.

Triangulator as Comparison Point

This fourth form of triangulation is similar to Thibaut and Kelley's (1959) Comparison Level and Comparison Level for Alternatives. People judge the quality of their relationships based on other available relationships and hence on their experience of a broader social world that encompasses more than simply the "difficult relationship." Participants in a long-distance relationship (LDR) may compare their partner to other potential partners (Sahlstein, chap. 7), or the receivers of money (e.g., the beneficiaries of a will) may judge the quality of their relationship with the giver (in this case, the deceased) by comparing the amount given to them against the amount given to others (here, other beneficiaries; Allan and Gerstner, chap. 5). This will cause a problem for the current relationship only if it is perceived as "less than" the comparison point. In other words, relationships appear difficult if they do not meet our triangulating expectations.

The chapters emphasize the importance of expectations by other people in other ways also. Although social norms are expectations, other sorts of "expectations" pervade social life (e.g., sexism, racism, and prejudice). "A man has to be Joe McCarthy to be called ruthless. All a woman has to do is to put you on hold" (Marlo Thomas, as qtd. in Levine & Lyons, 1980). As a further example, Erin Sahlstein (chap. 7), talking about long-distance relationships, indicates that part of the problem is that people experience their LDRs in the context of what could be expected in proximal relationships *and they know it*. Part of the difficulty, therefore, is knowing that what they are getting in a LDR is less than they would be getting in a proximal relationship. This problem of course is not unique to LDRs, though it is important there and particularly prominent in the minds of the partners involved. Any difficulty in relating can be contextualized by triangulation—other relationships—and in their relative lack of choice about whether to see other relationships as alternatives. People do not have a choice about their observation of other relationships all around them, all being conducted differently from their difficult relationship.

The modification of expectations, especially expectations about self, plays a key role in the management of difficulty. In the case of physical distress, disability, or illness, the management of changes in expecta-

tions about self has been well described by Lyons et al. (chap. 11). However, a shy person also has different expectations of self than do other
folks, and violent people have expectations of the self's role in controlling others. Long-distance relationship partners experience unhappy
expectations about the future of their relationship with consequent
negative inferences about the self's experience. One of the consequences
of hookups is the negative view of self that they evoke, and nonresidential parents experience themselves as "less than" a whole parent. One result of chronic illness noted by Lyons et al. is a tendency to feel
vulnerable and unsafe, and hence a tendency to distrust others during a
change in one's self-image. Throughout the book, we see that difficulty
is an inherently interactional concept; it stems from the ways in which
people perform relating as a consequence of broader contexts beyond
the person and the relationship.

Personalization.   Despite this fact, one essential element of "difficulty" is that it is personalized, that is, attributed to individuals rather
than to situations or processes. Foley (chap. 3) notes the tendency in
early literature to blame abused women for the violence perpetrated
against them and the tendency for abused women to blame themselves.
Allan and Gerstner (chap. 5) indicate that "poverty generates tensions
which are hard to accommodate, frequently resulting in attribution of
personal blame and inadequacy even though the underlying causes are
evidently structural." Paul (chap. 8) notes how "hookups gone bad"
tend to lead to assessment of self as incompetent or spoiled in some way.
Lyons et al. (chap. 11) note, "People will consider relationship issues as
their personal problem or another individual's 'fault' instead of attributing problems to the situation or circumstance of illness/disability." As
we indicated in the opening chapter, the immediate tendency to claim
that other people are difficult is one of the most dramatic and forceful
aspects that make difficulty interesting and perplexing.

This tendency to blame others has two implications. One interesting
and research-stimulating possibility is that by locating difficulty in
other people, we defend ourselves through victimage and scapegoating
in Burke's (1966) terms: The other person takes the whole rap for whatever may have emerged from faulty process between the two people.
The other implication is that by locating difficulty in people, especially
in others, we simplify the problem and make it more manageable. Just
as relaters tend to simplify by making the term *relationship* stand for a
whole series of separate experiences of interaction with a particular
partner, the term *person(ality)* stands as a simple summary for a range
of behaviors generated by one individual.

The effort to see one person as responsible for difficulties in a relationship draws attention away from the process and toward a supposed inherent fault—particularly, the inherent fault of others. Very handy! As
researchers increase their understanding of difficulty, it will be neces-

sary to form a sharper conception of why people use personalized vic-timage and scapegoating—that is, accept or distribute blame—when faulty process management and shared involvement may be more likely culprits. It is worth noting that the classic Heiderian model of attribu-tion (Heider, 1958) allows attribution to the person and the situation, but not to the process and hence misses the level of analysis that focuses on relating specifically. Accordingly researchers not only must ask themselves when it is appropriate to attribute fault to a relationship process, but also need to gain a fuller understanding of how externalizing and personalizing a responsibility contributes to the pro-cess of "difficulty" itself. To this end, Bradshaw indicates that, an impor-tant area to examine in future research on both shyness and other types or causes of difficulty would be how the 'difficult' person in a relationship is viewed by the relational partner.

Management

Because difficulty is a process, any difficulty with another person, however it is attributed, has to be managed. Difficulty may arise from several different sources and means, but the end result that makes diffi-culty interesting to relationship researchers is that it presents people with situations that must be dealt with relationally. Not all of these sit-uations are serious predicaments—although some are—but all require relaters' conscious and attentive effort (e.g., see Sahlstein, chap. 7). The issue of management of difficulty may overlap the issue of personaliza-tion in some ways, because it focuses the partners on one anothers' characters, rather than on the socially constructive processual dynam-ics inherent in their interaction. However, whether the persons blame each other or not, they still need to conduct and manage their future in-teraction in the light of the difficulties that exist.

The management of difficulty, of course, relates to our earlier obser-vation about triangulation. Just as difficulties themselves often result from triangulation, so too, managing difficulty occurs through trian-gulation. In part, we experience difficult people as difficult precisely be-cause we use external reference points for understanding them. One such point is to relate this person to others whom we know about. An-other reference point that helps us understand difficulty is relating pre-vious experience with the same person to our present experience. Some people are labeled "difficult" because their obstreperousness is predict-able from past examples; this particular instance of obstinacy triangu-lated with those past experiences confirms the other as "difficult." This suggests that responsibility for difficulty lies in both time and process as well as in people, and hence that one basis of "difficulty" is triangulated by the process of relating itself.

Interestingly, it appears that the interaction process that renders re-lating difficult is often outside the "difficult relationship" itself. We should be careful to recognize this as a social process that occurs between all three points of the triangle, and not simply reposition the "difficult person" outside the relationship. It is important to note that a Triangulator who perceives difficulty in the relational interaction is not necessarily bad or "difficult." For example, a woman's shelter worker who helps a woman reframe her experience as abuse ascribes difficulty with potentially liberating consequences. A residential parent may quite reasonably interfere with the nonresidential parent's visitation rights if the nonresidential parent has endangered or neglected the child in the past. Individuals may only inadvertently create difficulty for their spouse and parents in an attempt to foster positive relationships among the people they love. In all of these cases, it is clear that difficulty lies in an interaction process, not in the inherent qualities of an individual. Furthermore, it appears that difficult relating may serve important social functions for those who constitute it.

REFERENCES

Burke, K. (1966). *Language as symbolic action: Essays on life, literature and method.* Berkeley: University of California Press.
Heider, F. (1958). *The psychology of interpersonal relations.* New York: Wiley.
Levine, S., & Lyons, H. (Eds.). (1980). *The decade of women, a Ms. history of the seventies in words and pictures.* New York: Paragon Books.
Simmel, G. (1950). *The sociology of Georg Simmel.* New York: Free Press.
Thibaut, J., & Kelley, H. (1959). *The social psychology of groups.* New York: Wiley.

Author Index

Kanouse, D. E., 4, *13*
Kanuha, V., 15, *57*
Kapferer, J. N., 162, *179*
Karmiloff-Smith, A., 151, *158*
Katriel, T., 3, *13*
Kelley, H. H., 104, 105, 106, 107,
      108, 109, 110, 114, 117,
      117, 229, *232*
Kelly, F. K., 163, *179*
Kelly, L., 49, *58*
Kenny, D. A., 21, *39*
Kenrick, D. T., 16, *40*
Kerr, M. A., 27, 28, 33, *40*
Kim, H., 64, *80*
Kimmel, A. J., 162, *179*
King, V., 183, 184, 185, 194, *199*
Kipnis, L., 8, *13*
Kisser, C., 171, *179*
Knapper, C., 4, *13*
Knight, P. D., 20, *40*
Knoester, C., 191, *199*
Knox, D., 121, 126, *138, 139,* 145,
    157
Knox, J., 122, *139*
Koch, P. B., 34, *40*
Koper, R. J., 19, *31, 39*
Kouneski, E. F., 186, *199*
Koval, J. E., 49, *57*
Kowal, J., 223, *224*
Kurz, D., 89, *98*

L

Lacy, W. B., 76, *78*
Lake, E. A., 20, *38*
Lamb, M. E., 182, 183, 187, 196,
    200
Lamb, S., 45, 46, *58*
Lambert, J. D., 186, 189, 190, *201*
Lambert, T. A., 141, 142, 144, *158*
Lambert, W. W., 27, *40*
Lang, P. J., 151, *158*
Langston, C. A., 25, 28, *40*
Lawler, E. J., 63, *79*
Lawless, E. J., 45, 54, *58*
Leary, M. R., 17, 20, 29, 33, *40*
Lee, A., 223, *224*
Leigh, B. C., 146, 151, *158, 159*
Leimar, O., 161, 168, *179*
Lemaistre, J., 210, *224*
Lempert, L., 46, 49, 51, *58*

Lenski, G., 73, *79*
Leonard, D., 81, *98*
Leonard, S. A., 111, *118*
Levin, J., 164, *179*
Levine, S. 229, *232*
Levinson, S. C., 7, 9, *12*
Levitskaya, A., 148, *159*
Liddell, D., 120, *140*
Lindsay–Hartz, J., 150, *159*
Linsenmeier, J., 23, 24, *41*
Linton, M., 32, *38*
Lloyd, S. A., 44, 45, 46, 47, 48, 49,
    57, 58
Loudon, J., 170, *179*
Lovaglia, M. J., 62, 63, 66, 70, 72,
    73, 74, 79, *80*
Lucas, J. W., 66, 70, 76, *79*
Lukes, S., 97, *98*
Lund, M., 187, 189, 190, 194, *197,*
    200
Lupton, D., 189, *200*
Lyman, S., 47, *58*
Lyons, H., 229, *232*
Lyons, R., 203, 204, 216, *224*

M

Macdonald, R., 94, *98*
Madden-Derdich, D. A., 111, *118*
Madson, L., 143, 145, 149, *157*
Malone, J., 48, 49, *58*
Manning, P., 21, 22, *40*
Manning, W. D., 124, *139*
Mannix, E. A., 62, *79*
Marcoen, A., 102, 106, *117*
Marcus, G., 51, *58*
Markovsky, B., 63, 74, 75, 79, *80*
Markus, H. R., 143, 149, 149, 150,
    153, *159*
Marsh, C., 82, *98*
Marshall, J. C., 149, *159*
Marsiglio, W., 182, *200*
Mascolo, M. F., 150, *159*
Masheter, C., 192, 193, *200*
Maslow, A. H., 19, *40*
Mason, J., 84, 86, 87, 95, 97, *98*
Masson, J., 84, 86, *87, 98*
Matthews, S., 76, *79*
McCubbin, H. I., 122, 124, *139*
McDermott, M. J., 45, *58*
McKay, S., 90, *98*

Subject Index